REINHARD GEHLEN: HITLER'S SPYMASTER

REINHARD GEHLEN: HITLER'S SPYMASTER

FROM THE EASTERN FRONT IN WW2 TO COLD WAR CIA ASSET

NORMAN RIDLEY

FRONTLINE
BOOKS

REINHARD GEHLEN: HITLER'S SPYMASTER
From the Eastern Front in WW2 to Cold War CIA Asset

First published in Great Britain in 2025 by
Frontline Books
An imprint of Pen & Sword Books Ltd
Yorkshire – Philadelphia

ISBN: 978-1-03611-325-4

Typeset by Lapiz Digital
Printed and bound by CPI UK

The Publisher's authorised representative in the EU for product safety is Authorised Rep Compliance Ltd., Ground Floor, 71 Lower Baggot Street, Dublin D02 P593, Ireland.
www.arccompliance.com

MIX
Paper | Supporting responsible forestry
FSC® C013604

For a complete list of Pen & Sword titles please contact:

PEN & SWORD BOOKS LTD
47 Church Street, Barnsley, South Yorkshire, S70 2AS, UK
E-mail: enquiries@pen-and-sword.co.uk
Website: www.pen-and-sword.co.uk

Or

PEN AND SWORD BOOKS,
1950 Lawrence Road, Havertown, PA 19083, USA
E-mail: uspen-and-sword@casematepublishers.com
Website: www.penandswordbooks.com

'Accurate secret intelligence is a key to success, particularly in a period of complex tensions.'

Harry Howe Ransom,
The Intelligence Establishment,
Harvard University Press, 1970, p.6

CONTENTS

Preface ix

Chapter 1 Artillery Officer 1
Chapter 2 The War 22
Chapter 3 Same Foe; Different Friends 76
Chapter 4 The Gehlen Organisation 117
Chapter 5 The BND 190
Appendix 1 Attendees at The Himmerod Meeting, 4–9 October 1950 201
Appendix 2 The Structure of *Die Generalvertretung L* in 1950 202
Appendix 3 Known Members of Gehlen Organisation 203

Notes 209
Bibliography and Sources 217
Index 221

PREFACE

During the Second World War, Reinhard Gehlen had faced many situations before where, as head of German military intelligence on the Eastern Front, he had sat up late into the night writing his reports agonising over whether he had overlooked some crucial piece of information or drawn an unwarranted conclusion that might have unforeseen, catastrophic results. It was like that now in spring 1945, but he was no longer weighing up the fate of armies in the field. His priority at this moment, with the war playing out its final agony all around, was survival for himself, his family and his staff and it was in the deep, narrow valley of the river Valepp that weaved its way between the high peaks of the Stolzenberg and the Kreuzbergerkopf on the German-Austrian border in the Bavarian Alps, that he considered his options. With him were six of his officers and three female staff assistants and they were all, technically, deserters from the German armed forces. If caught by the *Schutzstaffel* (SS – German paramilitary organisation) they would be hard pressed to talk their way out of a peremptory firing squad. On the other hand, discovery by advance US forces would see them thrown in prisoner of war (PoW) camps where it might take many months before Gehlen could negotiate his way to an interview with the people he needed to contact and by then it might be too late. Capture by the Red Army was something that he tried not to think about at all. He was cool, analytical, pragmatic and a strategist by inclination, however, and he had a plan. It was a plan so fantastic that, if successful, it would have consequences way beyond any issue of immediate survival for him and ones that would underscore the political landscape of Europe for years to come.

He had spent many hours in the Bavarian Alps as a young military cadet in happier times and so was familiar with the surroundings. Now with his nine companions he climbed up a steep path through deep snow to an isolated alpine cottage sitting high above the valley floor at a place the locals called 'Misery Meadow'. A shepherd, Rudolf Kreidl, wounded and discharged from military duty, had shown them the way. It was exactly what Gehlen was looking for as a hideout with the narrow German-held territory being inexorably squeezed by Soviet tanks rolling through the streets of Vienna, Austria and US General George Patton's Third United States Army crossing the river Rhine. Here in the heart of the Alpine Redoubt some of the remaining *Wehrmacht* (German armed forces) and Nazi leadership planned to make their last stand and sue for peace but SS units were terrorising the region bent on rooting out and executing enemies of the state. In his madness and uncontrollable fury at what he saw as Germany's failure to live up to his demands, Adolf Hitler had ordered that his forces laid Germany to waste leaving only a scorched earth for the victors. It was a perilous environment and one made even more dangerous by the fact that Gehlen was planning treason on an unimagined scale.

He had travelled south from Zossen, near Berlin over roads now subjected to constant air attacks and choked with the desperate and pathetic mass of refugees fleeing bombed-out cities frantically trying to keep out of the clutches of Soviet forces in the east. Their nightmare journey took them through SS roadblocks where anyone even suspected of desertion or illegal activity was taken aside and shot, but although Hitler, in one of his insane rages, had relieved him of his command on 9 April 1945, Gehlen still carried documentation of a one-star Wehrmacht general that enabled him to reach Bad Reichenhall in Upper Bavaria, just a little more than 10 miles north of the Führer's Berchtesgaden.

Although the recent flight from Berlin had been catalysed by his dismissal, Gehlen was now playing out a scenario that had been some time in preparation. In February 1945, he had rescued his wife and four children from Liegnitz, now directly in the line of the Soviet advance, and instructed one of his staff, Major Hermann Baun, take them to a place of safety way to the south at Naumburg in Thuringia. They passed through Dresden only days before it was fire-bombed by 1,000 Allied aircraft but Baun's wife who ran a small hotel in the city remained and was one of the 30,000 people who died there on 13 February 1945. Baun had also taken with him two lorry loads of some fifty steel boxes containing the whole archive of Gehlen's intelligence files that included index files of Red Army personnel and Soviet politicians, aerial photographs of Soviet cities and industrial regions, and coded lists of German agents operating behind Soviet lines. Events now led Gehlen to believe that Thuringia would be in the Soviet zone of occupation so he quickly arranged for his family and the archives to be moved again this time to an isolated house, Gutmanning, at Cham on the Czech border and it was at this place where he held a short family reunion to celebrate his wife's fortieth birthday on 17 April 1945. When he left his family after a few brief days, there was no certainty that he would ever see them again but Gehlen stuck to his plan and headed for Valepp. There he waited until the time was ripe for him to take the world's most valuable espionage files gathered over three years of war against the Soviets and hand them over to the Americans.

Chapter 1
ARTILLERY OFFICER

Early Life

> As a young officer I stubbornly refused to learn a foreign language beyond what I had picked up at school, so that there could be no risk of my being posted to military intelligence work within the General Staff, let alone to the secret service.
>
> Reinhard Gehlen[1]

At the beginning of the twentieth century, the German Empire controlled by Kaiser Wilhelm II was at its peak politically and economically. It was a military superpower with global ambitions and sufficient self-confidence to earn for itself a not unwelcome soubriquet of arrogance. German technical innovations were admired around the world ensuring Germany had a leading position in the global economy promising increasing prosperity to nourish its growing population. It was into an emerging, power-conscious German middle class that Reinhard Gehlen was born on 3 April 1902, one of four children of Benno Erwin Felix Walther Gehlen and Luise (née Wiede). His siblings were Nathalie, Max and Theodora, who married Karl von Rabenau. Theodora and Karl had a son, Friedrich von Rabenau, who later became general of the artillery and head of the army archives in the Wehrmacht.

Family roots went back to Gaugraf Johannes Geylener, a man of Flemish nobility, who lived in Paderborn in the fifteen century, giving the Gehlen family a certain social status and it was this sense of historical entitlement that was instrumental in shaping young Reinhard's personality and confident manner. While his grandfather on his mother's side had served with distinction in the Franco Prussian

War of 1870 to 1871, his father, Walther, had not come from a military tradition and had been the first professional officer in a long middle class family tradition of civil servants and lawyers but he had been a less than successful officer in 1st Thuringian Field Artillery Regiment No. 19. The choice of field artillery was a common choice for middle class aspirants of the day and had been since the sixteenth century, but it did not carry the prestige of the elite cavalry regiments. It did, however, have the compensating benefit of making it a much less expensive career and it allowed him to develop his horsemanship skills.

Walther Gehlen was long overdue for promotion when, at the end of 1900, somewhat above his station, he married Katharine 'Käthi' Margarete von Vaernewyck. A photograph taken a day before his wedding shows a relaxed smiling Walther obviously unaffected by the somewhat embarrassing circumstance of a six-month pregnant wife to be. Exactly why the couple waited so long to hold the wedding has led to speculation that Walther was not the child's father and the marriage had been arranged somehow to save Käthi's reputation. After the wedding, the newlyweds went on honeymoon to Rome, Italy over the New Year and remained there until their son was born and christened Johannes, which, perhaps significantly, was not a traditional Gehlen family name.

Instead of returning home with their child, they immediately gave him away to be brought up by a German-Jewish friend of Käthi, Anna Baum, and her husband with appropriate regular financial support. This was not a particularly unusual thing to happen especially when parents did not have the resources to care for a child, but this was obviously not the case here and it suggests that it was the purpose was to hide embarrassment or shame when they returned home. It was obviously done this way to disguise the fact that there had ever been a child and poses the question of whether Walther was Johannes's biological father. Reinhard was born a year later, and, unlike his brother, he was given a traditional family name. A third son was born in 1905 and christened Walther after his father and a daughter, Barbara, followed in 1912.

Johannes proved to have an extraordinary talent for languages. He grew up in the Baum household speaking French, English and Italian perfectly, Swedish very well and having a level of proficiency in Spanish, Danish and Norwegian. It was only when he applied for a copy of his birth certificate to enroll at college that Johannes became aware of his biological family and not unnaturally wanted to meet them. When he travelled to Breslau, he was met at the station by his father Walther, who told him that on no account must young Barbara be told the truth about his upbringing. This condition was ostensibly to protect her from knowing that Johannes was conceived outside marriage, but it was also, no doubt, convenient to prevent gossip amongst Gehlen's family and friends who were unaware of the facts of his relationship to the family. He agreed to be introduced as an 'Italian cousin'. The truth was not kept from Reinhard, however. He later developed a close relationship with Johannes, whose marriage ceremony to a Swede, Agda Torborg Paulson, he attended in Rome in 1933. Johannes's wife brought a modest dowry to the marriage, which allowed him to continue his studies, gaining a doctorate in mathematics and physics from the University of Leipzig before going on to work with the eminent physicist Werner Heisenberg. He fully accepted Reinhard as head of the family after their father's death while Reinhard is said to have been very envious of Johannes's Italian lifestyle.

Just after Reinhard was born, Royal Lieutenant Walther Gehlen retired from the armed forces citing chronic rheumatoid arthritis for the decision but he seemed to be in good health at the time. The real reason may have been frustration at having become stalled in the promotion stakes. He was evidently fit enough to be listed as a reserve officer, assigned to 2nd Landwehr Division, first in Bitterfeld, then from 1904 in Halle an der Saale. Walther struggled to adapt to civilian life but his younger brother, Max, had married into a wealthy publishing family, Ferdinand Hirt & Son, and he managed to secure a position for Walther as the manager of the company's Breslau branch. Two years after Reinhard was born, his uncle Max and his wife had a son, Arnold, who became an important German philosopher and sociologist. Arnold would go on to join the *Nationalsozialistische Deutsche Arbeiterpartei* (NSDAP – Nazi Party) as a private lecturer in philosophy, but his personal creed remained free of anti-Semitism. Arnold became close to Johannes and although he was less close to Reinhard, he influenced his broad outlook with ideas that saw human beings as essentially 'deficient' requiring strong institutions such as family, church and state by which they must allow themselves to be 'consumed' in order to function efficiently. Reinhard and Johannes would find themselves working together after the First World War.

As a young child, Reinhard received only one serious beating from his father, who believed that every child should have at least one in their lives. This had a considerable effect on Reinhard causing him to shy away from personal confrontations and he rarely gave way to violence himself. He grew up in a liberal household where children were encouraged to take part in mealtime discussions about general political issues, which often centered on the obligations of individual citizens towards the state. Walther's view was that the fulfillment of duty should not be directed primarily at the monarch, as had previously been the case, but at the state now that the Kaiser had abdicated. It was this obligation to the state that the young Reinhard was imbued with during his formative years and to which he, alongside his family, developed an intellectual and political allegiance. It only went so far, however, with the patriarch setting an example by being careful to keep a discrete distance from right-wing nationalist extremist circles such as the Pan-Germans. He chose as a role model for his son Frederick the Great, a man who had described himself as the 'first servant' of his state. In political discussions with friends, who were amongst the local elite, Walther would often get animated, but the young Reinhard later recalled that arguments would be conducted in a very friendly spirit, which he recognised as being in contrast to his experience of political opposition among other Germans where disagreement very often degenerating into personal hostility. Here again, Reinhard learned the value of rational, controlled behaviour and followed his father's example of emotional restraint.

As a 10 year old, Reinhard grew up in the old university town of Breslau, a city with a large Jewish population and an intellectual centre that absorbed influences from all over Europe. He joined the conservative *Jungdeutschlandbund* (Young Germany Association), which was a kind of boy scout movement where boys hiked, slept out in tents, ate meals and sang songs around campfires very much as the *Hitlerjugend* (Hitler Youth) would do more than a decade later. This was Gehlen's first experience of group activity and collective action. In it he discovered the emotional security of camaraderie and shared experience which later became the essence of his total commitment to a military lifestyle. At around the same time, there were celebrations in Breslau on the occasion of the 100th anniversary of the Wars of Liberation when a magnificent exhibition hall was opened by the Prussian Crown Prince. This pageantry of Prussia's glorious military history and victory against Napoléon engendered in him huge respect for the military which was, for him, becoming the very embodiment of the German spirit.

Reinhard was moved to the renowned König-Wilhelm Gymnasium in Breslau in 1912 where he thrived as a shy but above average, hard-working student, especially in mathematics and classics, but he was never a 'bookworm' remaining at all times alive to the world around him. Relationships with his classmates, however, were not easy. He was

> 'narrow-chested and slight … never taller than five feet four [163cm] … with sallow, peaky face, myopic eyes, protruding ears and mousy hair.[2]'

A schoolfriend, Herbert Urban, remembered him as 'cold … with a passion for figures and formulae.' He had a reputation as a loner but someone whose intellect shone through once drawn into discussion when he would become an animated and formidable debater.[3]

Although devoting many hours to his studies, he also found time to take up dancing lessons and developed a love of horses and horse riding. Another great friend of his at this time was a Jewish boy called Theodor Eckstein whose father had died and whose mother worked long hours to pay for the Theodor's education. Eventually, Theodor would be forced to move to a less expensive school and the friends lost touch. Later Theodor went on to study mathematics and physics at the University of Breslau before emigrated to Palestine in 1936. The two would be reunited in the 1980s.

When the First World War broke out in 1914, Reinhard's father was called up at the age of 43 as adjutant of 22nd Silesian Landwehr Brigade but Käthi returned to Eisenach with the children where 12-year-old Reinhard worked as a helper for the Red Cross. It was shock for the young man, when, after a long absence, he returned to school in Breslau from Eisenach to find he had fallen behind in his studies to the extent that he was downgraded. It was a humiliation and his first real setback in life. His reaction was characteristic. He worked in what he later described as possibly the most intense period of his life to catch up with his work and regain the favour of his teachers. He was actually suspected of cheating in his exams and forced to re-sit in an empty classroom because the teachers found it hard to believe that he had made up for lost time so quickly. They could not doubt the second result, however, and awarded him a high mark and promotion to a higher class in which he rapidly became one of the star pupils.

As he approached early manhood in his formative years, he was inevitably influenced by the national mood that was dominated by the First World War and, despite his 'puny physique', he volunteered to join his father's former regiment, 19th Field Artillery Regiment, but defeat of the German army at the Second Battle of the Marne had seen the last hope of German victory vanish.[4] Field Marshal Paul von Hindenburg accepted the Allies' armistice terms and the Kaiser fled to Belgium. German civilian morale was crushed and when Gehlen's father returned from active duty, he refused to permit Reinhard to pursue his military ambitions and insisted that he complete his studies. The whole political structure of eastern Europe was becoming unhinged as the three former empires, German, Russian and Austro-Hungarian, collapsed and cities all across the region were consumed with revolutionary, nationalistic and ethnic violence. Communists and paramilitary ultra-right-wing *Freikorps* (irregular military volunteers) battled for control of the streets in German cities. The country was gripped first by the fear of, and then by the reality of, revolution. Reinhard experienced the turbulence together with his mother and his younger siblings at home on Breslauer Königsplatz. Large crowds collected in the streets in the evenings, and there were gunshots all through the night.

Along with all the rest of the German middle class Gehlen's mother had become fearful of revolution. In such dangerous times, with rioting in the streets all around, she struggled to understand what was happening and did her best to protect her family. She took Reinhard with her to public meetings, which often erupted into fighting between nationalists and communists. Returning from one such meeting at the Great Hall of the Breslau Theatre, they became embroiled in a street battle in the Gartenstrasse and took refuge in a cellar from which they were eventually rescued by the communist member of parliament Max Gruschwitz.

When he turned 20, Gehlen completed his education at the König Wilhelm School and passed his final *Abitur* (examination) with a report describing him as 'a shining example to other pupils'.[5] Having been dissuaded from taking up a military career that might have given his life stability and direction, Gehlen turned to a career in medicine or physics, which his older brother Johannes had taken up and which his own son would later follow but it was hard to see a path into the future with German civilian life racked by so much instability.

To the Gehlen family the worst threat to Germany was the 'new twentieth-century gospel' of 'Pan Slavism' that sought to unite the peoples of eastern and east central Europe in a common cause.[6] The only things preventing a Bolshevik revolution destroying what was left of the social fabric, was the rump army, massively depleted after Versailles, and the paramilitary *Freikorps*. Motivated by a deep discontent with the chaos of the world around him and a desire to see order restored to a society where his family could live in peace, he turned again to the military and this time his father did not intervene. He did warn his son, however, that life in the army was a daily grind with poor promotion prospects but Gehlen was sure that the *Reichswehr* (German armed forces) was his spiritual home, a solid foundation for his life and a refuge from the confusion and mayhem that threatened to consume the continent. It was a decision taken

> 'coolly, clearly and purposefully and [with] mathematical precision and inevitability'

wrote Herbert Urban.[7] It was an indication of the way that Gehlen would approach every crisis in his life.

Early Military Career

> Gehlen kept piles of books about Russia in his room and used to go to bed at night with a heavy volume of statistical yearbook on the Soviet Union.[8]

On 20 April 1920, Gehlen took the oath,

> I vow that I will behave as a brave and honour-loving soldier, that I will dedicate all my strength to the defense of the German Reich [empire] and my home state at all times and in every place, and that I will protect the government appointed by the people and want to obey my superiors.

He then joined 1st Division of 6th Light Reserve Artillery Regiment under Colonel Brüggemann, which was then in the East Border Guard near Breslau. Fealty of the armed services was no longer to the Kaiser but to the elected government. He was content to remain clear of politics, as required to do so by the military law of 23 March 1921, at least while he was undergoing his four-year training period at the old Silesian garrison town of Schweidnitz not far from Breslau where his regiment sat alongside 7th Infantry Regiment. This would remain Reinhard's main location for the next fourteen years. His room commander was Lance Corporal Hasler, who maintained a long friendship with Reinhard and who later recalled:

> Nothing was given to us. I came straight from school and the physical strain of daily service also had its advantages. My body was toned. The food was anything but lavish. But at least I gained twenty pounds in a short time.[9]

On 1 January 1921, Gehlen joined up with No. 1 Battery of the newly formed 3rd (Prussian) Artillery Regiment under commander Colonel Viktor von Aigner. Then, on 10 August of that year, he went to Jüterbog, south of Berlin, to take the officer candidate examination. There he undertook artillery training, which was actually forbidden by the terms of the Treaty of Versailles, meaning that the guns had to be hidden in the forests near Markendorf during visits by the International Control Commission.

After passing the final exam, Gehlen was appointed as an officer candidate and assigned to the Munich Infantry School for one year. Here, at the newly established central training centre of the *Reichswehr*, he met officer candidates from all branches of the armed forces for full infantry training. It was a time of high political tensions in Bavaria where right-wing extremist groups were staking their claims for power. One such was the NSDAP led by Adolf Hitler but Gehlen continued to steer well clear of politics.

His training was intense and left little time for diversion. According to the new modern army doctrine, an officer was expected to show initiative and be able to do everything he asked of his men. All officers were expected to be able to ride and Gehlen took lessons with Captain Georg Lindemann, who, as commander-in-chief of Army Group North during the Second World War, also retained a close professional relationship with him. It was during his period of training, on 1 March 1922, that Gehlen learned that his mother had died as the result of complications after a gallbladder operation.

One month later, he was promoted to sergeant and returned to his original unit in August of the same year where he was quickly made up to ensign. At a regimental ball he met and fell in love with a medical-technical assistant called Helene. She rode and climbed, was self-confident and cheeky. Three times he proposed and three times he was rejected but he never forgot her and was able to help her much later in February 1945, when she, with two children and heavily pregnant with her third, was able, with Gehlen's help to take the last hospital train out of Breslau ahead of a Red Army attack on the city.

The Reichswehr was a volunteer army in which the soldiers were highly motivated with a comradely spirit and it was during this time that Gehlen was able to indulge his passion for horses. On 1 December 1923, he received a commission as second lieutenant with 3rd (Prussian) Artillery Regiment in which he, like all other recruits, found himself following a conventional military routine with responsibility for cleaning out stables and feeding two horses every day before breakfast.

Gehlen became friendly with a number of officers at this time who would play a part in his future career. One of them was a first lieutenant in his regiment, Andor Hencke, who later became personal secretary to the German ambassador in Moscow, Ulrich von Brockdorff-Rantzau. Through a career in the Foreign Office, Hencke rose to the position of undersecretary of state. He was later greatly valued by Gehlen as an expert on Eastern Europe during the Second World War.

Two others who went on to play a part in Gehlen's wartime agency were Lieutenant Horst von Mellenthin and Lieutenant Colonel Wolfgang Langkau. A third, Rudolf Bamler, was six years older than the others and perhaps not quite as close to Gehlen but he also maintained a close relationship with him after he became head of the newly created *Abteilung III b* (German Military Intelligence Department III – counterespionage) under Admiral Wilhelm Canaris.

Bamler, described as ambitious, intelligent, agile and with great organizational talent, was later an avid supporter of the Nazi Party in an agency that was certainly less enthusiastic than he was, but he resisted all attempts by Reinhard Heydrich to lure him into the *Sicherheitsdienst* (SD – SS Intelligence Service). Bamler became a lieutenant general, was captured by the Soviets in 1944 and worked assiduously on their behalf thereafter. He joined the National Committee for Free Germany spying on German prisoners of war helping to bring to trial in a Soviet court the German defector General Walther von Seydlitz-Kurzbach. Returning to Germany in 1950, he became a major general in the *Kasernierte Volkspolizei* (KVP –Barracked People's Police People's Police) in the German Democratic Republic where he helped to set up a central Ministry for State Security.

A year later, in the run-up to Christmas, an election was held in which the officers of Gehlen's regiment met under the leadership of the commander to vote on the admission of the senior ensign to the officer corps. If elected, the man must commit himself to twenty-five years of service. A candidate was ranked to determine what his career path might turn out to be. Gehlen was placed fourth out of forty-two and with an annual salary of 978 gold marks was promoted to lieutenant. The salary was adequate but not particularly generous and since it was important that young officers did not incur any debts and he could not rely on financial support from his family, he was, of necessity, required to follow a frugal and moral lifestyle. The codes of behaviour were laid out in the training manuals that called for

> men who are imbued with love for the fatherland and for our wonderful profession, who want to help rebuild the fatherland and who are determined to protect the homeland and its lawful institutions, if necessary, to the last drop of blood.[10]

The 'Professional Duties of German Soldiers' were laid down in fifteen articles not all of which rested easily with Gehlen, however. Being called upon to 'Strive diligently to fulfill duties faithfully and conscientiously' was never a problem, neither was a requirement to show respect and obedience to superiors but he would struggle to 'consider honour as the highest good' in the service of the General Staff during the Second World War and later when he became a master spy. With a totally honourable outlook Gehlen would not have got very far in a profession often requiring subterfuge, adaptation and willingness to compromise. The young lieutenant, however, like most of his comrades, had no problem following Article 9, which demanded that

> The soldier may not be politically active, may not belong to political associations and may not take part in political meetings.

After completing his officer training, Gehlen became a gun commander, fire control officer and company officer in command of four guns of the battery. As a lieutenant, he received further training through courses in ammunition and radio systems and when he was sent to the artillery school, he received special training in surveying and artillery observation. The firing procedures and tactical operational patterns required a high level of technical and mathematical knowledge where the commander was required to be adept at systematic thinking and careful calculations. Artillery officers were amongst the elite. Many leadership and top positions in the future Wehrmacht would be filled by men who had risen through the artillerymen regiments.

Gehlen was always very conscious of his status and went out of his way to ensure that he won and held the respect of those around him. With this attitude he acquired a personal authority that stood out even alongside older and more experienced officers. When his brother Walther joined as a recruit in Gehlen's unit, he committed an offence that required his older brother to punish him. According to regulations, he asked the team's representatives what they suggested as punishment, and they recommended giving the young Walther just a warning but Gehlen disagreed, believing that such a course would leave him open to accusations of favouritism. He had his brother locked up in prison for three days instead.

On 17 August 1926, four years after his mother died, Gehlen's father married a widow Helene von Hörner, née Markiewitz, the widow of a colonel in the Imperial Guards. Gehlen's stepmother was of Jewish descent but died suddenly only five months later. His father married again very soon afterwards, this time to Klara Elisabeth Kopp who was divorced from her first Jewish husband, Otto Schneemilch. Klara was head of a secondary school for boys and girls and brought to Reinhard's family two stepbrothers.

In that same year, Gehlen escaped from the dreary routine and sluggish promotion trail of an artillery regiment when his personal qualities were recognised and saw him transferred to the Hanover Cavalry School. Artillery regiments were still very much reliant on horses for transport and Gehlen had been able to spend a great deal of time with horses but now he found himself surrounded by them. Tournament sports became the norm but his salary was not sufficient to pay for a first class competition horse. However, his promotion to first lieutenant on 1 February 1928 brought a modest rise in income and life continued to be good for him. Beyond the lecture theatre, his days were filled with horse riding in drag hunts, long convivial lunches and social evenings often in the company of foreign dignitaries. Riding so much, he suffered frequent falls and injuries, one of which was presumably caused by excessive drinking because afterwards he swore off alcohol except for certain formal occasions. Eventually the lifestyle began to pall a little, partly because he could never quite afford a reliable horse and also because he was getting bored with the routine that failed to stimulate him intellectually. Ambition was once more driving him on.

He was not altogether pleased to be returning to his former regiment on 1 November 1928 where he joined the staff of 5th (Equestrian) Division as an adjutant and after just a few months moved to 1st Division in Schweidnitz. From there he transferred to 14th (Right) Battery, becoming adjutant to the division commander, Colonel Herbert von Ondarza. Indulging his love of horses, Gehlen continued to organise riding tournaments and drag hunts, which were important training exercises for young officers in the field artillery much as they were for the cavalry regiments. At this time, he worked with officers who would go on to hold high positions during the Second World War, including Friedrich Fromm, later colonel general and commander of the reserve army, and Field Marshal Günther von Kluge.

All this time Gehlen continued to follow military tradition by avoiding political associations unlike three of his fellow officers who were accused before the Reich Court in Leipzig in 1930 of preparing to commit high treason. The accusation was that they had colluded with Hitler's NSDAP, distributed literature for them and called for a national popular uprising all of which, according to the military code, was classified as strictly unconstitutional. They were sentenced to a year and a half in prison.

Gehlen was now well on the way to a successful military career and had little time for a social life so it was left to his stepmother to suggest to him that it was the right time for him to get married. She had already got someone lined up for him. Two years younger than Gehlen, Herta

Charlotte Agnes Helene von Seydlitz-Kurzbach came from an old Silesian military family. She earned her living as a secretary at the military district command, something that was not uncommon for the daughters of officers. Her father was retired Lieutenant Colonel D. Friedrich Wilhelm von Seydlitz-Kurzbach who had served in the prestigious 8th Cuirassiers but the family had fallen on hard times having lost the family fortune in the global economic crisis. Although lacking a dowry, Hertha brought to the marriage connections to the high ranking von Lettow-Vorbecks and von Reichenau families. They were engaged on 20 March 1931 and were married on 10 September the same year in the garrison church at Glogau. Gehlen now began preparing for the military district examination, which was essentially an entrance exam for the shadow *Kriegsakademie* (war academy), an institution which in theory did not exist having been banned by the Treaty of Versailles.

Meanwhile, the political environment in Germany was undergoing seismic shifts. Prussia was becoming more and more under the control of the NSDAP and Gehlen's father as a publisher of educational textbooks was anxious to be on the right side of history. From a purely business perspective, it was economically convenient to show strong allegiance to the new power in the land, which also helped the business to distance itself from its Jewish connections. As a family too, Walther and his wife, Elsa, saw membership of the Central Silesia Gau Authority in Breslau as essential to maintain their social and political status but their application became stalled because of the large number of applicants that had overwhelmed the party administration. To speed up the process, the family turned to old friends who had reached high positions in the Nazi Party. Walther called on Heinrich Lammers the former court assessor in Breslau who had become state secretary and head of the Reich Chancellery. Lammers took the case to Martin Bormann but it was far from easy in such turbulent times to be heard above the clamour, and even Bormann could not do very much. Elsa, however, managed to get through to Rudolf Hess, deputy head of the NSDAP who was able to force through the application and was even able to backdate its acceptance to allocate them an early membership number. This gave the family significant political security.[11]

It was at this time that Ernst, the brother of his old school friend Theodor Eckstein, was arrested. He had become a lawyer and one of the leading figures in the Socialist Workers' Party of Germany (SAP). In the immediate aftermath of the Reichstag (German Parliament) fire in 1933, he was arrested and died under torture in the Breslau-

Dürrgoy concentration camp. If Gehlen was aware of this, he never made reference to it.

Gehlen was, at the time, preparing for his military district examination, which would decide whether or not he would be assigned to General Staff training. Officially, the German General Staff did not exist having been banned under the Treaty of Versailles but it had continued to exist under the guise of the *Truppenamt* (Army Troop Office) and the Staff College, for similar reasons, was referred to as the *Wehrkreise* (Military Districts).

It was precisely because the German General Staff had held such a dominant position in the life of the state that the Western Allies had disbanded it. Its members had traditionally been a powerful, venerated, aristocratic breed of men and, had it not been for its catastrophic capitulation in 1918, someone of Gehlen's background would have been hard pressed indeed to get anywhere near its hallowed portals. It was a sign of the changing times that he could even think about being accepted and it would be a measure of his character and ability, not to mention his ambition, that he eventually was.

For his specialist subject of study, Gehlen chose Bismarck's foreign policy with special consideration of the reinsurance treaty with Russia. Knowledge of at least one Eastern European language was a distinct advantage but Gehlen spoke only German. He passed the examination with ease and on 1 October 1933 was put at the disposal of the chief of Army Command, which essentially meant that he was accepted into the *Kriegsakademie* at *Wehrkreis III* in Berlin. Soon afterwards his wife became pregnant. This put him on a career trajectory pointing to the *Oberkommando der Wehrmacht* (OKW – German High Command).

Living in rented accommodation in a twelve-apartment block at Suarezstrasse 24 in the middle class Charlottenburg area of Berlin, Herta Gehlen gave birth to a daughter, Katharina Margarete, on 19 January 1934. The marriage appeared stable and strong with Herta tending towards an old-fashioned domestic order while Gehlen was now completely absorbed in his military career. Despite never acknowledging awareness of the murder of Ernst Eckstein, he would have been acutely aware of the huge political upheavals taking place in the streets, but he made no attempt to criticise the NSDAP and showed no inclination to comment on politics.

Gehlen passed out of the *Kriegsakademie* with distinction and saw further promotion on 1 May 1934. Signed by Reichswehr Minister Werner von Blomberg, on the authorisation of the President of the Reich, a document appointed First Lieutenant Reinhard Gehlen as captain in service of the chief of the Army Command

> in the expectation that the person appointed, true to the imperial constitution and the laws, fulfills his professional duties for the good of the empire and justifies the trust demonstrated by this appointment. At the same time, [he is] assure of the special protection of the Reich.[12]

It would be of rather more significance, however, when, on 29 October 1934, he, like all other members of the armed forces, had to take an unconditional oath of loyalty to the 'Führer' – Adolf Hitler. Gehlen showed no reluctance to comply. From his perspective, what the new regime was offering was pride in the renewal of the German state and the reemergence of the German army as a modern elite organisation that guaranteed a bright and rewarding future for him. He was particularly influenced by a lecture given by Lieutenant Colonel Fritz Lindemann, which emphasised the military's historically claim to be the very embodiment of the state and poured scorn on the totalitarian claims of the NSDAP which, although in power, was still politically insecure.

Towards the end of his time at the *Kriegsakademie*, Gehlen had attended a seminar on the Soviet Union where he distinguished himself by knowing more about Marxism, the Soviet regime, the Comintern, the Red Army and the Soviet espionage system than all the other participants.[13] His interest in the Soviet Union had first been stimulated by textbooks published by his father, which asserted the rights of Germany to re-occupy lands occupied by ethnic Germans that had been illegally stripped away at Versailles. His growing belief in the need for Germany to expand its borders in the east merged with a deep fear and hatred of Bolshevism, which would, if Germany remained passive, spread west and perch itself with menace on Germany's borders. He had studied Soviet government and administration. The Red Army organisation under Leon Trotsky held a fascination for him but it was head of the Joint State Political Directorate (OGPU), Vyacheslav Rudolfovich Menshinsky, in whom he had the most interest. An intellectual who reputedly spoke twelve languages including Chinese, Japanese and Arabic, Menshinsky had almost limitless powers over millions of lives.[14] Despite his expertise in Soviet military systems, however, Gehlen claims never to have had any special interest in the Soviet Union or intelligence work at this stage in his career.

In 1935, he was invited to attend a meeting between Chief of the British General Staff General Sir John Dill, Director of British Military Intelligence Major General Sir Bernard Paget and Chief of German Foreign Armies Intelligence Colonel Carl-Heinrich von Stülpnagel. Years later, Paget would recall meeting a 'pale little captain' who was proudly introduced by Stulpnagel as 'one of our brightest young experts on Russia'. Paget would later recall how he had been struck by

> how little [Britain] knew compared with the knowledge the Germans had about Russia.[15]

General Staff Appointment

> But we can also see something of the inner bearing of a man, something that stamps him as a soldier, and, moreover, as a General Staff officer.[16]

Gehlen's training at this time would have accentuated the need for clear, systematic thought as opposed to wishful thinking and inspiration, no matter how clever or ingenious that may seem to be. Officers were instructed to follow the path of logical conclusions and that was something Gehlen would do throughout his life. Neither was there a place for politics or morality. When called on to exhibit a 'joyful commitment to the National Socialist worldview', he made sure not to draw attention to himself by demurring, but Nazism was not a noticeable component of his personal *Weltanschauung* (world view).[17] When he was asked, as were all officers, which department of the General Staff he would prefer to work in, he responded with guile and intelligence by requesting the prestigious Operations Department (Ia) but added that he considered himself to be in no position to judge his suitability. It showed ambition and humility which, combined with excellent results in the final examination got him accepted to the *Reichswehrministerium* (Reich War Ministry) on 10 July 1935 and afforded him the honour of wearing the coveted red braid of a General Staff officer.

Gehlen was seconded as adjutant to Lieutenant General Erwin Erdmann von Witzleben who would become one of Hitler's most vociferous opponents. After the failed Stauffenberg bomb plot to kill Hitler on 20 July 1944, von Witzleben would be arrested, tried and hanged, in Plötzensee Prison on 8 August 1944, from a hook with a thin hemp rope, sometimes erroneously referred to as 'piano wire'.

Gehlen joined the General Staff at a time when operational thinking was moving away from defence of the Reich and towards offensive considerations as a result of Nazi foreign policy. His move was made a little more comfortable because of his distant relationship, through his wife, to, now, Lieutenant General von Stülpnagel, who served as chief quartermaster II in the General Staff. As part of his duties, Gehlen's range of contacts widened. Alongside von Witzelben and von Stülpnagel, he often met foreign military attachés, amongst them the British military attaché's assistant, Major Kenneth Strong, whom Gehlen would meet repeatedly after 1945, when Strong had become the first director of the Joint Intelligence Bureau of the British Ministry of Defence.

After a year as an adjutant to von Wietersheim, on 6 October 1936 Gehlen was transferred to the Operations Department of the General Staff, which was responsible for operational planning and therefore for all related questions that affected the German army and its war-focused peacetime development. This included training, armament, equipment and organisation, as well as border protection, national fortifications, transport and mapping. He worked under Colonel Erich von Manstein who would go on to be considered the greatest operational talent on the German side during the Second World War. Under von Manstein were three more outstanding officers who would also have a strong influence on Gehlen. These were Siegfried Westphal, Henning von Tresckow and Bernhard von Loßberg.

Initially, Gehlen was assigned to the Fortifications Section, which was in line with his training as an artilleryman but was far from the position he really yearned for in operational leadership.[18]

The Fortifications Section was commanded by a man who would play a significant role in Gehlen's career trajectory. Small of stature, modest and reserved, Major Adolf Heusinger had many qualities that Gehlen admired. He was a very intelligent, calm, confident and tireless worker. Major August Otto Winter of this section, a pompous man with few redeeming qualities would go on to become chief of the Wehrmacht command staff alongside Heusinger. It was Winter, as senior OKW general in southern Germany towards the end of the Second World War, who authorised Gehlen to pursue his wartime exit strategy and, as a reward, would become one of Gehlen's leading employees in the *Bundesnachrichtendienst* (BND – Foreign Intelligence Service of the Federal Republic of Germany).

Gehlen's department was galavanised into a hectic planning programme when Hitler's Four Year Plan drawn up in 1936 called for Germany to be ready for war within four years. Their task was complicated by not knowing what eventualities to plan for. The lessons of history had shown that Germany could not sustain war on two fronts for any length of time so, at that time the General Staff were basing their plans on the assumption that, allied with Italy, Hungary and Austria, their primary target would be Czechoslovakia with the Western Powers remaining neutral. The Czechs, however, had strong defensive positions on the German border and it became Gehlen's responsibility to survey these fortifications. The scenario envisaged that after defeating the Czechs, Germany would come under attack from the Soviet Union moving through Romania which would necessitate Germany taking up a temporary defensive posture before going on the attack by driving into Ukraine. The *Anschluss* (annexation and occupation of Austria) on 12 March 1938, however, would, at a stroke, totally undermined Czech defenses leaving Prague praying in vain for Western intervention.

Hertha gave birth to a second child, Felix Christoph, in Berlin-Wilmersdorf on 11 February 1937 and their economic circumstances now allowed the family to employ a nanny. During all this time, however, Gehlen had little time for anything but work, which he immersed himself in with great energy seeing less and less of his family. Working under intense pressure, many Wehrmacht officers resorted to using the stimulant Pervitin and it is documented that Gehlen himself used it after 1942 but there is no evidence that he did so at this stage of his career.[19] He was transferred to the newly created 10th Department with Group 2 of the Operations Department under Colonel Kurt Wilhelm Gustav Erdmann on 8 July 1937. This was another rung up the ladder for him and even more advantageous was his frequent call to fill in for his superior who was often too ill to work.

In his new role, Gehlen was sent on a short visit to Finland where he made study of the country's border defences against the Soviet Union. A secret study by the 5th Abteilung of the Abwehr (military intelligence and counterintelligence) had concluded that large Soviet troop movements through northern Sweden towards the Norwegian coast would be almost impossible to carry out due to logistical difficulties which meant that a major German offensive against Narvik and the Swedish ore mines might be possible without interference from the Soviets. In 1945, while in United States captivity, Gehlen would later write of an interview with a Finnish officer who told him that Soviet military-political goals were focused on Europe. 'You are standing here on the borderline between Europe and Asia,' he said

> but you shouldn't think that today's Russia is something new; Russia's development towards Bolshevism only means that it has shed its Western European whitewash, reflected on its Asian essence and returned to the methods of one of its most important rulers, Ivan the Cruel, which corresponded to the characteristics of the Russian people.[20]

With focus on Czechoslovakia, now intensified by Hitler's *Hossbach* Protocol (Hitler's expansionist policies) of 5 November 1937, there were serious rumblings of discontent inside the Wehrmacht. Commander-in-Chief of the Army Werner von Fritsch and Reich War Minister Werner von Blomberg argued that an attack against the Czechs would lead to a wider conflagration for which Germany was, as yet, ill prepared. For Hitler, it was the time to stamp his authority on the army. On trumped up charges, both von Fritsch and von Blomberg were removed from office and a new, more malleable, commander-in-chief of the army, Walther von Brauchitsch was installed. War clouds were gathering on the horizon and Gehlen was drawn inexorably into the heart of planning. The role of the SS and SD in the plots to remove the two commanders had not gone unnoticed by him and he began to perceive the insidious rise of the leader of the SS Heinrich Himmler within the Nazi hierarchy.

Gehlen received the Wehrmacht Service Award, second class, on 20 April 1938 in recognition of eighteen years of loyal service and was now transferred to accelerate the expansion of fortifications in the reoccupied areas west of the river Rhine. It was essential that the border with France could be held with small forces while German plans for Austria and Czechoslovakia were enacted. The Western defences were under the command of Lieutenant General Wilhelm Adam. Despite Hitler having called for the reoccupation of the Rhineland as early as 1933, little had been done to 'close the hole in the west' as he put it and now there was extreme urgency to make up for lost time. When Luftwaffe (German air force) Chief Field Marshal Hermann Göring made a tour of inspection, there was an eruption of damning criticism of the army's dismal efforts. Hitler furiously demanded immediate construction of fortifications and airfields that Adam said would take 'decades' to complete. In a private note, Gehlen recorded Göring's 'very sharp criticism' and saw his intervention as a deliberate ploy to further his own ambitions towards acquiring much more control over the Wehrmacht leadership. It was noticeable also that Göring took little heed of Adam's warnings about the supreme inadvisability of waging war on two fronts. Instead, he reported back to Hitler criticising Adam for weakness. Gehlen felt obliged to defend his commander and, for his trouble, suffered a curt rebuke from Göring who insulted him by calling him a *Kriegsschulversager* (war school failure).[21]

Gehlen remained silent before Göring but was not willing to allow this confrontation to define his relationship with him. He turned to Inspector General of the Air Force Colonel General Erhard Milch and Göring's representative to explain that it had been his duty to represent the army's point of view factually and exactly and desperately asked Milch to plead his case. It was a risky thing to do and could easily have ended Gehlen's career there and then but Göring was apparently impressed by his bravado and harboured no ill feelings. Adam was not so lucky. Brauchitsch quietly removed him from post and forced him into retirement.

Planning for a later, German occupation of Poland, Gehlen was also required to design a line of fortifications to hold against a Soviet attack with particular attention to anti-tank defences.[22] Never allowed to rest, Gehlen was then called on as a fortification officer, to help prepare the war game *Generalstabsreise* in 1938, which rehearsed an attack against the massive Czech fortifications. When the results were reported at the end of June 1938, there was a clear difference of opinion between Brauchitsch and Chief of the General Staff General *der Artillerie* (of the Artillery) Ludwig Beck. Beck was criticised for his exaggerated fears of a wider conflagration and was bluntly told by Hitler that he did not understand *die neue Zeit* (the modern political environment). Beck responded by calling for the collective resignation of the General Staff. Soldierly obedience has limits, he told them, and history will burden them with blood guilt if they did not act according to their conscience. Beck was a very powerful and influential figure, but his words were not fully supported by his own personal commitment. He seemed to shy away from a final confrontation with Hitler and was thereby found himself unable to gain the confidence of his fellow officers. None would follow unless all followed. To take a stand only to find oneself in the minority was professional suicide.

The crisis came to a head at Jüterbog military training area on 15 August 1938 when Hitler called together the senior generals. To ensure secrecy, Hitler personally assigned staff officers to guard the doors and windows. He turned sharply against Beck and declared that he was determined to solve the Czech question by force. Beck saw no way back and submitted his resignation to be replaced by Halder. It may have been the stress of these events that saw Gehlen struck down with gallbladder trouble, the same issue that had brought an end to his mother's life. He was operated on at the beginning of September 1938 and remained for two weeks in the Hindenburg hospital in Berlin-Zehlendorf, near his apartment.

Meanwhile, British Prime Minister Neville Chamberlain was making great efforts to avoid war by meeting Hitler for discussions to solve the Czech crisis. For two weeks at the end of the month, while Gehlen was recuperating from his operation, the political situation threatened to spiral out of control and tension reached a high point but shortly after his release from the hospital, the Sudeten crisis came to an end with the surprising conclusion of the Munich Agreement on 30

September 1938. Britain and France agreed to the German annexation of the area populated by the Sudeten Germans hoping it would end Hitler's expansionist ambitions.

When Gehlen returned to active duty on 10 November 1938, it was the very same day that *Fremde Heere Ost* (FHO – Foreign Armies East) was created. That was the military intelligence department of the *Oberkommando des Heeres* (OKH – German Army High Command). Gehlen was moved to the newly built Scharnhorst barracks as head of 8th Battery of Artillery Regiment 18 in Liegnitz. His family followed him from Berlin and moved into an official apartment at Dovestrasse 14, which remained their home until January 1945.

The regimental commander, Colonel Kurt Anger was not particularly impressed with Gehlen and gave him only an average assessment but Gehlen's department commander was Lieutenant Colonel Ralph Graf von Oriola, an old acquaintance, who would rise to command a division during the Second World War. Gehlen was much more experienced than his fellow officers and was keen to set a good example by strict adherence to regulations and by handing out severe punishment for indiscipline.

As the calendar turned to 1939, Gehlen was busier than ever, preparing for and taking part in war games. One planned exercise was conducted on 23 February under the gaze of Divisional commander Colonel Erich von Manstein. In it, Gehlen's mastery of horsemanship shone through. He commanded a battery of four six-horse gun squadrons and four four-horse ammunition squadrons. After he paraded around the grounds, the audience was stunned into silence when Gehlen suddenly set off with his eight squadrons at full gallop towards a ravine at the edge of the parade ground. It appeared to be madness that could only end in disaster with men, horses and equipment crashing in a catastrophic melee but Gehlen successfully took his troops over the lip and down the steep slope then up the other side without mishap. It was an outstanding manoeuvre that Gehlen had been secretly practicing for weeks. Anger was not amused but von Manstein beamed his approval. He was so impressed that he ordered similar feats of bravado must be practiced by other squadrons to be performed whenever foreign visitors were present at German military parades. After this, Gehlen's promotion to major with effect from 1 March 1939 was little more than routine.

When the Munich Agreement fell apart, the occupation of Bohemia and Moravia followed on 15 March 1939 and two weeks later the Germans also occupied the area around Memel on the Baltic coast. Gehlen's position did not allow him to be informed of the intensive preparations that were taking place for the attack against Poland but when he was assigned to receive trainloads of Czech weapons that were pouring in to arm new regiments it was clear that military action was far from over. Gehlen was then assigned to Chief Quartermaster II Major General Friedrich Sixt von Arnim, the man responsible for training in the Army General Staff, where Gehlen met his adjutant, Captain Hans-Heinrich Worgitzky, who would later become one of his leading employees at the BND.

Chapter 2
THE WAR

'Without my intervention, from that point on my life took a turn towards the unique and extraordinary.'

Reinhard Gehlen[1]

Poland and Fall Gelb

Mobilisation ahead of the expected attack against Poland saw Gehlen given the job of setting up an intelligence section of the new 213th Infantry Division at Glogau in August 1939. This gave him scope to employ his organisational talents to a much greater degree. He was fortunate in that many of his men had seen service before in the First World War but few of them were familiar with modern intelligence practices. There was little time to bring the division up to combat readiness, but Gehlen tackled the problem with his customary flair and moved his section into Poland as part of the German 10th Army on 3 September 1939 getting as far as Łódź in the first week without coming under fire. Being held mostly in reserve, the division saw little fighting and had what Gehlen later called 'a comfortable' time, which was not exactly what he wanted. He would have preferred to have been more in the main action to gain combat experience. By the end of the month, the division was in the Posen area acting in the role of an occupation force but still Gehlen received the Iron Cross, second class, on 2 October 1939, which was little more than a routine decoration for his four-week frontline probationary period and a few days later he returned to his General Staff post as head of the fortifications department under General Alfred Jacob. Through his important work, he was now coming into regular contact with men at the very top of the German High Command and he was impressing them with his grasp of detail and ability to express himself clearly. His appetite for hard work and long hours saw him still at his desk hours after conferences had dispersed to the refreshment lounge. The next day his reports would be a model of clarity that encapsulated the decisions of the previous day but, often, in ways that reflected his own slant on the issues. It was a very effective way of influencing powerful men without them knowing it and, importantly, in ways that would not reflect on him or bring him into the limelight. It was this efficiency and his ability to get to the heart of issues rather than his quiet manipulations that saw his reputation grow and which would bring him promotion to lieutenant colonel on 1 July 1941.

Hitler wanted to turn west and immediately subdue the French so allowing him to move further east without having to worry about a two-front war. Understandably, his General Staff were horrified by the idea, given that they had no operational plan for such an eventuality. The French Maginot Line was thought impregnable and the political consequences of an advance through the Low Countries were barely worth thinking about, but Hitler was determined that an attack should take place on 7 November 1939. It was a logistical impossibility, of course, and eventually he was persuaded to postpone it but only for a few weeks. A hurried plan was drawn up to attack through Aachen via Liège to northern France. Halder sent Gehlen to act as liaison officer to the German 4th Army, which was stationed on the border with Belgium at Eupen and Malmedy. This suggested that he could expect to play a central role in the attack.

It was an indication of Halder's growing respect for and reliance on Gehlen that, as part of his responsibilities, he, a mere artillery major with no experience of construction, had been sent to inspect and report on the west wall defences. Impressed by Gehlen's report at the end of January and confident in his ability to manage the extra workload, Halder then requested that Gehlen perform the same function along Germany's eastern border with the Soviet Union, which now ran down the centre of Poland. An attack by the Soviets was thought most unlikely, given the Molotov-Ribbentrop Pact but it was certainly not beyond the realms of possibility, so fortifications to prepare for such an eventuality had to be at least planned even if not actually constructed along the Vistula. In the west, the prospect of a stalled offensive and the emergence of a war of position meant that here, also, contingency plans had to be made for a fortified defensive line. After six weeks of intense activity Gehlen produced his report on the eastern and a further report on the western borders that were both received with much praise. After this point, Gehlen's name began to crop up with increasing frequency in Halder's war diary.

In occupied Poland, Gehlen was developing his acumen at navigating politically treacherous waters. Most Wehrmacht resources were being deployed in the west to prepare for the attack there but Gehlen argued strongly for more manpower to fortify the Narew-Vistula-San line with the increasing probability of the fragile German-Soviet peace agreement breaking down. Himmler suggested using more than 2 million Jewish forced labourers to dig anti-tank ditches, which precipitated long and heated debates about responsibility for the work. Gehlen would have been keenly aware that Himmler's plan would result in the death of many thousands of Jewish slave workers forced to work beyond endurance but he, like the rest of the High Command had no wish to get involved in another battle with Hitler and his newly installed governor general of Poland, Hans Frank, and simply backed off leaving the SS to supervise the work. Leaving the 'dirty work' to the SS, however, would prove to be no more than a temporary measure in the face of the growing power struggle between the SS and the Wehrmacht over control of German military strategy.

The attack against France and the Low Countries was postponed again and again and again over the winter months as arguments raged between Hitler and his General Staff. When it was eventually launched on 10 May 1940, Gehlen was assigned to work under Army Chief of Staff of 16th Army on the Luxembourg front General Walter Model. This force was covering the left flank of the Kleist Panzer Group, which included the XIX Panzer Corps led by the headstrong Heinz Guderian, the arch proponent of mobile warfare. As it happened, Gehlen and Guderian would become close friends and work closely together during the later stages of Operation Barbarossa.

Model's force was a crucial pivot for other armies to the north and south and it was vital that it did not race too far ahead. Guderian, who had so impressed Hitler with his theories of *Blitzkrieg* warfare, was not an easy man to restrain, however. His breakthrough at Sedan after only three days completely destroyed the cohesion of French defences forcing Allied armies into a hasty retreat all along the battle front. Guderian's subsequent race to the Channel coast, cutting off the British Expeditionary Force and Allied armies in Flanders was a military master stroke that impressed Gehlen greatly. Guderian had annoyed Halder during the Flanders advance by deliberately delaying his reports because he knew that if he was giving an up to date assessment of where he was and Halder knew just how far he had stuck his neck out, he would have been immediately ordered to halt and he had no intention of doing that. Gehlen embedded himself with Guderian's

Panzers on their subsequent crossing of the river Seine and their drive towards the Swiss border before the French surrender on 22 June 1940.

Halder had been disappointed by the performance of his adjutant Captain Heinrich Eduard Nolte during the French campaign and replaced him with the ever impressive Gehlen who had proved himself to be an efficient liaison with Guderian whom everyone considered difficult to deal with. Halder's relationship with Gehlen was said to be 'open and comradely' and Gehlen became an indispensable assistant to the general. His boss spoke to him candidly and without reservation. Years later, Gehlen would describe 'a close fatherly friendship'.[2]

Operation Barbarossa

> The main psychological problem was the traditional lack of regard for the military intelligence branch, particularly for intelligence procurement. I was originally not entirely innocent myself in this regard.
>
> Reinhard Gehlen[3]

Despite having no official brief to do so, Halder now turned his attention to planning the attack against the Soviet Union. Gehlen was involved at every level especially given the work he had done on eastern fortifications. During the planning stages, he was to come across the man whose place he would take some twenty months later, Lieutenant Colonel Eberhard Kinzel, head of the FHO. Gehlen's star was now clearly in the ascendent since Halder chose to take him to the Berghof on 13 July 1940 when Halder laid before Hitler his plans for the invasion of the Soviet Union.

Gehlen's burgeoning reputation, however, brought increased responsibility and an ever-expanding workload when, in October 1940, Halder put him in charge of the *Ostgruppe* (Group East) in the operations department where, under Heusinger, who had been promoted to colonel, he would assume joint responsibility for the development of one of the largest undertakings in the history of war. His particular responsibility was overall strategy in the eastern area and the south-east area north of the river Danube where he worked under Generaloberst Friedrich von Paulus who would go on to command the German 6th Army at Stalingrad. This included the deployment and transportation of reserves along with the drawing up of dividing lines between the advancing army groups. It was a key position offering immense potential for career advancement. A measure of his importance was that Gehlen was one of only nine people who received a copy of Hitler's

Directive No. 21, dated 18 December 1940, calling for preparations for an attack against the Soviet Union to be ready by 15 May 1941. The guiding principles of the attack were to destroy the Red Army

> by deeply penetrating armoured spearheads and the erection of a barrier on the general line Volga-Arkhangelsk followed by elimination of industrial areas in the Urals by the Luftwaffe.[4]

Heusinger, only five years older than Gehlen took to him immediately describing him in a confidential report as

> All that a staff officer should be. Far above average in personality, ability, and industry. Of pronounced operational ability and capable of thinking ahead.[5]

Gehlen, in return, had great respect for Heusinger and would later find temporary accommodation for him in his organisation after the war enabling him to make a fresh start and become inspector general in the Bundeswehr (armed forces of the Federal Republic of Germany) in 1956.

Gehlen's experience of working on the Vistula defences now stood him in good stead and it was at this point that his intelligence career started to take on a character that reflected his own personality. He gathered around himself a secret, selected staff of mostly young officers of low rank to collect and evaluate intelligence quite separate from Canaris's Abwehr. Within a week he furnished a delighted Halder with a document entitled *Draft of Transportation and Logistics for Barbarossa*. He then went to Bucharest and, without giving too much away about German intentions, discussed with Romanian military authorities the extent to which they could be relied upon to support the German army if it moved into the Balkans. Working at a frantic pace, Gehlen drew up plans for the occupation of northern Greece to be followed by an attack against Yugoslavia, all of which would be a prelude to the attack against the Soviet Union. Within three weeks, Halder was reading Gehlen's final report on preparations for the Balkan campaign, Operation Marita. By 12 May 1941, the Panzers had smashed through Hungary, Romania and Greece and were poised to drive into the Russian Steppes. As a token of thanks, Hitler sent Gehlen a leather-bound copy of *The Life of Frederick the Great* inscribed 'for your excellent work.'[6]

In early June 1941, as preparations for Operation Barbarossa intensified, arrangements had been made to take advantage of the intelligence opportunities that would present themselves once the attack went in. It was assumed that it would become easier to establish agent networks and this, together with interrogation of PoWs and analysis of captured documents, would yield a great deal more information requiring rapid assessment and analysis. Unfortunately, the German capacity for carrying out detailed evaluation, especially of documents, was never developed to a sufficiently high standard to derive maximum benefit.[7]

The first phase of Operation Barbarossa went well and Halder took Gehlen on an inspection tour of Field Marshal Fedior von Bock's Army Group North in Smolensk. Here, on 22 July 1941, Gehlen met Hitler in person and was presented by him with the Gold Cross of Merit with Swords and allowed the honour of attending one of the Führer's conferences.

The Red Army had been generally perceived by the German High Command as a 'colossus of clay'; clumsy, incapable of operational initiative at all command levels, habituated to mechanical military planning and operational conduct, and in general unprepared to wage modern warfare. The general consensus was that it would collapse under a swift, strong blow from the outside.[8] Up to this point, FHO had seen no reason to disabuse OKH of that notion. By Christmas, however, it was an entirely different story. The German army had failed to achieve its main objective, which was the occupation of Moscow and it was facing a Russian winter in the open. Gehlen had not seen his wife and children for months.

Operation Barbarossa would later be shown to have serious flaws. Hitler had forbidden any active pre-invasion intelligence gathering against the Soviets or the infiltration of agents into the leadership in Moscow in order to avoid and risk of exposure, which would have been a huge embarrassment given the existing non-aggression treaty between the two countries.[9] It was thought, also, that after the great Moscow purges of many top military commanders, those left in charge were 'uneducated' and the mass of troops 'needless and dull'.[10] This proved to be a serious error. As a result, the strength and capabilities of the Red Army was consistently underestimated. Not only that but the lack of reconnaissance and intelligence gathering meant that the Germans had completely failed to notice that the Soviets had introduced the formidable T-34 tank into their ranks even though this had already been used in the Khalkin Gol campaign against the Japanese in summer 1939, but was not shown at military parades and had not been used in the Russo-Finnish 'Winter War' of 1939 to 1940.[11]

Much of the blame for the intelligence failures was placed on Kinzel whose removal Halder demanded saying he 'no longer meets my requirements'.[12] For months, Hitler and his generals had complained about the tardiness and ultimate inadequacy of his reports. Kinzel was an expert on east Europe but he was of the old school and had never really caught up with the new modern methods of intelligence gathering. Neither was he adept at inter-departmental intrigue and he found himself the object of Canaris's criticism as Canaris tried to undermine the FHO in his bid to have other departments of his Abwehr take it over. The FHO had been established, on 10 November 1938, as *12 Abteilung des Generalstabes des Heeres*, under *Oberquartiermeister IV* (O. Qu. IV) and from the start had been under Kinzel's control. It was given responsibility for the collection of statistical data and military and technical information and essentially answer the question that was always on the lips of the OKW; 'What is the enemy thinking and doing?' The Soviet Union had not been given much attention until 31 July 1940, when Hitler called on the General Staff to draw up preliminary plans for Operation Barbarossa when it shot up to the top of the agenda. The United States remained well down the agenda until even later. Up until the mid-1940s, the FHO had relied heavily on reports from agent and military attachés in Moscow and Helsinki, *Abteilung Fremde Luftwaffe Ost* (aerial reconnaissance) and *Leitstelle fur Nachrichtenaufklärung Ost* (signals reconnaissance), and merely passed on the information to the *Operationsabteilung* of the General Staff for analysis. Even Kinzel's own staff complained that their

> knowledge of Soviet Russian weapons and armaments [was] extraordinarily sketchy.[13]

Some like General Alfred Jodl seemed content with the FHO output but Major Heinz Hiemenzof of Group II was candid and decidedly unimpressed when he said

> *Die Masse des Nachrichten-materials, das wir erhielten, war Mist.* [The bulk of the news material we received was crap.][14]

At the start of 1941, Kinzel had very little idea of what was going on in the Soviet Union. His estimate of army manpower was well below the actual figure and his analysis of their distribution proved to be seriously wrong. The High Command desperately needed someone who could provide solid facts and analyses instead of Kinzel's superficial assessments. The challenges facing the German High Command towards the end of 1941 were immense. Should they adopt a defensive posture and build up reserves now that the Soviet counterattack had taken them by surprise, or should they bow to pressure from Hitler to launch a new offensive in the Caucasus? They certainly did not have the resources to resume the offensive on the entire front. There was an urgent need for information about the Red Army's potential forces and operational capabilities.

Hoping to take advantage of Kinzel's plummeting reputation, Canaris had given the chief of *Abteilung III b*, a typical old-fashioned Prussian despite his Italian name, Colonel Franz Eccard 'Benti' von Bentivegni, authority to set up three highly mobile FAK forward reconnaissance groups on the Eastern Front. These infiltrated spies into the Soviet lines to set up radio outposts and opened camps to interrogate prisoners of war. The counterespionage aspect of FAKs work was taken up with detection and apprehension of Soviet agents. Maps were drawn at regular intervals showing the location and concentration of enemy agent incursions along with their mission details. This density map was a good indicator of forthcoming enemy operations.

FAKs were not the only challenge to Kinzel. Under an agreement with Canaris in March 1942, which gave it legal standing, Himmler had also reached out and established his own SS reconnaissance and intelligence operations in Russia under the 'university-educated intellectual gangster' SS-Brigadenführer Walter Schellenberg's *Amt VI*.[15] Schellenberg's boss, Heydrich, piled on the pressure by forcing Canaris to agree that 'Counterintelligence shall in future be an additional function of the Security Police and SD.'[16] It was a concession that progressively weakened the Abwehr's standing vis-à-vis the SD and would prove to be the first act leading to Canaris's downfall in 1944. Himmler's right-hand-man was Heydrich, and it was he who had told Dr Albert Filbert that foreign intelligence would no longer rely on 'newspapers and radio news' and he would only accept reports 'acquired through direct intelligence work'.[17] This was threatening to turn into a three-way intelligence turf war between Canaris, Schellenberg and Kinzel, which would have serious detrimental effects on any intelligence gathering and evaluation going forward especially with Himmler's insidious influence growing inexorably. When Heusinger recommended that Halder find a replacement for Kinzel, who was now slipping into a personal miasma of despair, Halder was in no doubt that Gehlen was the man to defend the position of FHO but the head of the Army Personnel Office Major General Bodewin Keitel would take some persuading.

Gehlen would later say that, up until this point, there was

> little ... that would distinguish my career from that of a thousand other General Staff officers.[18]

He was certainly no expert in military intelligence and did not even speak Russian. He was, however, highly thought of as an outstanding officer who had been thoroughly trained in all fields and was supremely capable of quickly familiarising himself with new situations. Any possibility of replacing Kinzel, however, was abruptly put on hold when, in mid-January, Gehlen, after months of incessant sixteen-hour working days under extreme pressure took their toll, was admitted to Reserve Hospital in Karlsbad for urgent treatment to his damaged gallbladder. He remained *hors de combat* for a month.

When Gehlen returned to active duty, he was certainly not short of admirers. Heusinger pushed hard for his appointment to replace Kinzel by describing him as

> a modest, likeable personality. Very ambitious. Fully proven before the enemy. A general staff officer who is far above average and has exceptional operational talent, forward thinking and a passion for the tasks assigned to him that is rarely found. Commits himself to his work to the limit of his ability.

Halder chipped in with his own addendum to the assessment by saying that Gehlen

> Combines excellent technical skills and unusual work ability with strong creative power and soldierly drive. Created for leading positions in the general staff.[19]

Chief of OKW Keitel eventually agreed and Kinzel was dismissed to be replaced by Gehlen on 1 April 1942 three days before his fortieth birthday. Gehlen had arrived. The trouble for him was that he knew very little about intelligence work at this stage of his career and he would have to learn quickly because commensurate with his appointment was the transformation of the FHO from a purely statistical organisation to a fully operational department of the General Staff and the *Operationsabteilung* (operations department) of the OKH. This gave Gehlen authority to make judgements in relation to planned German offensives and *Feindlagebeurteilung* (enemy situation assessments). The FHO was tasked with the processing and evaluation of data into statistical intelligence concerning the Red Army to produce a general estimate for OKH of the enemy situation, capabilities and intentions on the Eastern Front.

Gehlen would later claim that it had never been his ambition to become a 'spy'. Traditionally, the Abwehr was looked upon with disdain and paid little attention to by the German General Staff who tended to rely on their own in-house intelligence officers. For a career-minded officer, it appeared to be very much a dead end but when the call came, Gehlen could not refuse and he met the challenge with characteristic determination and total commitment. As a new man with few qualifications for the post, he immediately saw that he would need to work extremely hard to get the OKH to take his department seriously especially after the way it had scorned Kinzel. His first act was to address the whole personnel of the FHO and make it quite clear to them that things were going to be very different going forward and he emphasised to them that in future they would be operating under a cloak of strict secrecy. He saw no benefit in keeping Kilzel on for a transitional period, and after a week, he made it clear to him that his presence was no longer required.

Kinzel had allowed his FHO staff to become too set in their ways and Gehlen saw that new men had to be brought in without delay to quickly create a new ethos. All existing section heads were replaced by younger men of high intellectual ability, initiative and drive mostly from outside the organisation but those who had only recently joined and had shown promise and had not yet had been subdued by the heavy hand of tradition were given a chance to impress. One such was Captain Gerhard Wessel, a 'reserved, impenetrable personality' who, like Gehlen, had been trained as an artilleryman and had little previous intelligence experience. Gehlen considered him to be 'ideologically sound [and] suitable for [a] command position.'[20]

Other potential leaders, such as Major Heinz Danko Herre, were brought in from outside the FHO to fill senior posts. Herre was also an avid horseman, which was an immediate boon to his relationship with Gehlen but it was his extensive knowledge of the Soviet Union that had made him one of the Abwehr's leading Soviet experts. Wessel and Herre would remain working with Gehlen throughout the war and well beyond.

The tall, athletic Herre, a fluent Russian speaker, was appointed Gehlen's senior staff officer and Gehlen introduced a new three-part structure for the FHO's Russian department. Wessel was put in charge of *Führungsgruppe I* with Captain Albert Schoellner as his deputy and given responsibility for *Lage-Bearbeitunge* (daily situation reports), situation maps, and statistics, which included the daily haul of Soviet prisoners. Herre took on *Führungsgruppe II (Russland/Militarische Gesamtlage)* to evaluate secret reports and maintain an up-to-date assessment of the Soviet Union's capacity to wage war. *Führungsgruppe II* reported on the economic and military potential of the Soviet Union and evaluated the strategy and operational intentions of the Stavka (Soviet High Command). It collected information from press and radio, *Nachrichtenaufklärung* (communications intercepts), prisoner reports, for which there was a special branch 'Albert', *Bandenlage* (Soviet partisans), and captured enemy documents. Based on interrogation of Soviet prisoners of war, a Soviet order of battle was complied with details of unit histories, equipment, personnel, casualty rate and battle readiness. This group maintained the main card index containing everything known about Soviet formations and Red Army officers from divisional commander upwards.[21] Herre gathered information from other agencies and kept permanent files which would go on to form the basis of Gehlen's post-war organisation.

Führungsgruppe III was under the authority of Lieutenant Colonel Alexis Freiherr von Rönne but, in practice, run by Captain Ernest Petersen. It was a somewhat dissolute rabble of Russian experts, mostly Baltic Germans, whose operational efficiency, fortunately, belied their reputation. Von Rönne was responsible for translating propaganda materials, captured documents, radio broadcasts and press articles. The latter would often include the names of meritorious commanders and their units after major battles had taken place, information that was important for knowledge of the Soviet order of battle.

Von Rönne was a man of deep Christian belief and 'superior air of a schoolmaster addressing pupils on a matter that was far beyond their comprehension', the tall, fair-haired bespectacled von Rönne performed his duties in a way, which he felt helped to thwart Nazi ambitions.[22] It is believed that, on occasions, he deliberately promoted what he knew to be false intelligence in ways that favoured the Western Allies. One such instance was where he was instrumental in persuading OKH to fall for Operation Mincemeat, the plan to deceive them over the Allied landings in Sicily. He would later ally himself with the failed Claus von Stauffenberg plot to assassinate Hitler and he was hanged in Plötzensee Prison on 12 October 1944.

Von Rönne had been one of Kinzel's men whom Gehlen not only kept in place but promoted to head a new department, *Dolmetschergruppe und Unterlagenbeschaf*, designated *Führungsgruppe*. This unit dealt with the Soviet economy, trying to make daily assessments of its industrial resources and output and determining Soviet military and industrial strategy as well as the Soviet Union political and social developments especially in occupied zones.[23]

From this, Gehlen compiled reports for distribution within the OKH (*Gesamt Beurteilungen der Feindlag*) about Soviet strength, deployment, organisation and defences. With a small army of translators, he was also tasked with monitoring Stalin's relationship with his Western allies, especially the US. His department covered such a wide remit, becoming almost a miniature foreign office, that Rönne became probably the most important operative in the FHO. It was he who liaised with the Abwehr and ensured smooth relations with Heinrich Himmler, Joachim von Ribbentrop and Alfred Rosenberg, which he managed with some difficulty given his anti-Nazi sympathies. Two signals intelligence offices shared information on reconnaissance with *Fremde Luftwaffe Ost* (FHO – German Air Force Intelligence) and *Leitstelle für Nachrichetenaufklärung Ost* (OKH – Signals Intelligence).

Gehlen now consulted all the army personnel departments looking for men to fill the ranks of the rapidly expanding Soviet sections, especially those who might have experience of living in or working with the Soviets over the previous decade. The requirement to speak Russian meant that often he would draft in civilians. It mattered little to Gehlen whether these men were fiercely pro-Nazi or non-enthusiasts like Wessel and Herre as long as they met the criteria for the job. He he undertook to improve FHO analysis and estimates by bringing in standardised procedures for the continuous, systematic collection and evaluation of intelligence about the Soviet order-of-battle, troop movements and deployments and organisation down to the level of unit strength, casualties and equipment losses.[24]

The whole of FHO was revitalised in a number of sweeping initiatives. Situation reports were updated more frequently to maintain a continuously up-to-date assessment of the enemy's position. Aerial reconnaissance reports were sent in by telephone and Gehlen arranged with Canaris to have closer liaison with front-line reconnaissance units called *Walli*. As a means of presenting his intelligence reports to OKH in a more dramatic fashion, Gehlen made use of coloured maps showing enemy positions and recent movements. Often blocks of colour would vary in size according to the concentration of forces. It was a startling innovation and one that immediately caught the attention and approval of his superiors.

Walli

> The enemy intelligence expert, especially in the higher echelons, had to think with two brains at once if he was to perform his assignment properly. It was not enough to know the precise military units and equipment opposing him, he had to be able to forecast the enemy's intentions.
>
> Reinhard Gehlen[25]

The German intelligence services consisted of the Abwehr (military intelligence and counterintelligence) run by Admiral Canaris, and the *Sicherheitsdienst* (SD) under the control of Heinz Jost until March 1942 when it was taken over by Walter Schellenberg. *Amt VI* (foreign intelligence desk) was the SD component of the *Reichssicherheitshautamt* (RSHA – State Security Main Office) of the SS.

Frontline intelligence networks, called *Walli,* were set up from *Abteilung I*'s eastern groups to head up Abwehr's participation in Operation Barbarossa. *Walli I,* under Major Hermann Baun. A 'short, thin, chain-smoking ex-infantryman',[26] Baun had been born in the Black Sea port of Odesa and grew up speaking Ukrainian, Russian, English and French and was Canaris's foremost Russian expert. He was responsible for espionage, sabotage and counterintelligence with forward headquarters, *Befehlstab Walli,* at Sulejówek near Warsaw. This was described as an 'invisible army' of agents trained in Abwehr camps in preparation for deployment in the Soviet Union ahead of the armed forces. Schools for training Russian *Walli* agents were opened in January 1942 and began recruiting volunteers, mostly former Red Army officers or captured young radio operators, from among Soviet PoWs. A course lasted between six and twelve months, and students spent ten hours a day in classes. As students graduated, they were dropped in the Red Army rear, frequently dressed in Red Army uniforms to contact local informers and interrogate PoWs collecting military and economic intelligence at the Soviet-German front.[27]

Walli I was broken down into *Frontaufkldrungsleitstellen I, II* and *III,* four *Frontaufklrungs-kommandos* (FAKs) and the twelve *Frontaufkldrungstrupps* (FATs). FAKs and FATs would carry out reconnaissance in occupied Russian territory and up until mid-1942 proved to be one of the best sources of operational intelligence. After that time, however, they became increasingly overrun by the sheer numbers of Soviet counterespionage groups. It has been estimated that there were well over 100,000 trained Soviet agents working behind German lines.

In charge of *Walli II* was Major Seeliger, an 'irregular warfare' specialist who would be killed by Soviet partisans in 1943. *Walli II* sent motorised columns deep behind Soviet lines to carry out sabotage, subversion, and reconnaissance missions. The broken nature of the frontline meant that infiltration was comparatively easy. An OKW directive to *Walli II* demanded that they 'promote rivalries and hatred between the various peoples of the Soviet Union'. Typical of *Walli II* assignments were securing bridges just before the German attack, sabotaging telephone and telegraph cables, electricity and water supplies, and reporting the locations, operations, and movements of Soviet troops.

Lieutenant Colonel Heinz Schmalschläger's *Walli III* was an *Einsatzkommando* unit operating behind enemy lines concentrating on capturing Soviet documents. Numbering some 500 men, they were subdivided into 5 groups. In small groups, which included Abwehr officers, translators and radio operators, they moved with the troops, often even ahead of them with the forward tank units. *Stab Walli* received intelligence and counterintelligence materials from these operational units in the field and, after a preliminary evaluation, sent the materials Abwehr headquarters in Berlin and to the FHO. The most important success of *Walli III* in 1941 was the acquisition of a relatively complete picture of the Soviet intelligence and security services based on captured documents and the interrogation of captured Soviet agents and intelligence officers.

The most valuable source of *Walli* intelligence on the Soviet order of battle was *Nachrichtenaufklärung* (signals intelligence). This was vital for the understanding of grouping of Soviet forces and the interrelationships within the chain of command. Vital breakthroughs were made by unbuttoning the Soviet ciphers and the use of *Funkpeilung* (radio direction finding). German cryptanalysts were also able to break some NKVD, railways and shipping codes but Soviet signals security was significantly improved after 1942 restricting the scope of surveillance. The Red Army also quickly learned to impose strict radio silence before major offensives. Nevertheless, signals intelligence remained the basic source of all FHO estimates of the enemy situation. Then came *Funkaufklärung* (radio reconnaissance) and *Drahtaufklärung* (telephone reconnaissance) for tactical intelligence. Radio intelligence was variously described as 'the most important means for clarifying the enemy picture', 'the darling of all intelligence' and 'the most copious and best source of intelligence'.[28] As the contribution of aerial reconnaissance was reduced, so signals reconnaissance took on a more critical role with increased training of specialists and more sophisticated equipment. Techniques were rapidly improved through experience. The two most important lessons learned were firstly to spread intercept stations over as wide an area as possible and then bring all the information together quickly at high level headquarters to get an overall picture before disseminating its evaluation to the various commands. Gehlen arranged with Canaris to have *Walli I* and *II* reporting their intelligence directly to FHO to speed up its exploitation but on the clear understanding that he would not interfere in any way with their operations.

The cream of Gehlen's new recruits went into *Führungsgruppe I* that was now split into three sections to correspond with the three army groups active on the Eastern Front. Each head of section was required to produce daily situation maps, based on *Luftaufklärung* (aerial reconnaissance), showing changes in enemy forces. After signals intelligence, *Eisenbahnaufklärung* (railway reconnaissance) and *Strassenaufklärung* (road reconnaissance) were the agencies that FHO most relied on. While *Luftaufklärung* could reveal only part of the enemy's activity at any one time it had the distinct advantage of being completely up to date and was usually the starting point for evaluation of intelligence from other sources. Aerial photographs provided data on troop movements, tank assembly areas, artillery positions and the location of forward airfields. Its disadvantage, of course, was weather and its weakness was interdiction by enemy aircraft. The two other limiting factors were shortage of suitable Luftwaffe reconnaissance aircraft and the growing aptitude of the Red Army for camouflage and concealment of its forces. After the first few disastrous months of Operation Barbarossa, the Soviets perfected night transportation of troops, which again reduced opportunities for monitoring strategic and tactical manoeuvres.

Another of the innovations Gehlen introduced was a significantly expanded questionnaire to be employed when interrogating prisoners of war at a *Vernehmungslager* (special centre). Previously the single page document had asked for name, rank, regiment, division and information about movements prior to capture. Now prisoners were grilled about their home life, civilian employment, training, chain of command, location of ammunition dumps, fuel depots and extent of casualties. Although background was still recorded, intelligence gathered with the new questionnaire was of a more tactical nature and could be put to immediate use on the battlefield.[29]

With some urgency, Gehlen put his people under constant pressure to realise his ambition for a new invigorated organisation that produced 'a picture of the enemy even more comprehensive than mere duty requires'.[30] New instructions were issued almost on a daily basis with Gehlen's own frenetic work rate setting the pace for all the others. Every single report was to be graded as either reliable, credible, possible, questionable or improbable.

For his first few weeks in office, Gehlen had no choice but to rely on evaluation reports that Kinzel's staff had prepared. In March 1942, Kinzel had reported

> Only a meagre reserve is available over and above the [Soviet] armed forces already existing.[31]

Gehlen felt the pressure after only days into his new role when he reported that

> Russian forces at the front have suffered so severely from battle wastage and the weather that scarcely a single formation can be described as fully battle-worthy.[32]

In his first major assessment, *Evaluation of the Total Enemy Situation and Its Possibilities of Development*,[33] on 1 May 1942, Gehlen was still forced to base his report on somewhat flimsy intelligence that he had not had time to substantiate. Nothing he had learned so far allowed him to make a new assessment of Soviet leadership intentions, so he played it safe by saying that

> there are no signs of a major operation with far-reaching objectives yet.

It was way off the mark, and it would not be long before he was proved wrong.[34]

Even though the report is considered to be a masterful discussion of the enemy's theoretically conceivable options, FHO reconnaissance had completely failed to detect Soviet reserves concentrated between the Caspian Sea and Moscow. Therefore, it was a total surprise when, eleven days after he submitted that report, Marshal Semyon K. Tymoshenko broke out from the Izyum 'bulge' to make a pre-emptive strike north and south of the strategically important Kharkov communications hub with 12 infantry divisions and 300 tanks in a ferocious attack that threatened to decimate von Paulus's 6th Army. Within two days, the Soviet armies broke through to the south and north-east of Kharkov. Unfortunately, based on flawed intelligence about German strength, Tymoshenko delayed the second phase of his attack. This had crucially allowed the Germans to call up massive air support to strike just as the first wave of Tymoshenko's attack was subsiding. General Major Fyedor M. Kharitonov's 9th Army was hit so hard that the German forces were able to almost totally surrounded it and the Soviet offensive collapsed just four days after its start. Stalin ordered the second wave to go in but they not only failed to breach the German lines, they also failed to prevent von Paulus counterattacking and completing the encirclement of Kharitonov's force. By 28 May 1942, the Germans had taken some 250,000 Soviet prisoners and were able to start their own offensives in the Crimea, capturing the fortress of Sevastopol. Despite the near disaster of the Kharkov attack, OKH wase still basing its plans, to some extent, on Kinzel's historic, unsound assessments.

The turnaround in fortunes brought about by von Paulus and Gehlen's short time in place had to some extent saved him from criticism but the seriously flawed report of 4 May 1942 was clear proof that reorganisation of FHO had to be accelerated. Gehlen was again working himself almost to the point of exhaustion and exacerbating his stomach problems but he was given no respite. In fact, his workload was further increased after Hitler's furious rant against Gehlen's equivalent at *Frende Heere West* (FHW), Colonel Ulrich Liss, for his failure to provide him with up-to-date intelligence about the United States. Liss was generally considered to be a first class intelligence officer but Hitler was incensed by the lack of information about the United States' war potential. It had hardly been part of Liss's brief up until the time of the Japanese attack on Pearl Harbor and Hitler's subsequent declaration of war against the US. Indeed, Hitler had shown little interest in the US at all until then but when he did, Liss had disappointed him.

The US counterintelligence agencies had been virtually non-existent until the exposure of the Griebl-Lonkowski spy ring in 1938 and only slowly thereafter acquired the necessary powers to deal with foreign agents. By 1942, however, things had changed and infiltration of espionage agents into the United States became something of a farce. The best they could do was Operation Pastorius, which had seen eight spies landed by U-boat in June 1942, only to find themselves in US custody within days. It was the complete failure of this elaborately planned operation, which had enraged Hitler and had him looking around for someone to blame.

It was around the same time that Halder had called Gehlen a 'born leader' in a document that had caught Hitler's eye and he asked for all reports concerning the US to be prepared by FHO henceforth. Gehlen probably knew less about the subject than Liss but he wasn't going to let that stop him giving Hitler what he wanted. He gave Halder a bulky report on US strength and strategic intentions including shipping tonnage available for transporting troops to Europe, the latter confirming his view that the Western Allies would be unable to open a second front for at least twelve months.

Having been appointed to the task by Hitler personally, there could be no resistance when Gehlen called for a number of Liss's staff to be assigned to FHO. Von Rönne was given responsibility for intelligence about the United States but once the furore over Operation Pastorius had died down, Hitler seemed to lose interest. When Liss was reassigned to a regimental command on the Eastern Front, Gehlen saw a chance to unburden himself somewhat of the US responsibilities by arranging for von Rönne to take over FHW completely.

On 30 June 1942, Gehlen was invited to Halder's birthday celebrations held in an atmosphere of quiet confidence about the campaign in the east. Even Hitler turned up to present Halder with a signed picture, which was poor reward when he had been anticipating promotion to field marshal.

Of course, Gehlen could see that any report he presented to the High Command, which could have significant impact upon the course of the campaign was based on somewhat flimsy intelligence. When he delivered his June 1942 appreciation it is clear that the Kharkov debacle had taught him an important lesson in presentation. He had learned to give what appeared to be an optimistic evaluation but one cloaked in caveats that were not always obvious but which could be referred to later if operations did not go well.

> It is clear that the enemy has suffered major losses in the defeats of these last twelve months. The fighting so far has shown the German soldier to be justified in feeling he is superior to the enemy, and we have seen that *where an assault is launched in force*, success is guaranteed. But the enemy's numerical superiority in manpower and equipment *must not be underestimated*. If we are to carry the impending operations in the East through to final victory, *we shall have to make a supreme effort*. [Author's italics.][35]

It was much easier to re-organise the FHO than it was to generate new and reliable sources of intelligence. Gehlen was confronted by historical constraints such as the low esteem in which intelligence work, generally, was held by OKH. This had starved it of resources. Much of what intelligence he had to work with he had to 'beg steal or borrow' from rival organisations the most accommodating of which proved to be the eastern desk of the Abwehr, run by Major Baun, who had intelligence officers with all frontline units sending back reports by radio. Gehlen found Baun's intelligence to be 'of considerable interest' but usually accompanied by poor evaluation. The Abwehr, as a whole, had no staff employed to analyse intelligence, it was circulated in its raw state to whomsoever seemed most likely to be interested in it and its usefulness depended solely on the judgement of its recipient.

Baun's *Walli I* operation had seen agents dropped behind enemy lines in the Baltics where results were encouraging as the region was quickly occupied in June and July 1941. The same cannot be said for operations further south along the main front, however. There were far too few agents to produce any worthwhile intelligence and the Abwehr was obliged to fall back on prisoner interrogation for the bulk of its information and this proved to be of little use for compiling all but the most superficial assessments. It was clear that more attention would have to be paid to developing sophisticated interrogation methods. As a result of these shortcomings, the OKH poured scorn on Baun's efforts but Gehlen, although never having total confidence in Baun, knew that Canaris had described him as having 'a special gift for intelligence work' and believed that *Walli I* had the potential to form the basis of a new agency capable of being modified to serve a vital role for FHO and one that might be able to divert it from its current path leading it to a place of irrelevance.[36]

Baun was essentially a disorganised man governed more by emotional intelligence rather than logic or military discipline. It was a flaw that Gehlen noted and would later exploit to his advantage.

He saw that Baun had suffered a humiliating blow and he gave him an opportunity to salvage his reputation. Unhappy at losing his 'Russian expert' but knowing that he might be made better use of elsewhere, Canaris reluctantly agreed to the transfer of Baun to FHO where he set up a new headquarters in Vinniytsia in central Ukraine. The FHO was now effectively run by four men, Gehlen, Wessel, Herre and Baun who would go on to be the founding members of the BND in 1956. Baun accepted the challenge with enthusiasm. Like Gehlen he was a reclusive, secretive man known personally to only a few inside FHO. With Gehlen's encouragement he revitalised *Walli I* with new agents, new training methods, and new equipment.

At the same time Gehlen had to meet the expectations of the Chiefs of Staff without coming into direct conflict with Hitler's directives, certainly no mean feat on its own. As befitting someone who had just been elevated to a position of great importance, he adopted a cautious approach when making assessments of the options available to the enemy and remained as reserved as possible when trying to anticipate which of them they would take. The question to which the High Command wanted an answer was whether or not the Red Army would be sufficiently replenished to withstand a major German offensive on the Eastern Front in spring 1943. Such an answer involved knowledge of Allied aid deliveries and whether the Soviet leadership would be able to get them in place on time.

The Max Organisation

> ...the events since mid-November ... have resulted from a sequence of basic command errors on our side as to whose extent and effect the military authorities were perfectly aware from the moment they were committed.
>
> Reinhard Gehlen[37]

Taking over at FHO, Gehlen was thrown in at the deep end. He had to come up with reliable figures and deployment of Soviet forces without delay. Meanwhile, Hitler was relying on a study that the OKW's Military Economics and Armaments Office had prepared about the military strength of the Soviet Union. In this study, the Soviet potential to manufacture aircraft, tanks, fighting vehicles and guns was based on economic data from 1938 concerning raw material imported into the Soviet Union. This meant that he was failing to take account of US aid that had started pouring in. The figures on which Hitler was basing his decision in 1942 underestimated Soviet military power in some areas by a factor of three. Intelligence was little better when available Soviet manpower was estimated on the basis of the 1939 census. Before quitting his office, Kinzel had predicted that, based on the losses they had suffered up to early 1942, the Red Army's performance would deteriorate, and its manpower reserves would be depleted to the extent that they would be unable to sustain any offensive before 1943. Halder, however, had no confidence in Kinzel's analysis and rejected it out of hand. He looked to Gehlen for more reliable intelligence but in the short time that Gehlen had been sitting at Kinzel's desk, he had not yet been able to come up with anything better. Kinzel had relied almost exclusively on intelligence reports from Abwehr agents in the field. Gehlen would change that but it would take time. After only days in post and based on Kinzel's evaluation, he produced an appreciation of enemy strength in which he said

> Russian forces at the front have suffered so severely from battle wastage and the weather that scarcely a single formation can be described as fully battle-worthy ... any counter-offensive on a broad front in the areas of Army Groups Centre and South is improbable.[38]

It would prove to be anything but a promising start.

Soon FHO would settle into an exhausting daily routine. All through the day, intelligence flowed in from all the army groups on the Eastern Front and would be analysed to create an overall picture of the day's events. Then, in conjunction with Abwehr Ic intelligence and counterintelligence officers, an assessment was made of the enemy's probable intentions for the following day. In the evening, there would be a conference in Gehlen's room when all the latest reports would be discussed around the map table. Each group leader would be invited to give his views and on the basis of that, Gehlen would produce a report which he took to the 10.00 hours daily meeting with Halder. Present at the meeting would be the heads of the operations FHO, organization, and rail transport branches, the quartermaster general, the chief of army signals and sometimes representatives of other branches. After each had made their report, Halder would decide on the orders and other measures to be issued. The next morning there would be a further situation conference in Gehlen's office to review reports that had come in overnight followed by a 10.00 hours situation conference with Halder who would then proceed to the midday conference at Wolfschanze, Hitler's headquarters. Gehlen only rarely met Hitler, he was of far too low rank for direct contact. There are only four recorded instances of him actually being called into the Führer's presence, the last of which was on 27 February 1945.

With efficiency and application that had come to typify Gehlen's performance, FHO produced a mass of detailed reports during his first months in charge. Mostly they were designed to provide frontline commanders with the most up-to-date intelligence and not particularly for the attention of the OKH but Gehlen would present a *Kurze Beurteilung der Feindlage* (brief estimate of the enemy situation) to the chief of the General Staff on a daily basis. On top of this he would produce a periodic *Zusammen-fassende Beurteilung der Feindlage* (comprehensive estimate of the enemy situation) in which the daily reports were amalgamated to make forecasts about the enemy's intentions and possibilities.

Much of this intelligence was incorporated into a series of booklets called *Surveys of the Formation, Composition and Distribution of the Red Army* based on the *Lage-Bearbeitunge*. There were also a number of comprehensive individual reports of subjects such as the Soviet defensive constructions to the east of Moscow that had been created in late 1941 in anticipation of the fall of the city to the Germans. While the majority of his reports pertained to immediate concerns, there were some that would have longer term value and play a role in Gehlen's post-war career. Examples of these were reports entitled *Characteristics of Higher Political and Military Leaders of the Soviet Union*, which included character sketches of Josef Stalin, Minister of Foreign Affairs Vyacheslav Molotov and Nikita Khrushchev, who would succeed Stalin as first secretary of the Soviet Union in 1953, and another called *The Red Army and the Peculiarities of its Structure, Leadership Principles and Method of Fighting*. One of the weightiest offerings was the meticulously detailed *Great Survey and Statistics of the Economy of the USSR*.

Gehlen was undoubtedly a brilliant and tireless organiser with a large number of sources of information, which he jealously protected and he efficiently managed a complex structure of responsibilities. His great communication skills gained for him a reputation for efficiency, which underlay his claim for having always made correct forecasts with *Fleiß, Gründlichkeit, Fachkenntnis und Schnelligkeit* (diligence, thoroughness, expertise and speed). It was only Hitler's *geheimnisvoll umwitterte Hexerei* (mysteriously shrouded witchcraft), Gehlen said, that prevented the OKH from taking full advantage of his output.

Reports from the front soon made it clear in the course of the summer offensive how far Kinzel's forecasts fell short of reality. Gehlen reported at the beginning of August 1942 that the Red Army had set up fifty-four new rifle divisions and fifty-six new tank divisions and its strength was steadily increasing. The numerical strength of the Red Army was estimated to be at least twice that of the Germans but German morale remained high on the assumption that German soldiers were much better trained and much more efficient.

Gehlen was a disappointment to Halder who expected more than daily reports about Red Army position and movements. The German's had seen plenty of evidence of the Red Army's ability to disguise its planned operations. It was not possible to make a judgement about Soviet intentions based solely on the position of its forces but Halder very badly needed more. The new German summer offensive was going to be limited to the southern wing of the Eastern Front and it would only succeed if the Red Army could be encircled and destroyed. Gehlen, however, was still hampered by the obsolete structure of his FHO.

He failed to interpret Soviet strategy in response to the German offensive in the Ukraine. Based on an agent report, he advised OKH that the Soviets would execute a massive, planned withdrawal movement to the river Volga as a result of the advance of Army Group South. They did carry out such a strategy but it was not a precipitate retreat forced upon them by the German attack. It was all part of a deliberate carefully planned Soviet strategy of in preparation for the defence of the Volga region. Rather than finding themselves facing a disorganised Soviet front disorientated by a sudden retreat, von Paulus's 6th Army would find itself up against a well-constructed and well-supported defence at Stalingrad.

On 1 July 1942, Gehlen had received intelligence from what he considered to be a reliable source, a Viennese Jew called Richard Kauder, a man

> of middle height, with a round face, well fed and well dressed ... who spent his nights in restaurants and cafes dining well and dating women.[39]

Born in Vienna in 1900 to Jewish parents, Kauder's early career had seen him working as a sports journalist, first in Zürich, Switzerland then Paris, France and finally Berlin, Germany. After the Nazis came to power he moved to Budapest where he honed his multifarious talents as a high-class pimp and procurer of documents such as residence permits and travel visas and as an unofficial foreign exchange dealer. Organising the latter two, which were especially important to members of the Jewish community, brought him to the attention of the US consul in Zagreb, Croatia, John J. Meily, with whom Kauder developed a shady business relationship. Meily was an avid collector of antique weapons and Kauder was able not only to point him in the direction of dealers but arrange for illicit currency exchanges so that he could purchase them. In this way Kauder inveigled himself into Meily's confidence sufficiently to be given special access to the US embassy in Zagreb. Not one to look a gift horse in the mouth, Kauder took advantage of this privilege by raiding Meily's personal and diplomatic files. This inevitably found him making arrangements with other agencies who were active in Budapest, especially the Abwehr and the SD.[40]

Kauder found himself in Vienna in 1941 where he was approached by an Austrian friend, Joseph Schultz, with a proposition to run a network of 'friends' he had in the Soviet Union who were willing to report on Soviet military movements. Kauder took the idea to Rudolf Graf von Marogna-Redwitz, the Abwehr chief in Vienna who passed it up the line to Berlin. Canaris approved the scheme and gave it the codename 'Klatt'. Kauder's Jewishness was less of an issue than it would have been in Germany and he was an uneasy fit into the intelligence community. Canaris protected him as best he could and set him up to operate independently of the main Abwehr station in Sofia run by Colonel Otto Wagner who, not surprisingly, viewed him with a jaundiced eye and took a hard look at his organisation.

Along with Ira Longin (Iliya Lang), a ex-White Russian Cossack officer and an ex-White Russian general Anton Turkul, Kauder established *Dienststelle I* or 'Klatt Bureau' in a villa in the central part of Sofia, Bulgaria in 1942. This is significant because Bulgaria was the only German ally that continued to have diplomatic relationships with the Soviet Union, a country that maintained a huge staff at the Soviet Embassy in Sofia including many political and military spies. Turkul claimed to control a fascist group of White Russian military emigrants in Europe and had his own intelligence network centred in Rome.

Kauder had taken over the running of Turkul's radio network codename 'Max'. This was said to consist of a network of wireless agents in the Red Army signals staff. Kauder told the Abwehr that the reports were collated in Russia at one or more centres and then transmitted via intermediaries to Istanbul and Samsun, Turkey, whence they were radioed to Sofia.

Wagner discovered that Kauder's radio communications with 'Max' were tortuously routed through Spain and Turkey rather than directly to Moscow and he was not impressed by Kauder's explanation that it was all subterfuge to avoid detection. Kauder would be in daily radio contact with Marogna-Redwitz but his communications were intercepted in December 1941 by British intelligence whose clear-eyed analysis of their content led them to suspect that Kauder was playing a double game.

Gehlen had no such doubts, however. He considered the 'Max' reports to have high value and used them liberally when presenting the OKH with his estimates of Soviet deployments. It was, perhaps, a measure of his inexperience in intelligence that he did so. Kauder came with excellent credentials and his apparent access to the Kremlin was probably too important to question for someone like Gehlen who had just been drafted in. At the time, Kauder's sources were believed to be a senior staff officer working at the front or army headquarters of the Red Army and a colonel in the Red Army signal troops. It was Wagner, finding himself in the shadow cast by Kauder' brilliance, who persisted with his scrutiny of the 'Max' set-up and went to Canaris and Marogna-Redwitz with his concerns. Kauder's intelligence seemed to be comprehensive and usually tallied with other sources but on close examination they showed a lack of detail and tended to be cloaked in generalisations. How was it, Wagner asked, that Kauder's Kremlin source was able to transmit extended radio reports without being detected. Anyone spending such an amount of time sending illicit signals in German territory, for instance, would be discovered very quickly. It was a bit of a turf war between Wagner and Marogna-Redwitz who insisted that the Luftwaffe rated Kauder's intelligence as first-class and vital to their operations and, they claimed, almost always proved to be accurate. It was a ringing endorsement and one that it was difficult to argue against, but a wary Canaris realised that although the 'Max' input was generally sound it added little to what was already known and, in fact, nothing much would be lost if it did not exist. He, himself, occasionally relied on 'Max' intelligence when briefing Hitler. Hedging his bets, he took Wagner aside after the meeting and advised him to keep an eye Kauder, but he was told definitely not to interfere with his work.

The story of Vladimir Vinishkiy (Minishkiy) is related to the 'Max' network and illustrates how difficult it is to differentiate between fact and fiction in the realms of intelligence. He was captured on

13 October 1941 by a unit of *Walli I* during the Battle of Vyazma and identified himself as a Red Army captain. After nine months in Luckenwalde PoW camp, he was interviewed by FHO officers and appeared to be a broken man worn down by captivity. He now identified himself as an undersecretary of the Soviet Central Committee who had later became a political commissar on the staff of Marshal Georgy Zhukov, which was when he was taken prisoner. Such men were a godsend to intelligence agencies. Gehlen had him brought to his headquarters at Angerburg and interviewed him personally. Vinishkiy seemed amenable to coercion and agreed to act as a spy (agent 438).

He was smuggled back into the battle lines where he gave himself up to the Soviets. His story of escape from German imprisonment seemed to satisfy the commander in the field and he was sent to Moscow where he gave the Soviets important 'intelligence' about conditions in the German occupied sector. This was highly unusual since it was generally the case that anyone who had been in German captivity was treated with contempt by the Soviets and Vinishkiy's avoidance of punishment is untypical It is frankly incomprehensible that FHO should take what happened next as truth.

Vinishkiy reported, through Kauder radio network, that he was subsequently assigned to a desk job at Stalin's Supreme Headquarters at which point he began sending intelligence back to FHO in what was called Operation Flamingo. His major coup was a report on a War Council meeting of 13 July 1942 between Soviet, British, US and Chinese delegates. The Red Army, he claimed would retreat to the river Volga with a 'scorched earth' strategy leaving a barren landscape behind them but would make a stand at Stalingrad. While much of the report proved to be accurate, Gehlen actually marked it 'fully credible', it contained little of real value to OKH and post-war analysis shows that details about persons reported to be present at the meeting were inaccurate in many respects.[41] Three months later, Gehlen engineered Vinishkiy's extraction from the Soviet Union and assigned him to *Walli II*. Very little about Vinishkiy's account rings true, however. Searches revealed no Alexander Vinishkiy or Alexander Minishkiy anywhere in Red Army records or in the Central Committee of the Soviet Union. The implication is that the story was fabricated to protect the real source of the Flamingo report which, at the time, was taken to be wholly accurate.

Kauder had clearly been central to the Flamingo operation and continued to have Gehlen's full backing. His group of cypher clerks and radio operators continued to grow to the point where he was given his own Abwehr station in Budapest *Luftmeldekopf Südost* (air intelligence outpost, south-east). Then, on 12 February 1945, two days before the Red Army took Budapest, his group relocated to Vienna at which point Austrian customs officers confiscated from him his three boxes containing cash, an expensive stamp collection and jewellery. He was arrested by the SS but, after two months in detention, he was released only to be taken prisoner by the Allies.

Kauder, his Hungarian mistress Ivolia Kalman, Ira Longin and General Anton Turkul were taken prisoner by the Allies in 1945 and interrogated at Oberursel detention centre, where the Germans had interrogated Allied air crews during the Second World War, while Smersh, the Red Army Counterintelligence Agency, arrested members of the Klatt Bureau, including Kauder's wife, Gerda Filitz. Filitz told the Soviets that the Klatt Bureau worked for Luftwaffe-1 Abwehr [Ast] in Vienna where Kauder had been first employed by the Abwehr in 1939. His contact there was Lieutenant Colonel Roland von Wahl-Welskirch but he also had a direct line to Berlin through Schellenberg. It was Ira Longin's people, Filitz said, who supplied Kauder with the bulk of his intelligence about the Soviet Union. Kauder had no direct contact with them. Valentina Deutsch, one of Kauder's radio operators further claimed that Longin worked for Turkul.

The matter is further complicated by a report written by the Soviet People's Commissar for Internal Affairs, Lavrentiy Beria, to Stalin in 1944 in which he stated that an analysis of Kauder's radio traffic between Sofia and Budapest during the years 1941 to 1944 showed them to be 'pure fantasies'.[42] Furthermore, Smersh had no evidence of any illicit radio communications between Soviet territory and Sofia at this time. The implication is that Kauder was fabricating the bulk of his information from what he had been able to pick up or buy from Soviet exiles, military attachés and corrupt Nazi agents. That none of the Klatt members taken captive by the Soviets was executed and only one, Otto Hatz, is reported to have received a lengthy prison sentence and he was released after only four years supports the notion that Smersh might have been behind the Klatt network all along.

Stalingrad

> While it is so far not possible to investigate the tactical situation in the breakthrough locations in detail, it appears probable that a major crisis is now upon us [at Stalingrad].
>
> Reinhard Gehlen[43]

On 22 July 1942, Hitler issued Directive No. 44 in which he ordered a direct attack on Leningrad and then, a day later, issued Directive No. 45 calling on the OKH to take Stalingrad before occupying the Caucasian oil wells. Halder was appalled at the thought of ordering von Paulus's 6th Army to advance with its northern flank dangerously exposed to counterattack. Hitler was anxious to strike against Stalingrad at the earliest opportunity, but Halder wanted to stabilise the Kharkov front first. Naturally, Hitler knew best and he ordered the Army Group South to split and advance in two directions simultaneously to the river Volga and the Caucasus believing that the Soviets had few reserves left. All Gehlen had to support Halder were reports from the front Ic intelligence officers, the sparse counterintelligence reports and conjecture. He was wary but at the same time he understood perfectly well how unwelcome doubters were within the leadership and one serious error could see the end of his career.

Advance headquarters for the offensive were now in Vinnitsa, in the heart of Ukraine where the SS had previously 'cleared' the village of Jews, even in the villages, 'all Jews had been shot completely, small children, women, everything', wrote Oberleutnant Georg-Heino Freiherr von Münchhausen.[44] Staff officers and generals, including Gehlen could not have been unaware of what was going on chose to turn a blind eye to the utter depravity of the massacres.

Gehlen had lectured the graduates of the *Kriegsakademie* in June saying that the Red Army would have less reserves in the coming winter and that the sense of superiority of the German soldier was fully justified meaning that success was assured. Gehlen's confidence was not shared by all his staff, however. Wessel, who would work alongside Gehlen throughout the rest of his career eventually taking over from him as head of the BND in 1968, was sceptical. The German forces were not sufficient to carry out all the tasks demanded of them, he said. Stalingrad and Leningrad could be taken but the cost in men and materiél would be too high and a Soviet counteroffensive would probably succeed. Gehlen's own strategic preference was for the German forces to stabilise the front and eliminate, as far as possible any weaknesses, take up defensive positions, conserve strength, reorganise and wait until 1943 before resuming the attack. Naturally, this was rejected out of hand by Hitler who responded by ordering Operation Blue (*Fall Blau*), a summer offensive in southern Russia to destroy the enemy west of the river Don and then occupy the Caucasus oilfields.

Three months later, Gehlen's lecture at the *Kriegsakademie* was somewhat less bombastic. The summer offensive had failed to realise its most important objectives. He would soon regret telling the students that German forces would succeed in taking the oil region of the Caucasus and on the river Volga near Stalingrad before the onset of winter.

Halder took Gehlen with him when he tried to persuade Hitler that it was a time for consolidation and not headlong assault against an enemy whose strength was unknown with another Russian winter in prospect. Hitler was tired of playing the pupil while this ascetic, aristocratic Junkers schoolmaster lectured him on strategy, however, and he cut Halder off with one of his ferocious rants. Frothing at the mouth and flailing his bunched fists he called Halder's objections 'idiotic twaddle'. The Red Army had been decimated, he roared, there were no Soviet reserves worthy of the name.[45] Halder tried to get Gehlen invited into the discussion but Hitler, who had no time for the FHO at the best of times, gave him short shrift as well saying that he was in no mood to listen to a *Märchenerzähler* (storyteller). It was a chastening moment for Gehlen and a warning about how fragile the position was of anyone who got on the wrong side of Hitler, especially when telling him things that contradicted what he had already convinced himself to be the facts. Gehlen's own report just a month earlier had identified fifty-six new Soviet armoured divisions and an equal number of new infantry divisions, but Hitler had refused to acknowledge it. Gehlen realised from this moment that he would have to take great care to protect himself and the FHO by maintaining a low profile and by keeping a detailed archive of his reports that would later stand as evidence of his own assessment and analysis of Soviet capabilities. Already he was sensing that the war would not go well for Germany and that there would be a reckoning at some point when he might have to defend himself against any number of wild accusations.

Gehlen was well placed as Halder's adjutant having spent a year and a half as group leader east in the operations department and nine months as head of FHO. He was now the General Staff officer with the greatest operational experience in the OKH but his career trajectory plateaued a few weeks later. The meeting with Hitler had been a defining moment for Halder also. He was crushed by Hitler's constant rejection of his advice and the knowledge of what it meant for his soldiers on the frontline and when Hitler removed him from office on 24 September 1942 and installed the 'bustling, stocky, bald-headed, dynamo of action'[46] Kurt Zeitzler as chief of the General Staff in his place, it came as no great surprise. For Gehlen, however, it was a setback to lose his most supportive mentor. It might not have been so bad if Heusinger had been the one to replace Halder but Zeitzler was a 'force of nature' noted for his dynamist and fervent enthusiasm for Nazism, qualities which he expected his subordinates to exhibit in equal measure.

Gehlen must have been contemptuous of Zeitzler's sycophantic devotion to Hitler and his totally unwarranted criticism of the General Staff who 'make sad faces at every unforeseen event', but the evidence shows that Gehlen was able to adapt to Zeitzler's rough and ready manner in a way that says much for his adaptability and forbearance.[47] Fortunately for Gehlen, Zeitzler was not in the habit of taking department chiefs into his audiences with Hitler. As much as possible, the other members of the General Staff deliberately kept Gehlen away from Hitler also. They had come to value his judgements far too much to risk seeing him removed for telling Hitler what he didn't want to hear. On the rare occasion that he was called in to address Hitler, however, Gehlen claimed always to have

> expressed [his] opinion unequivocally [but] taking care that it should be consistent with Hitler's way of thinking,

a somewhat roundabout way of saying that he was clearly anxious to avoid contradicting the Führer.[48]

The most important source of FHO intelligence about Red Army order of battle, the position and grouping of Soviet forces, and Soviet operational intentions was signals reconnaissance. The most productive of which were radio and telephone reconnaissance. Up until the summer of 1942, FHO had achieved considerable success by breaking low-level Red Army codes using *Funkpeilung* (radio direction finding), *Verkehrauswertung* (traffic analysis) and *Inhaltsauswertung* (content evaluation) but Soviet signals security was undergoing significant improvements and, crucially, the Soviets had begun imposing strict radio silence before major offensives. Signals intelligence usually offered immediate tactical appraisals but was often sidelined where it contradicted strategic indicators upon which existing plans were based. The limitations of radio reconnaissance were soon exposed by its failure to reach deep into the Soviet rear where reserve formations were assembled.

The highest level of encryption of Soviet signals was never broken meaning that FHO could never get inside Soviet communications in ways that British and American signals intelligence did with the Germans. It is true that *Walli* succeeded in placing agents in Soviet military headquarters at the divisional and army level but never above or any high-level department of the Soviet government. Furthermore, not only had *Walli III* failed to penetrate the headquarters and main field offices of the Soviet security services but it is certain that nearly every report concerning high-level Soviet military and political plans transmitted by agents of Abwehr I contained Soviet disinformation. Gehlen was certainly aware of that the Soviets practiced deception but he was never able to rid himself of the sense of superiority of the German military over the Soviets, which caused him consistently to underestimate them and make assessments on the basis of unfounded opinion.

This weakness of FHO analysis was exposed in brutal fashion on 11 October 1942, when *Leitstelle fur Nachrichtenaufklärung* signals intelligence reported a wholesale regrouping of Red Army forces between the river Don and the river Volga with the establishment of a new forward headquarters. FHO interpreted this as 'defensive enemy behaviour'.[49] After Kharkov, this was Gehlen's second serious intelligence failure. He had placed too much importance on reports that the Red Army was planning a massive withdrawal of forces to the river Volga and failed to realise that it was a deliberate strategy to stabilise the line and actually try to prevent the Germans reaching the river Volga. A few short weeks later signals intelligence reported a build-up of Soviet forces behind Serafimovich on the boundary between the Romanian and Italian armies to the north of Stalingrad. Even when Army Group B intelligence pointed towards a Soviet offensive on the river Don, Gehlen refused to change his advice, which was that the Soviets did not have the manpower to launch a winter offensive on two fronts and if they did make any attempt at all it would be against German Army Group Centre. Aerial reconnaissance added little to the argument either way because the Red Army had become very efficient at camouflage while weather conditions hampered the already limited Luftwaffe reconnaissance capability that, even in the best weather, could not reach far enough to monitor the Soviet strategic build-up. Shortage of Luftwaffe reconnaissance aircraft also meant that routine flights were cancelled, and missions were only flown when specifically requested. Soviet air power had forced the Luftwaffe to heavily arm their reconnaissance aircraft which, in order for them to defend themselves, were flown by combat crews rather than specialist reconnaissance personnel.

In his first major test as head of FHO, Gehlen had to provide intelligence that covered a wide range of eventualities but was still within the limits of OKH strategic objectives and expectations, and which related directly to their ambitions. The main problem was that the Soviets were perfecting their strategy of keeping reserves well beyond aircraft range and launching them towards the centre of gravity at the last minute with a massive rail operation. Gehlen faced the same sort of dilemma that had got Kinzel dismissed. Hitler saw a Soviet offensive north of Stalingrad against weak Romanian troops as a possibility and he repeatedly expressed concerns about the stability of the German front there with German reserves in the area being bled into grinding machine that was Stalingrad.

Even though signals intelligence was the basic source for most FHO estimates of the enemy situation, when the results of signal reconnaissance contradicted the strategic indicators of enemy intentions upon which FHO had already based its assumptions, FHO, increasingly aware of the Soviet penchant for misinformation, would often refuse to modify its existing evaluation. This was clearly the case at Stalingrad. Gehlen had anticipated that any major offensive would come in the direction of Smolensk and in the north towards the Baltics, but he had little hard intelligence to back up his assessment. At the time, he thought any Soviet attack towards Rostov unlikely as this would involve dispersal of Soviet forces and wherever the attack was to come, Gehlen could give no worthwhile opinion about timing.

Even in late October 1942, FHO's advice was still that there were no indications of an imminent Soviet offensive to the north of Stalingrad but Zeitzler had picked up an unsubstantiated rumour that Stalin had authorised an offensive before the end of the year. Gehlen looked at the evidence and reaffirmed his opinion that the Soviets did not have sufficient strength to do any such thing in that area. The entry of reserves to the south of Stalingrad was seen as nothing more than replacements for exhausted troops and the build-up of the armoured divisions was beyond the range of the *Luftaufklärung* who failed to detect it. Gehlen had dismissed from his mind the possibility of a Soviet pincer to surround the German 6th Army at Stalingrad and had consequently been less that assiduous in looking for evidence of it. As late as 6 November 1942 with his *Estimate of the Enemy Situation in Front of Army Group Centre*[50] he still stubbornly refused to change his advice saying

> it was evident that Soviet preparation for the attack in the south had not proceeded so far that it was necessary to expect that a large operation would be conducted in the near future simultaneously with the expected offensive against Army Group Centre.[51]

He was stuck with his early assessment and clearly did not accept that there was enough reliable intelligence to warrant a change of view. Clearly, others were of the same opinion. Hitler had withdrawn his headquarters to east Prussia and FHO had moved back with him. Heusinger was confident that nothing much would happen now that the Russian winter was setting in. As early as August 1942, FHO had foreseen the possibility of a Soviet counteroffensive against Army Group B at Stalingrad but discounted it in favour of an attack in the centre. Gehlen in his assessment *Thoughts regarding the Further Development of the Enemy Situation in the Autumn and Winter*, made the fundamental assumption that the Red Army would be unable to mount more than one winter offensive, because of insufficient manpower reserves after the summer campaign season.[52]

By 3 November 1942, there were clear indications of early preparations for an attack on the Romanian 3rd Army but FHO was unable to say whether the object was an attack designed to lure German forces away from Stalingrad, or an operation with a much broader objective. FHO did, however, report on 12 November 1942 that there indeed was evidence of a possible imminent attack against the Romanians to cut the railway links to Stalingrad but concluded that the available Soviet forces would be too weak for 'far-reaching operations'.[53]

Gehlen's *Brief Estimate of the Enemy Situation* of 18 November 1942 suggested that attacks north and south of von Paulus's 6th Army 'could not be excluded' but overall there was no sense of urgency or crisis but then on the very next day, with complete tactical and strategic surprise, the Soviets launched Operation Uranus with a ferocious artillery barrage but still it was not interpreted as an overture to a counteroffensive. Gehlen later said that the attack took place precisely where he had predicted but by the time OKH realised what was happening a few days later, 500,000 Soviet troops and 900 tanks had completely surrounded von Paulus's 6th Army, which was completely cut off in Stalingrad with little hope of reinforcements.

There were massive rows at the highest level about how this had been allowed to happen. Gehlen had failed to anticipate the Soviet attack but then so had everyone else in the OKH and it had been Hitler, himself, who had ordered the 6th Army to advance beyond what the OKH advised. Hitler did not purge his generals as he had done after the failure to take Moscow and instead, to save face all round, it was agreed that the disaster had been the fault of the Romanian Army that had been covering von Paulus's left flank. When Soviet 21st and 65th armies and 5th Tank Army had followed up the artillery barrage with an all-out attack through thick fog and a fierce snowstorm the Romanians had quickly fallen back in disarray. The German 48th Panzerkorps tried to come to their aid but suffered catastrophic losses.

Hours later the Soviet 64th Army attacked south of Stalingrad against the Romanian 4th Army which disintegrated in similar fashion to the 3rd. It was the first time that Hitler chose to point a finger of blame at his allies but it would be far from the last. After the encirclement of Stalingrad, Gehlen understood that the whole collapse of the Eastern Front became a possibility.

By 10 December 1942, in his report *Possible Indications for a Beginning Russian Shift of Main Effort from the Middle Front Section of the Don Front,*[54] Gehlen still refused to acknowledge his mistake and held to the belief that the main Soviet winter offensive would be directed against Army Group Centre towards Smolensk with only a modest, careful operation on the Don front. It's true that Soviet radio silence severely hampered German signals intelligence and poor flying conditions in October and November 1942 together with Soviet operational and strategic *maskirovka* (camouflage) greatly reduced the effectiveness of aerial reconnaissance but, ultimately, FHO must bear the final responsibility for the intelligence failure at Stalingrad. By the end of October 1942, FHO had been in possession of enough tactical and operational intelligence to form a timely and correct assessment of Soviet intentions on the Don-Volga front. Gehlen's obduracy in the face of the evidence was astonishing.

In his defence, he began to document his misgivings with Hitler's leadership. In a note written on 10 February 1943, just two days before his father died, Gehlen said that almost all German moves since mid-December 1942 had 'resulted from a sequence of basis command errors on our side'. It was the Soviet commanders who had 'adopted German tactics' by showing initiative and had been given the freedom to exercise it whereas German commanders had been 'discouraged' under threat of court martial from doing the same. They had therefore

> forfeited one of the fundamental requirements of a successful and versatile military command.

The German army had become 'benumbed and incapable of strategic action'.[55] This was essentially a pessimistic assessment, in direct contrast to earlier, unfounded optimistic estimates and had the effect of unnecessarily reducing confidence by underestimating German capacity for effective resistance and exaggerating the ability of the Red Army to sustain its offensive in Ukraine. Morale was restored somewhat, however, by Erich von Manstein's Donets counteroffensive, known as the Third Battle of Kharkov, in February and March.

Gehlen's poor performance did not improve his career prospects, which seemed to have stalled. If he wanted to make general, the only avenue for advancement now was through a transfer to one of the combat units on the front but like all frontline leaders, Gehlen was haunted by the terrifying prospect of being taken captive by the Soviets. It would become one of the fiercest motivations for German forces in battle to do all they could to avoid encirclement and capture on the Eastern Front. It is therefore an illustration of how desperate the situation had become inside the Stalingrad enclave that on 2 February 1943, the surviving 90,000 German soldiers of von Paulus's 6th Army laid down their arms and trudged into Soviet captivity. How long could the German Eastern Front now hold along the Dnieper? Not very long Gehlen though. He made every effort to influence military decisions from the background but avoided direct confrontation with Hitler.

Naturally, there was enormous disquiet within the German High Command and Gehlen had heard rumours and speculation about a growing internal opposition to Hitler. Minister of Armaments and War Production Albert Speer, along with Zeitzler hoped to persuade Hitler to step back from military control and leave the generals to run the war. There were also whispers of assassination but that would not necessarily improve the immediate military situation in the east. Of course, in the wider diplomatic environment if Hitler was eliminated there might be scope for beginning a negotiated end to the war with a combined Allied-German front against the Soviets but to put faith in that was ambitious to say the least. Gehlen rejected all approaches to ally himself with the plotters.

Citadel

> From the point of view of the general war situation, there is not one ground that could justify launching Operation Citadel at the present juncture.
>
> Reinhard Gehlen[56]

Without definitive intelligence, the High Command was dithering but Hitler, in usual fashion, was pathologically unable to sit back and wait for the enemy to take the initiative. His decision was to launch a pincer attack, *Unternehmen Zitadelle* (Operation Citadel), with the newly deployed Tiger and Panther tanks against the Kursk salient in Russia with the objective of capturing large quantities of Soviet equipment and troops and shortening the battlefront by around 150 miles, but that was exactly what Stalin anticipated that he would do. Then Hitler had second thoughts. Guderian urged postponement until there were sufficient spare parts for the tanks and it was still not clear what armour the Soviets could bring to bear.

On 23 March 1943, Gehlen wrote another FHO *Assessment of the Enemy's Intentions on the German Eastern Front on a Large Scale* in which he said that

> the Red Army had decided to revert to the defensive on the southern front in the face of German counterattacks. On the basis of the high Russian losses during the winter, it must appear doubtful whether the enemy was in the position at all to conduct a war-deciding summer offensive.[57]

Gehlen came under extreme pressure to come up with numbers of Soviet tanks but he was way off the mark when he estimated that the Red Army had 4,300 armoured vehicles with another 1,900 available by the end of April 1943. His estimates of Soviet tank numbers proved to be a massive 10,000 short of the actual number they were able to deploy at the beginning of July 1943.

He did, however, come up with a timely and correct analysis of the difficulties that the Wehrmacht would face in executing Operation Citadel and of the consequences of this operation, including the Soviet counterattacks against the northern and southern flanks of the participating German forces. His *Comprehensive Estimate of Overall Enemy Intentions Before the German East Front* of 21 May 1943 proved to be more reliable when it predicted correctly that the Red Army was, after all, planning to launch a large-scale summer offensive against the right wing of Army Group Centre.[58] This would prove to be a high point of FHO analysis. On 5 June 1943, Gehlen advised Zeitzler that German forces should remain on the defensive in the east and let the Soviets attack and run down their reserves but any hope the High Command had that Hitler would actually call off Operation Citadel was unfounded. One leading observer openly wondered why the German army bothered to have a General Staff at all for all the influence it seemed to be having on the progress of the war.[59]

On 4 July 1943, an FHO report stated that Operation Citadel had lost all strategic and tactical surprise and could no longer be justified 'by any reason' given that the two main prerequisites for success were absent. The Germans did not have superiority of forces and had forfeited any possibility of surprise. In fact, the Soviets had been preparing for months to defend the Kursk salient and had built extensive defensive lines while holding large reserves in the rear beyond the range of aerial reconnaissance. Luftwaffe surveillance was having more success further south, however, and was bringing back clear evidence of a Soviet build-up opposite Army Group South against Kharkov and Belogrod. An attack now, said the report, would lead to 'a high consumption of forces'. Gehlen wrote a personal note,

> I consider the intended [German] operation to be a very decisive mistake that will take a heavy toll

with heavy underlining. Of course, he had no expectation, by this time, of influencing events but was determined that his criticisms would be on record. He was also at pains to go on the record with a defence of his own position. 'In recent days,' he wrote somewhat disingenuously

> the course of the fighting on the eastern front has once more proved the accuracy in every detail of the enemy appreciations elaborated by [FHO].[60]

It was clear to Gehlen that his advice was having little or no influence on Hitler's decision making and, like some of his superiors, was beginning to realise that the war could not be won in the face of irrational and arbitrary disregard of the facts.

As things turned out, on the morning that Operation Citadel was to be launched, Soviet bombers attempted a pre-emptive strike on Luftwaffe airfields indicating prior knowledge of Operation Citadel. The attack was driven off by Luftwaffe fighters but it had disrupted the German plans, which went ahead regardless although with much reduced efficiency. Four days after the battle began Allied forces invaded Sicily forcing Hitler to divert reserves, that had been held in France to support Operation Citadel, if required, to the Mediterranean area. A massive Soviet counteroffensive had first stalled the attack then driven German forces back. After only seven days, Hitler called off Operation Citadel but the Soviets pressed home their advantage.

Gehlen saw the possibility of follow-up attacks 'beyond the local areas' but predicted that the Soviets would essentially limit them to consolidating territory in preparation for a further assault at some future date. Nothing in his reports suggested that only two weeks after the end of Operation Citadel, the German forces would face a massive Soviet assault and be pushed back over 100 miles as far as the Dnieper river. By the autumn, Gehlen was forced to admit that he had very little upon which to base any assessment of future Soviet intentions other than that Soviet planning over the following few months would depend essentially on the course of the weather, and the arrival of the 'mud season', which stubbornly failed to materialise.

The obvious improvement in Soviet leadership and the general competence of the Soviet soldiers was seriously eroding the previous advantage that the Germans had held in both regards. The latter, Gehlen said, was the result of a massive propaganda coup made possible by what he called the

> frequent unnecessary use of violent means [and] blatant injustices on the German side against the population of the eastern territories.[61]

The tone of his reports now began to contrast markedly with his previous ones. A powerful and continuous Soviet offensive was now to be expected but while he no longer believed in a German victory, Gehlen was careful not to betray this particular personal thought to OKH.

Gehlen was army through and through. The Wehrmacht had rescued him from the treacherous revolution-ravaged streets of Germany in 1921 and given him a refuge and a philosophy. He had responded with total application, dedication and sheer hard work. His reward was acceptance into the heady ranks of the German General Staff, probably the single most important and transforming event of Gehlen's life. After the German defeats at Stalingrad and Kursk, it became glaringly obvious to him that Germany could not win the war against the Soviet Union in the east. The question was how would the war end? How crushing would be the defeat? What would remain of Germany and the German High Command to which he had devoted his working life and which, for him, epitomised everything that was good about Germany? How could he save his wife and four young children? How would life go on? Hitler's insane refusal to apply rational military strategy in the face of the Soviet counteroffensive suggested that defeat, when it came, would be total and crushing. He had experienced the disastrous aftermath of the 1918 armistice and that did not bode well for his future now.

There were several possible outcomes for Gehlen personally, most of which he would have little control over. The most likely were transfer to a frontline unit, which would probably result in his death, assassination by SS death squads if he tried to flee or, if he survived the war, capture and immersion in the mass of PoWs. As early as May 1944, he and Wessel had discussed the consequences of defeat. Later recalling their talks at this time, Wessel made no mention of a political dimension in relation to their Nazi overlords. The primary consideration was to prevent Germany falling under the yoke of communism and if the German forces were unable to do that then the battle against Bolshevism must be fought by other means. Every effort must be made to ensure that the Western Allies were given all necessary support to do that if and when Germany could no longer do it alone. To this end, the vast resources of FHO must be preserved and placed at their disposal. Amongst these was the huge card index that had been built up recording not only the personal and professional details of the Red Army leadership with character studies and psychological profiles but masses of data about the industrial and social fabric of the Soviet Union. For instance, there were numerous street maps and town plans showing the location of all main services.

Gehlen and Wessel revisited the issue of the post-war landscape as the OKH was reeling from the defeat at Kursk and they agreed that defeat for Germany was now certain and that all their efforts must be focused on preserving the German armed forces and not allowing them to be stripped by the victorious Allies as had been the case at Versailles. There were encouraging indications that the Western Allies were also thinking ahead and contemplating a future confrontation with their current allies, the Soviets. At the end of 1943 Britain and the US had scaled back their bombing of civilian centres such as Hamburg and concentrated instead on the Ruhr river. Their sense was that continued attacks on civilian populations would have such a catastrophic effect on German morale that the whole Eastern Front might collapse completely and it was no part of the Western Allies' plans to allow the Soviets a clear path to occupy Europe ahead of their own invasion, which could not be launched before mid-1944. It was a fine calculation for the Western Allies to mount aerial attacks in the West without weakening the German Eastern Front more than necessary. The ever-astute Gehlen was already planning out his future as part of a continuing crusade against the hated communists.

That was the future, but it was the present that demanded his attention. He did not slacken his pace or allow the FHO to relax its efforts to keep its data banks on the Soviet Union up to date but the extent to which Gehlen subsequently influenced the progress of the war may be determined by the fact that from this point until 22 March 1945 his name does not appear in a single Hitler briefing. Gehlen insisted that his assessments were sound but the historian Hans-Heinrich Wilhelm believes that, had OKH and Hitler taken more notice of them than they did, the results may well have been even worse. On the big question FHO was quite unable to say which of Stalin's options he would pursue. There was a possible incursion into the Balkans, an advance via Poland to the Baltic Sea or a decisive breakthrough in the middle towards Minsk, Belarus. Evidence suggests that Gehlen now adopted a reticent approach by keeping as far away as possible from the central decision-making within the confines of his responsibilities. As far as possible he restricted the FHO to providing information with only minimal assessment of Soviet intentions and offered no hint of criticism of Hitler's leadership.

In his memoirs, Gehlen says that, at this point, both he and Canaris had concluded that the Soviets had a source of intelligence at the very heart of the German command structure. He recalled a meeting at Angerburg when Canaris told him that he suspected Martin Bormann, by this time Hitler's personal secretary, of operating a clandestine radio station sending intelligence to Moscow. Since Canaris was arrested and executed in 1945, it is impossible to verify this but Gehlen claimed that he had harboured similar suspicions for some time and indeed, after the Second World War, he went on to say that he subsequently received 'conclusive proof' to confirm the suspicions. While this suggestion was received with great acclaim at the time, no evidence has ever been produced to support the idea. Analysis of Bormann's whereabouts after his escape from Hitler's bunker on 2 May 1945 in my book *Hitler's Gold* suggests that Bormann was either killed hours after his escape or, more likely, eventually fled to South America.[62]

Hitler fired Canaris on 12 February 1944, ostensibly for 'professional and personal failures', which had 'risen to an intolerable level'.[63] Canaris would end his life in the most brutal fashion hanging from the end of a 'piano wire' on 9 April 1945 at Flosssenbürg concentration camp. Hitler then issued a proclamation making it clear that Himmler would be taking command of all Abwehr departments. Schellenberg would be Gehlen's boss now, but Schellenberg, although a 'skilful political manipulator' was 'a sorry specimen of an intelligence officer'.[64] Gehlen urged Keitel to fight for some degree of FHO independence from SS control otherwise it would suffer what he called serious disadvantage. Keitel was anxious to do anything to prevent the total takeover of OKH by the SS but when he made his protest to Himmler, it was muted saying only that the move threatened disruption and a threat to frontline intelligence gathering. Schellenberg tried to take over the running of *Walli I* and *Walli III* but was persuaded that it was a step too far and Gehlen improvised an ad hoc relationship with both Baun and Schmalschläger to try and ward off any future moves by Schellenberg. When Hitler fired von Manstein on 30 March 1944, Gehlen lost one of his mentors. It made him even more anxious to retain the leadership of FHO, which gave him the best hope of coming out of the other side of what was surely now a complete breakdown of German hopes for a negotiated peace.

The stress was taking a toll and Gehlen's health was failing. Every day he was required to make assessments of the military situation upon which he could put no semblance of a gloss. All he had were assumptions about Soviet intentions and strength. He advocated strategic withdrawals to natural defensive positions, but this was unacceptable since Hitler was stubbornly refusing to allow his armies to give ground. Gehlen's stomach problems were getting worse, and he was forced to take sick leave at his home in Leignitz at the beginning of May 1944 leaving Wessel to run the department. Just before he left, Gehlen had issued his *Comprehensive Appreciation of the Enemy Situation before the German East Front and Presumes Enemy Intentions in General,* which nowhere mentioned the Soviet offensive that, days later, pushed the Germans out of the Crimea. Instead it had concentrated on predicting a Soviet offensive towards Lublin, Poland and Brest, France, which never actually materialised.[65]

When he returned, the situation map showed a concentration of Soviet forces in the north directly threatening the German homeland. FHO intelligence had failed on three crucial occasions: Moscow in 1941, Stalingrad in 1942 and Kursk in 1943 but the timely use of reserves had staved off catastrophe for Germany. Now there were no reserves left for countermeasures against the anticipated Soviet offensive. They were all being sent to France to meet the challenge of the Allied D-Day landings.

While Gehlen can be commended for the sheer volume of material, concerning the Soviet Union, that FHO was able to accumulate during the war, the reputation for competence and prescience, which he assiduously constructed in his memoirs does not reflect the extensive equivocation he applied when giving his advice. He rarely predicted the timing of enemy actions and usually included a variety of possibilities in any scenario, which meant that whatever happened he could claim to have predicted it. Often reports could be interpreted in a number of ways according to the preference or prejudice of the reader. His mistakes, however, are clear for all to see and now the scene was set for Gehlen's final and most consequential failure, admittedly at a time when his health was critically poor.

The *Comprehensive Estimate of the Enemy Situation* issued by FHO on 3 May 1944 had discerned two possible Soviet offensives.[66] The first could start from the sector Kovel-Lutsk on the southwestern edge of the Pripyat Marshes, designed to strike behind Army Group Centre north-west to Warsaw and on to the Baltic. According to FHO, this would require a level of tactical proficiency, which was beyond Soviet forces leaving them with a second option of an offensive directed at the Balkans. The FHO, doubted that the Red Army possessed sufficient forces to conduct a wide-ranging offensive in the general direction of Minsk leaving them convinced that the main Soviet offensive would be launched against Army Group North Ukraine.

Gehlen made a number of assumptions about future Soviet intentions upon which he based all subsequent FHO evaluations relating to the expected Soviet summer offensive. One was that the Soviet summer offensive would be directed against Army Groups A and South and another that the Red Army would attempt by every means to drive strong forces deep between the Carpathian Mountains and the Pripyat region before the construction and fortification of a continuous German defensive front.

From around 10 June 1944, intelligence showed a build-up of Soviet forces that appeared to threaten Army Group Centre but it did not alter FHO assessments believing that it was a diversionary manoeuvre. Deputy Chief of the Red Army General Staff General Sergei Shtemenko would later say that

> [The Soviet] system of operational deceptive measures [meant that] the enemy was profoundly misled concerning our real intentions.[67]

This Soviet subterfuge was the most sophisticated and thoroughly organised of the whole war. On 14 June 1944, Gehlen reported a Soviet build-up in front of Army Group Northern Ukraine but he was unable to locate the position of the Soviet strategic reserve, which had actually been built up behind the front facing the German Army Group Centre.

'Credible defensive reports [and] radio reconnaissance' pointed to a 'staggered attack' towards the Balkans expected to begin between 15 and 20 June 1944.[68] Gehlen emphasised the need for 'a really smooth defensive success', which was almost completely devoid of either tactical or strategic advice and which the OKH could interpret any way they wanted. Three days later, Gehlen reaffirmed his belief that the main attack would be in Ukraine, and he did not change this opinion even after the Soviets smashed through the German Army Group Centre on 22 June 1944 with a thoroughly organised and strategically sophisticated attack that destroyed more than thirty German divisions.[69] Operation Bagration saw four complete Soviet armies and one tank army achieve total operational and strategic surprise. Nothing in the record shows that Gehlen had any idea that the Soviets had amassed such a force.

Only in late July 1944, by which time a 250-mile gap had been ripped in the German front, did he finally admit that Operation Bagration had been a major Soviet offensive and a strategically crushing blow with catastrophic consequences. He was forced to admit that radio and aerial reconnaissance, which alone could obtain reliable information about strategic reserves, had almost completely failed.

The blame game got into full swing and all the General Staff now tried to have as little as possible to do with Hitler. Having failed to persuade Hitler to allow Army Group North to fall back in the Baltics, Zeitzler offered his resignation. When Hitler refused to accept it, Zeitzler simply stopped attending the daily audiences at the Berchtesgaden and left Heusinger to face the music. Heusinger was privately saying that the war could no longer be won but he urged all officers to continue doing their duty. His hope now was that Zietzler would be relieved of his post and he would be able to slip away unnoticed alongside him. Gehlen also cried off sick with what he called a 'rather unpleasant suppuration of the pine sinus'[70] At the beginning of July 1944, he was admitted to the hospital in Lötzen with sepsis and remained for several months, first to Angerburg in East Prussia, then in his native Breslau. Once again it was down to Wessel to deal with the crisis on the Eastern Front.

The Russian Army of Liberation

> It was Vlasov's dream to lead a Russian national army of liberation into the Soviet Union.
>
> Reinhard Gehlen[71]

During summer 1941, Field Marshal Fedor von Bock, commander of Army Group Centre had working under him a German-Russian Balt called Wilfried Strik-Stirkfeldt who was organising a group of Soviet collaborators, ex-Red Army officers and Soviet PoWs who would form the nucleus of what he saw as a puppet military government to take control of the Soviet Union after Stalin's defeat. The sheer enormity of the ambition made the possibility of bringing the plan to fruition distant enough but it really had no support from the Nazi political leadership. For Alfred Rosenberg, Hitler's head of the Reich Ministry for the Occupied Eastern Territories, the idea of setting up in Russia a facsimile of the Vichy government in occupied France was anathema. The Eastern European populations would be treated as *Untermenschen* (sub-humans) and those who survived the war would be subjected to virtual slavery.

Others took a less barbarous approach but the fate of a subjugated Soviet population was far from decided. Ever since the occupation of Poland, German *Einsatzgruppen* (SS paramilitary death squads) had been active in occupied territories of the east carrying out slaughter of civilian populations on a massive scale. German army commanders repeatedly protested on the grounds that it was motivating huge partisan resistance making control and administration of the occupied areas extremely difficult. Hitler grew tired of their complaints and von Bock was one of those who spoke out once too often and had been relieved of his post on 18 December 1941. The concept of recruiting Soviet PoWs into an auxiliary army did not die with von Bock's dismissal, however. The general idea was to deploy them in auxiliary roles to replenish the German forces who had failed to take Moscow and were now suffering in the open during the bitter winter weather but Hitler would not hear of it. He would later moderate that view somewhat.

A few months later, when Gehlen had taken charge of FHO, having previously carefully followed the arguments put forward by Strik-Stirkfeldt, he picked up the idea of a Russian army of liberation. He had no stomach for Rosenberg's vision for an occupied eastern Europe brutally stripped of its inhabitants and personally believed that Rosenberg's views would not prevail. It was well known that Rosenberg was a favourite of Hitler, not for his intellect, which was limited, but for his sycophancy and ruthlessness and while the Führer indulged him with titles, he took very little notice of his opinions. Gehlen envisaged an eastern Europe under German administration with a subjugated, docile indigenous population into which German emigrants could realise the goal of *Lebensraum*. Order would be maintained by auxiliary units commanded by a Soviet military leadership made up of dissidents and PoWs all of whom had been recruited, motivated and 're-educated' to serve the Reich. Since part of FHO duties was the routine interrogation of Soviet PoWs, the organisation was ideally placed to carry out the selection process. His ideas won the approval of Halder and many within the FHO ranks including another Balt, Rönne, to whose Group III, Strik-Stirkfeldt was now assigned. Captured Soviet officers were sent to a training camp at Wulheide, essentially part of Joseph Goebbels's ministry, where they underwent indoctrination and instruction. Halder was prepared to indulge Gehlen's ambitions, however, but he was not convinced that his plans would work. Gehlen looked elsewhere and found the very man whom he believed could bring them to fruition.

Lieutenant General Andrey Andreyevich Vlasov had never been a fervent Bolshevik. Born into the Russian peasantry, he claimed to have joined the Red Army and Communist Party when he was 18 purely as a means of self-advancement. He thrived in a military environment and not only managed to survive Stalin's purges in the 1930s but by December 1941, he found himself a general commanding the Soviet 20th Army in the defence of Moscow where he distinguished himself by dislodging the Germans at Solnechnogorsk. He was subsequently given command of the Soviet 2nd Shock Army to relieve the siege of Leningrad but when he advanced on the Volkhov front in May 1942, supporting armies failed to keep up with him and his force was faced with encirclement. Denied Stalin's permission to retreat, Vlasov's army was cut to pieces at Myasnoi Bor. When he scorned the opportunity to escape by aircraft, Vlasov was taken prisoner by a German tank unit and brought first to Vinnitza, where he was interviewed by Strik-Stirkfeldt and then to Himmler's eastern headquarters at Zhitomir. Strik-Stirkfeldt reported back to Gehlen, who arranged meetings with both Heydrich and Canaris to prepare the ground for Vlasov's exploitation.

Gehlen now concluded an agreement with Heydrich whereby the SS would furnish FHO with intelligence gained by their *Sonderkommando* units in return for copies of FHO's evaluation reports based on that intelligence. Making one of his rare visits to the east, Canaris was happy to put his and Heydrich's mutual animosity aside and agreed to allow Bentivegni's Abwehr Group III to cooperate with the FHO. It should be remembered that, despite Gehlen's later claim that he was in charge of the German espionage organisation in the east, right up until spring 1944, the FHO was under the ultimate control and supervision of the Abwehr and his relationship with the admiral was of the utmost importance to him.

These agreements gave Gehlen the negotiating room to secure exclusive access to Vlasov and set up a small group under Strik-Stirkfeldt, who all came under Rönne's FHO Group III. Vlasov was taken to a comfortable house in Victoria Straβe in Berlin under military police guard. Gehlen's men now scoured the PoW camps for other Soviet collaborators while Gehlen, himself, negotiated directly with von Ribbentrop and Goebbels to prevent interference from their quarters. Soon, the Jewish Colonel Mileti Zykov, General Vasili Feodorovich Malyshkin and Major General Georgi Nicolaievich Zkilenkov joined Vlasov in Berlin where they remained under house arrest, but they were always treated with military courtesy and respect.

A special interrogation unit was set up as part of Herre's Group II at Boyen in East Prussian under Major Adolf Wicht who had been drafted in from General Erwin Rommel's North African theatre of operations.

Wicht's responsibilities were the compilation of all available current information about the Soviet Union derived from captured documents and forwarding it other departments. He persuaded Gehlen to put his unit on an equal footing with Rönne's Group III, whose own interrogation centre was at Lötzen in Poland. Soviet PoWs were evaluated for technical skills and potential for defection. Suitable candidates then underwent intensive indoctrination and prepared for integration into the Russian Army of Liberation. Prisoners of other nationalities were separated out to other camps. Ukranians, Cossacks, Tartars, Turks, Georgians and Kazbeks were treated in a similar fashion to the Soviets but were prepared for recruitment into ethnic *Osttruppen* units who would go into battle led by German officers.

As part of his drive to recruit Soviet dissidents, on 23 May 1942 Gehlen authorised Operation Hanover and sent 350 men dressed in Red Army uniforms behind enemy lines to carry out sabotage and set up clandestine radio posts. These men were part of a special unit of some 3,000 Russian exiles called *Graukopf*. Hanover's primary objective was to capture members of Soviet General Pawel Belov's staff. The operation was a dismal failure with almost three-quarters of these men killed or taken prisoner during heavy fighting and *Graukopf* was soon dismantled due to its 'unreliability'.

While Hanover had been a disappointment, the idea of insurgency was given a high priority. With rather better planning and training. Operation Schamil was staged by a unit of special forces in response to intelligence indicating that Stalin had ordered the destruction of the Maykop and Baku oilfields if Soviet troops were forced to abandon them. *Unternehmen Zeppelin* (Operation Zeppelin) had been set up by Schellenberg in 1942 under SS-Sturmbannführer Erich Hengelhaupt, head of the Eastern Group of *Amt VI*. Using Soviet defectors its aim was to drop agents deep behind enemy lines to carry out intelligence and espionage operations. Gehlen rightly suspected that *Zeppelin* was heavily infiltrated by Smersh. His own plan was to parachute a small detachment of some fifty men behind enemy lines to take control of the Grozny oil refinery in preparation for the advancement of 1st German Panzer Army. The German advance was halted, however, and they were forced to withdraw but managed to bring back a number of Soviet defectors. Other operations saw agents infiltrated into the Caucasus and even Leningrad to establish radio posts and send back intelligence.

Vlasov was allowed to form a political organisation that trawled the PoW camps for recruits to the Russian anti-Soviet ranks but it was, of necessity, a low-key operation. It was widely known that Hitler had described the idea of a Russian army fighting on the side of the Germans as a 'fantasy of the first order' and Himmler had threatened to end any further efforts but Gehlen managed to get Rosenberg onto his side and for a while the argument that Vlasov's army would be a vital part of FHO intelligence gathering won the day.[72] Given the military setback of Stalingrad, FHO needed all then help it could get in early 1943.

In Operation Silver Streak, Vlasov's recruits were filtered into the Soviet front lines spreading propaganda and misinformation, which saw over 6,000 Soviet deserters cross over the lines. This success went to Strik-Stirkfeldt's head unfortunately and he sent a memo to Hitler's office, no less, to request permission to set up a Russian government in exile under Vlasov. It had the unfortunate effect of nourishing Hitler's suspicions that Vlasov's army was a 'trojan horse' that would eventually be deployed against his forces. This brought Gehlen under suspicion also and he began to dismantle the experiment but not before he had been able to get some sense of the level of dissatisfaction many Soviet soldiers and their families felt under Stalin's dictatorial rule. It was an idea he would hold and return to in later years.

In some ways, though, the Vlasov experiment had weakened FHO. When it became clear to Beria that the FHO was actively and aggressively trawling for Soviet defectors and spreading propaganda he quickly organised Soviet countermeasures in the form of Smersh (*smert shpionom*, death to spies) whose officers were attached to every command to take the place of political commissars and root out dissent. One of their main tasks was to take control of all partisan operations especially those behind German lines and in this way quickly became a thorn in the flesh of FHO.

When the Germans had launched Operation Barbarossa, they had little idea of the complexity of the war they would be getting involved in against the Soviet intelligence and security services. As a result, OKH and the Abwehr grossly underestimated the threat they posed to the Wehrmacht. The Soviets would go on to win the intelligence war on the Eastern Front by means of espionage conducted by Soviet agents at every level of operations including penetration of the German High Command and German intelligence organisations. After 1941, the NKVD had infiltrated hundreds of agents into the rear of the German army, and large numbers of Soviet agents penetrated the German civil and military administrations. The partisan movement, in particular, had been organized before the war and been prepared for action in the enemy's rear. *Walli III* soon understood the extent of the threat posed by these groups, but by the time they convinced OKH, it was already too late, and it was never possible for the Germans to allocate sufficient resources to combat it.

The Stauffenberg Plot

> I played no active part in the conspiracy, but it would be untrue were I to deny I knew that one was afoot.
>
> Reinhard Gehlen[73]

Just how much of a dissident Gehlen was, has been much debated. Throughout his career, he had kept out of politics, but politics would not keep out of FHO and the issue that roused Gehlen to take a view was not the military aspects of the war against the Soviets, which he always supported, but the *Gleichschaltung* occupation policies of Himmler's SS. Either by conviction or expediency, he came to believe that Hitler was unaware of the extremes of butchery and exploitation being perpetrated in the east by Himmler's *Einsatzgruppen*. Gehlen argued that Himmler's policies would make the occupied areas ungovernable and believed that Hitler could be persuaded to rein in the murder squads, but he did not want to do anything that even hinted at that FHO harboured anti-Hitler sentiments. While Gehlen had tried to foster an apolitical environment within FHO, there were many of his staff within whom the creed of Nazism ran deep but there were also some, like von Rönne whose written criticisms of Nazi policies towards the civilian population in the east Gehlen occasionally had to moderate before allowing them to go forward.

Eventually, the evidence of extermination policies was such that Gehlen, along with other senior military leaders, thought that Hitler should be confronted with the facts. On 25 November 1942, Gehlen had submitted a seventeen-page memorandum criticising the brutal German occupation policy and advocating Stirk-Strickland's idea of a Russian army of Liberation to govern. Hitler's outright rejection of the idea was a moment in which Gehlen's mood appears to have shifted towards a bitter resignation that it was Hitler, himself, who was the problem. There were others who though likewise and whispers of revolt against the Führer grew louder.

Gehlen knew how precarious the position of the German forces were with von Paulus's 6th Army bottled up and cut off in a bitterly cold Stalingrad and it was certainly not clear to him how a change of leadership right at the top would ameliorate the situation. It would probably lead to a direct confrontation between the OKW and the SS with a complete collapse of the Eastern Front. It was barely worth thinking about what the consequences would be for Germany and indeed for the whole of Europe if the Soviets were given a free hand to flood their forces across the Continent.

Gehlen would later say that it was his illness and subsequent hospitalisation that saved him from the 'witch hunt' that took place after the failed attempt on Hitler's life on 20 July 1944. That begs the question of the extent to which he was involved with Claus von Stauffenberg's bomb plot. Clearly, he knew about the conspiracy, he says so in his memoirs. One of the conspirators, Baron Wessel von Freytag-Loringhoven, visited him in hospital on 17 July 1944 to say that a move was imminent. Von Freytag-Loringhoven had taken over command of *Abteilung II* from Colonel Erwin von Lahousen in March 1943. Many of his FHO staff knew about it also but Gehlen claims that none played any active part in it. Early in 1944, Heusinger had alluded to it after which Gehlen concentrated on ensuring that FHO was staffed with men 'upon whom we could count in such an emergency'.[74]

When news of the explosion came through and it was clear that Hitler had survived, back at FHO headquarters, Gehlen says that Wessel broke into his private filing cabinet and destroyed all evidence of correspondence he had with Halder who was implicated in the plot. Unfortunately, it is not always productive to take what Gehlen writes in his memoirs as an accurate record of events. Gehlen was a careful, security-conscious man and it is unlikely that he would have kept anything incriminating where it could be found by the Gestapo.

Wessel, in fact, later made a point of asking Gehlen how much he had known about the plot. In his reply Gehlen said that he had been aware of 'certain efforts against Hitler's leadership' but had not discussed it with Wessel because he did not want to compromise him. Why then had he trusted Wessel to destroy the letters? At a meeting weeks before the bomb blast, Gehlen was reported to have said

> But even if it does not succeed, at least it will be recorded in German history that people risked their lives to eliminate this criminal.[75]

There is a suspicion that he was painting himself as much more of an anti-Nazi collaborator than he actually was at the time. On the other hand, after the war, Heusinger claimed that Gehlen had belonged to the circle of conspirators and said that he had been amazed at the time that he had avoided arrest. Heusinger had, in fact, been injured by the bomb blast and was later arrested and imprisoned by the Gestapo at Prinz-Albrecht-Strasse. Questioned personally by Hitler, who had a great admiration for, and need of, him, Heusinger was eventually freed. Any involvement he may have had in the bomb plot had probably been peripheral and no more active than Gehlen's.[76]

One War Ends...

> Hitler dismissed [my final intelligence digest] as 'absolutely idiotic' and defeatist, and on April 9 I was relieved of my position as head of Foreign Armies East.
>
> Reinhard Gehlen[77]

Some of Gehlen's friends were swept up in the purges following the failed assassination attempt. Von Rönne was arrested immediately but released only to be rearrested two weeks later and hanged in Plötzensee Prison on 12 October 1944. Gehlen reacted by clamping down on all anti-Hitler or anti-Nazi sentiment within FHO and, with the Abwehr gone, allowing it to come more and more under the control of the Schellenberg and the SS. Schellenberg, the urbane, charming schemer was so unlike Gehlen the reclusive, reserved and calculating workaholic, but the two men shared an instinct for self-preservation. Both were now focusing on survival after the inevitable defeat of German forces both in the east and in the west but, more immediately, planned to make use of Vlasov's Army of Liberation, which, by some estimates eventually numbered some 50,000 men.[78] Even Himmler gave it the green light in August 1944 by providing the resources to create two Russian divisions. Gehlen proposed that Herre become Vlasov's chief of staff and appointed Wessel to be his chief of intelligence.

When *Jagdverbände* (SS special forces) under Major Otto Skorzeny became involved, Gehlen saw opportunities to expand his intelligence network behind Soviet lines. Skorzeny, later famously referred to as 'Hitler's favourite commando', had been commissioned to establish a partisan organisation in November 1944 made up of Polish and Ukrainian resistance fighters, which is what brought him into contact with Gehlen in the first place. Gehlen saw an opportunity to bring together resistance movements, Vlasov's forces and FHO into a combined espionage strategy involving Russian and non-Russian agents working deep inside the Soviet Union in what would become the basis of his post-Second World War organisation. It is a matter of conjecture as to exactly what extent Gehlen's plans extended beyond the end of the war at this stage but he began the long process of deliberately laying the foundations of a post-war career by the careful accumulation of massive amounts of economic and military data on the Soviet Union. The war was certainly lost by this time and the effects of any new intelligence and espionage initiative could have had absolutely no bearing on that outcome. On 7 October 1944, Gehlen had written that the 'natural contradiction' in the political goals of the Western Allies and the Russians would create areas of friction and that Moscow was fully aware that

> only the German Reich can put a military and political stop to the Soviet Russian claim to Europe, and thus also become a valuable military factor for the Anglo-Americans later on, if it is necessary to keep the autocracy of Bolshevik imperialism away from Europe.[79]

Was now the moment when Gehlen finally began to formulate his ambition to continue the war against communism under a different flag? Gehlen described the new organisation thus

> For the purpose of collecting intelligence a new non-German intelligence network will be created by formation of the necessary number of efficient groups of agents in the enemy's rear areas; it will be known as the 'Secret League of Green Partisans' [*Geheimbund der grünen Partisanen*] and will ostensibly be under Russian leadership. The principle will be: the organisation to be constituted solely behind the Russian front; on this ide there will be only channels of intelligence. No affiliation to Vlasov.[80]

Whilst utilising Vlasov's men, the new movement would, crucially, sideline the Soviet general as a mentor or influencer. Up until this time, Vlasov, who claimed to know Stalin personally and who claimed to be able to predict the responses of the leading Soviet military commanders, had been lamenting the fact that he was 'sitting in his little house in Dahlem' playing cards instead of fighting the communists. It is a serious criticism of Gehlen that he had not made better use of Vlasov during his time in captivity. His decision to avoid learning to speak Russian came back to haunt him but even using interpreters his conversations with Vlasov were few. Probably the best source FHO had on the Soviet mind was virtually ignored until it was too late. Gehlen would later say that he had avoided Vlasov fearing that his Russian Army of Liberation was infiltrated by communist agents and could not be trusted. In May 1945, Vlasov was riding in a US convoy when his presence became known to the Soviets who demanded he be handed over to them. He was court martialled and hanged as a traitor by them on 1 August 1946.

For Gehlen, Schellenberg was a threat but also a potential lifeline. Gehlen knew full well that it was Schellenberg's driving ambition to take FHO under his SS control, but he also knew that, like him, Schellenberg was, by this time angling for a way out of the mess. Both men were focused on survival. To protect FHO, Gehlen employed subtlety. He invited Schellenberg to FHO headquarters where, over the course of a full working day, he saw first-hand how Gehlen's staff collected and evaluated the huge amount of intelligence that flowed in and out. Gehlen knew that Schellenberg's people were nowhere near the level of efficiency required to take on that sort of workload and, after his visit, Schellenberg knew it also. Not only that but while Gehlen's leadership was attuned to the 'dry, sober and brittle craft', Schellenberg's nature was much more flamboyant and mercurial, he would never allow himself to become bogged down with something so dreary as intelligence gathering and analysis. The two men came to an unspoken agreement to keep out of each other's way and concentrate on getting through the next few months alive and, crucially, out of the hands of the Soviets.

Gehlen, therefore, now gathered as much information as possible about partisan movements from the Wannsee Institute and other research institutes, which kept lists of existing anti-Soviet groups, predatory partisans and deserters. He was mainly interested in military frontline reconnaissance commando units that existed as remnants of the Abwehr. While he outwardly supported it, Gehlen had no faith in Skorzeny's underground *Werwolf-Organisation* (armed resistance), set up to terrorise the enemy, which he thought was bound to fail without the support of regular troops. OKH seemed to place great store by *Werwolf*, however.

Meanwhile, there was a monumental clash of armies around Budapest but Gehlen, who was promoted to major general on 1 December 1944, stuck to his assessment that the main Soviet thrust would come just south of Warsaw with Stalin waiting for hard frost to solidify the ground conditions. It was still not obvious what arrangements had been made between the Soviets and their Western Allies, stalled in the Ardennes, about how to exploit the present situation. Clearly, Britain and the United States would dearly like the Soviets to expedite their attack to force the repositioning of German forces from west to east. Guderian, who was now commander-in-chief of the German forces, took Gehlen's figures of Soviet build-up and advised Hitler that the Ardennes defences should be scaled down to reinforce the Eastern

Front. According to Guderian's account, Hitler called Stalin's move a bluff and called Gehlen's data nonsense. Himmler, who was present, is supposed to have agreed with Hitler, which made Guderian's opposition irrelevant. This placed blame for what happened next firmly on the shoulders of Hitler but neither he nor Himmler survived to give their version of the conversation. While Guderian praised Gehlen for the accuracy of his intelligence, subsequent analysis shows that he underestimated Soviet strength by a hefty 40 per cent for two reasons. Radio reconnaissance was constantly being degraded because of improved Soviet security and a retreating German army was taking less PoWs for interrogation.[81] For Guderian and Gehlen, it is another piece in the jigsaw of their post-war self-styled embellishment of their wartime record.

While Guderian was urging all members of the General Staff to stand by their Führer as loyal standard-bearers, Gehlen had spent Christmas with his family in Legnica and was secretly making preparations to have his wife and four small children moved west. It was fairly easy for an intelligence organisation to forge the travel permits. Hitler had strictly forbidden any officer from evacuating any family members to the west but Gehlen's plans would not allow him to be governed by that order especially given that rumours were rampant about atrocities committed by the advancing Red Army and Stalin, himself, had decreed that 'the German beast [was to] be stamped out in its kennel'.[82] It was widely accepted that all children in areas overrun by Soviet forces would be evacuated to the Soviet Union for indoctrination into communism. Baun took Gehlen's wife and four children to Dresden on 21 January 1945 and some of Vlasov's men loaded a few of their possessions onto a truck and followed. In his memoirs, Gehlen says that Baun had then moved 'several truckloads' of FHO files together with Gehlen's family to Rossbach near Naumburg and thus avoided being consumed in the firebombing of the city on 13 February 1945.[83]

The first sections of FHO were moved to Zossen in Bavaria on 15 February 1945 and a couple of weeks later Gehlen's family and the documents Baun had taken to Naumburg were moved again. The family went to Cham on the Czech border and the files to Bad Reichenhall. Gehlen says that only two trucks were used to take them from Naumburg to Bad Reichenhall.[84] Baun then secured his own files in a similar manner to those of FHO with the most important ones going onto microfilm. These were buried also.

From a future historical perspective Gehlen was anxious that he make his position clear in a memorandum *Conclusions from the*

Assessment of the Present Enemy Situation in the East for the Conduct of Combat on the Eastern Front without appearing to be defeatist. In this he employed his customary approach by being cautiously optimistic but ensured that this optimism was based on eventualities that were clearly unrealisable. When he said crises could only be averted by 'the use of sufficient reserves, especially in fast formations' he knew full well that such reserves no longer existed. When he said that the Eastern Front 'could not be considered secure at the moment' it was a rather understated admission of an obvious truth. By contrast, he was openly critical of the situation in the west, for which he bore no responsibility.

On 6 February 1945, Gehlen had been made deputy chief of the Strategic Group of the General Staff but he was soon to find himself out in the cold when Guderian fell foul of Hitler on 28 March 1945 and was advised to take 'six weeks holiday'. Twelve days later Gehlen received an order signed by General Hans Krebs, Guderian's successor, advising him that he had also been relieved of his command to be replaced as head of FHO by Wessel. Guderian and Gehlen denied it, but it is likely that their dismissal was the result of having given Hitler poor advice. Guderian had taken Gehlen's advice that the Red Army would make a direct attack on Berlin and not, as Hitler believed, in Pomerania. Hitler, however, had been correct to believe that the Red Army would not make a direct attack on the capital without covering their flanks, which is exactly the mistake that OKH had made in 1941 at the gates of Moscow. For Gehlen, it was a blessing in disguise. It now gave him time to pursue his primary objective of departure with his organisation and the full measure of its resources to a place of safety.

As early as February 1945, his position with the Strategic Group of the General Staff had already given him scope to commission a secret plan for the evacuation of FHO and its precious card index. By 4 April 1945, an instruction *Geheime Kommandosache* (secret command matter) had gone out to

> ensure that officers, NCOs, men and secretaries are instructed that the order for movement must be carried out within two hours at the maximum and that within this period the entire card index must be loaded.[85]

Gehlen says that

> we tried to duplicate the caches as far as possible so that we would have at least one set of everything at our disposal when we came to set up shop again.

Gehlen's survival strategy was getting into full swing. Documents revealing allied plans for occupation zones after the defeat of Germany had found their way to FHO and it was to the US zone where Gehlen planned to deliver himself up.

Chapter 3
SAME FOE; DIFFERENT FRIENDS

Surrender

> It was important for our plan that we should not be captured too soon.
>
> Reinhard Gehlen[1]

Transferred to the Führer Reserve after his 'retirement' from FHO on 9 April 1945, Gehlen was offered a command post in the frontline by the Army Personnel Office but he excused himself by saying that he was needed at FHO to facilitate the hand-over to Wessel. It's clear that this was a ruse because Wessel had proved himself to be more than capable of taking on the role, having done it recently while Gehlen was hospitalised. It was merely a deception to give him time to put the finishing touches to a plan drawn up on 4 April 1945, the same day those instructions had been issued for the evacuation of the FHO card index. It was in Bad Elster in Saxony where he and Wessel had met up with Baun in a hotel room to action a plan that, for Gehlen had been months in the making. It was a plan that could only work if Baun was able to maintain his intelligence networks intact through the chaos of the war's end and have them ready to be reactivated as soon as possible afterwards. The two main protagonists, Gehlen and Baun agreed to work together in a relationship with equal standing based on a broad secret verbal understanding of what was required knowing full well that the merest hint to the SD of what they were planning would bring an instant and brutal death sentence. What Gehlen suggested, and what Baun agreed to, was no less than the implementation of a strategy they hoped would put them at the heart of a post-war German state in a polarised Europe allied with the West against the Soviet menace.

With Third United States Army forces some 60 miles to the west and Soviet tanks on the streets of Berlin, Prague, Budapest and Vienna, the three men plotted their route out of the trap. Gehlen was certain that Germany could not hold out for more than another month, but he was not as confident about whether or not the war would actually end. He still felt there was an even chance that the uneasy alliance between the Soviet Union and its Western allies would break down leading to an immediate east-west confrontation. That begged the question of which of the Western Allies to approach and offer them the FHO archive. In his memoirs Gehlen said,

> it is the duty of every sophisticated intelligence service to keep open a channel of communication with the enemy's intelligence services.[2]

He then went on to say that the FHO had established a channel to the British Military Mission in Moscow in 1943 and again in February 1945 had communication with MI6 who furnished him with a copy of British Prime Minister Winston Churchill's political intelligence appreciation of the Soviet Union, which, incidentally, impressed Gehlen with its accuracy. The Germans were known to have high regard for British intelligence and his experience of them may have suggested to Gehlen that he might have a hard time getting them to take him seriously.

It was Churchill who seemed, at that time, to be more worried than the Americans about a strong residual Soviet presence in Eastern Europe. Gehlen says that he initially contacted the British offering his services post-war and received no reply but the fact that he had chosen to hide out in southern Germany in what would be the American zone of occupation shows that from an early stage he intended to surrender to them. The Americans were much less experienced in the intelligence field and probably much more anti-communist than the British, which would probably make them an easier target.

It seemed as if his only hope was to negotiate with the 'young, raw, recent arrivals in the world of politics' but there was really no way of knowing what value they might place on his 'treasure'.[3]

All FHO staff were to be moved from Zossen to south Germany, which was the occupation zone allocated to the United States. That would put them beyond the grasp of Skorzeny who was still trying to have *Walli* agents integrated into his *Werwolf* units. It would be there also that contact was to be made with US forces but the first problem was how to avoid all of Gehlen's men being swept up and hauled off to PoW camps before they could even begin to negotiate. To make it easier, when any one of the three men – Gehlen, Baun and Wessel – were taken into custody, it was agreed that each would be authorised to speak for the other two. When taken into custody, they would attempt to make contact with each other using codenames, Gehlen was 'Fritz', Wessel 'Horst' and Baun 'Otto'.[4] All other staff should give only name and rank with no mention of their unit. On the following day, Baun, dressed in civilian clothes, went to Wendelstein in the Allgäu taking with him all the treasures with which they planned to buy their futures in fifty steel cases packed with the FHO and *Walli I* card index of Red Army personalities, all German agents behind the Soviet lines, reports, and aerial photographs. Gehlen says that

> we tried to duplicate the caches as far as possible so that we would have at least one set of everything at our disposal when we came to set up shop again.[5]

This seems to imply that much of the archive, certainly the most important parts had been put on microfilm.

Meanwhile, the SS was ruthlessly dealing with anyone they suspected of failing to engage in the final battle for Germany. Old scores were settled. Canaris and von Rönne were peremptorily court martialled and hanged. Karl-Heinrich Graf von Rittberg had been Gehlen's right-hand man for the past couple of years and he too was executed on 12 April 1945. It was a desperately dangerous time for Gehlen who had already been dismissed from his post. Accusations from his own side of failure, sabotage or treason could easily follow.

When Allied and Soviet armies met up on the river Elbe, the German forces were split and the FHO establishment along with them. One small group went north to Flensberg whilst the majority moved south to Bad Reichenhall where Southern Command Staff of OKH had accumulated. Wessel prepared his last enemy situation assessment for the Wehrmacht on 29 April 1945 and issued all FHO staff with forged papers so that they could conceal their affiliation with the department and protect them from the SS. Schellenberg did something similar for his men but ordered the destruction of all his operational documents. Gehlen had chosen a different solution. He discussed has plan to take his FHO files to the Americans with Winter, now a lieutenant general. He told Winter that he already had Guderian's approval. Winter had no hesitation in adding his blessing and added that he hoped that it might be possible for him to be part of such a plan in the future despite what he described as the difficulties of foreseeing the events of the interim period.

Between 3 and 5 May 1945, the cases of documents were now split up and taken into hiding. One lot went to Reit-im-Winkel to the south of Lake Chiem, another to Wildmoosalm, north of Kufstein, but the bulk went to Valepp where, on 28 April 1945, the heavy containers were hauled up the mountain track to the chalet and buried in a clearing the locals called *Elends-Alm* (Misery Meadow). Gehlen and Wessel with five other officers and three female staff assistants ensconced themselves in a

> large low-roofed, wooden hut, with broad eaves, a tall brick chimney and a veranda.[6]

Having put themselves out of the reach of the German High Command, they were effectively deserters, and were now in great danger but their situation began to change on 30 April 1945 with Hitler's suicide. Gehlen's objective was still to protect himself and his organisation from condemnation and vilification along with all the other Nazi organisations and in this he was not without options. He had anticipated the new political dynamic emerging from six years of war and it was his plan to make use of his valuable assets and trade them if he could reach the right marketplace.

His three-week stay at Misery Meadow beyond the daily grind of war were an intense relief for Gehlen who described his time there as his

> last days of freedom [in the] great outdoors [that] were truly enchanting.[7]

During the hours of daylight, with the winter snow disappearing fast, some of the group moved up to a camouflaged camp in the forest to avoid being surprised by the Americans, leaving the three secretaries and two young, wounded officers who could not make the climb. He wanted to meet his prospective captors on his own terms.

Gehlen was experiencing a sense of wellbeing in the mountain air and enjoying a brief respite from the punishing daily demands he had been subject to for three years as head of OKH but was still anxious about exactly how his plan would play out. It was by no means certain just how long US forces would stay in Germany after the end of the war and that decision would determine their interest in buying what he had to trade. If he had guessed wrong, then he could easily end up with a long term in prison or he might even be handed over to the

Soviets. At best he would become a refugee with no non-military skills in a country ravaged by war.

It was complicated by the fact that he was sitting in the centre of the *Alpenfestung* (Alpine Fortress) along with other Wehrmacht personnel all hoping to contact the US Army in the hope of doing business with them to facilitate an effective cease-fire, demobilisation of German forces or perhaps utilising them as a reserve for a possible confrontation between the Western Powers and the Red Army.

The situation changed dramatically after Hitler's suicide and the German surrender on 8 May 1945, but it was still dangerous to risk exposure. Rumours abounded of both US and Soviet trigger-happy and war-hardened soldiers shooting German soldiers on sight whether they surrendered or not. Approaching any Allied forces was not going to be straightforward so Gehlen waited to see how things evolved hoping they would calm down and, crucially, waited to see which of the Allied forces were moving into the area. Then he received a vital piece of intelligence that indicated to him that the time had come to make his move. Two German-speaking US soldiers, Sergeant A. Kinghofer and Corporal H. Hickson, had discovered the chalet and questioned the occupants. Not knowing exactly what to do with them, the Americans had given the men documents saying that they had been questioned and discharged by Allied forces. When Gehlen returned to the chalet at night, he concluded that the day's events meant that the US forces were active in the region and had an orderly way of dealing with, which reduced the danger somewhat. He was sure now that he would be treated well if he gave himself up and could prove that he was a German officer of high rank.

Anonymity was the key to survival out in the open, however, so when the day came for action all indications of rank were stripped from their clothes and after three weeks in the mountains, Gehlen took his group west hoping to make contact with US forces, but it was French mountain troops whom they encountered first as they descended the steep slopes of the Maroldschneid. The French showed little interest in Gehlen's party believing them to be civilians and allowed them to continue on to Lake Spitzing in the Schliersee region. Here they split up. Wessel went with Nauck, Heimenz, Schoenbeck and Ritter, and gave themselves up to US forces at Ruhpolding while, on 23 May 1945, Gehlen walked into the mayor's office of the small town of Fischhausen with Goellnitz, Hoheisel, Hindesin and von Wangenheim, four of his staff officers. It was here that 42nd US Infantry Division had set up a local headquarters. It was a shock and a humiliation for him to be interviewed by a mere US captain, John Schwarzwalder, who did not even speak German. Since none of the five Germans spoke any English, an impasse ensued. The young American officer was unimpressed with these men in civilian clothes but obviously having a military bearing. To get them off his hands, he arranged for them to be sent to Captain Marian E. Porter, a G-2 officer in Wörgl. Gehlen tried to explain to him the importance of facing up to the communists and that he had vital information as part of that effort but, as far as US troops were concerned, the Soviets were still their allies and Porter was not interested in listening to talk of fighting them. Three days later, Porter had Gehlen taken to Salzburg PoW camp from where he went to Seventh United States Army's Augsburg-Bärwald interrogation centre (SAIC). There, he was questioned over a three-week period by Lieutenant Drake whose main interest was the organisation and staff of FHO. Drake reported that Gehlen

> talked freely and gave all information willingly; he is anti-Communist and anticipates a Russo-Allied conflict

but resolutely refused to respond to questions about FHO. Drake began to suspect that Gehlen may have had nothing at all to do with FHO and might well be SS so he had him thrown into prison in Wiesbaden.[8] Meanwhile, Baun and *Walli I* staff had also gone south to the Allgäu where they ended up in French custody but were able to arrange transfer to the US zone.

Frustrated beyond measure, Gehlen took it upon himself to try and impress upon his captors exactly how important he was by writing a report *Russische Expansionspolitik in der Vergangenheit und Gegenwart* (Russian Expansionist Policy in the Past and Present). Strik-Strikland came across him at this time and later said that he had found him 'confident and unbroken'.[9] Gehlen's report seemed to stir some interest and he was questioned on Red Army leadership and tactics but he was not taken very seriously by his captors until a fortuitous meeting with his old boss, General Halder saw a significant change in his fortunes. Halder was one of an elite group of prisoners that included Admiral Dönitz, and he was able to convince the camp authorities that Gehlen was who he claimed to be which saw him transferred to the Villa Pagenstecher, an interrogation centre at Camp King in Wiesbaden run by United States Forces European Theatre (USFET) under Colonel William R. 'Rusty' Philp. Here, Gehlen was met by the German-speaking military intelligence officer Captain John R. Boker Jr who had experience of interrogating captured German intelligence officers during the war and had gained a certain expertise in the Soviet armed forces.

Boker was one of the first Americans to be confronted with the issue of working with former Wermacht officers against a background of what he described as a

> military and political situation [giving] the Russians control over all of Eastern Europe and the Balkans [leading to] an indefinite period of military occupation.[10]

Even before coming across Gehlen in 1945, Boker had already acquired

> a vast fund of information of the Soviet Air Forces together with Aerial Photographs covering most of the Russian Industrial complex within the range of German reconnaissance planes[11]

that together with twenty-two German intelligence officers had been captured in Czechoslovakia. Boker immediately realised the importance of keeping the documents and personnel together to get maximum intelligence benefit but was unable to resist British pressure to take the five top Germans of the group to their interrogation centre leaving the rest to be dispersed to their homes. It was against this background that he had then come across Gehlen in Wiesbaden. He knew something of Gehlen but was amazed when Gehlen described to him details of the 'size and ramifications' of the FHO and the scope of its work. Word must have got out, because a request now came in from a Soviet officer, working with the British on a joint commission sorting out German PoWs, for any information about the former head of the FHO and any of his staff. Such special interest shown by the Soviets on a mere one-star general among the hundreds of high-ranking officers and war criminals in the PoW cages, impressed Boker who started to see Gehlen in a different light and decided to keep quiet about his whereabouts. Whether or not he could make use of him was problematical, though, given Eisenhower's directive not to elicit help or advice from former Wehrmacht officers.[12]

While Boker found Gehlen to be 'anxious to cooperate', Gehlen was immediately impressed by the 'cultivated manners' of the 'tall, handsome, slim and straight' Boker whose family had emigrated to the United States from Westphalia, although he was by now a third-generation American.[13] It was a great relief for Gehlen when, after only a few conversations, he realised that Boker needed little convincing of the Soviet threat, and he was not alone in that viewpoint. It was soon clear that others, including the top US intelligence officer in Germany at the end of the war, Brigadier General Edwin L. Sibert, chief of military reconnaissance (G-2) of 12th Army Group High Command and his chief of staff, General Walter Bedell 'Beetle' Smith, anticipated an imminent break in the anti-Hitler coalition. Gehlen impressed upon Boker the importance of not wasting any time locating and protecting as many former members of his FHO staff as he could.

Sibert was alert to the enduring legacy of Nazism and recognised the need for a through reform and re-education of a German society conditioned by 'hundreds of years of authoritarianism'.[14] At the same time, he was an early advocate of shifting the focus of the US Army's intelligence services towards the communist threat. Under Sibert, G-2 became the principal intelligence agency of the European Theatre and took over virtually all the operational functions leaving the Strategic Service Unit (SSU – Foreign Office Intelligence (S1) and Counterintelligence Unit (X-2) of the US War Department) with no significant operational role.[15]

In general, newly deployed US military intelligence officers had scant understanding of Second World War German intelligence and accorded it rather more respect than it deserved. After all, Gehlen had got every major assessment wrong in his capacity as the head of FHO. He had missed the Soviet pincer movement at Stalingrad, misjudged the strength of Soviet armour at Kursk and predicted a quiet summer on the Eastern Front in 1944 days before the Soviets launched their biggest offensive of the entire war.

Despite the British having a low opinion of Gehlen's wartime record, he enjoyed a good reputation with the Americans in 1945 because of the belief that he had transformed German military intelligence when he took over from Kinzel in 1942. It was difficult for them to make a definitive assessment, however, given that their own intelligence agencies lacked any great experience or understanding of how the intelligence game was played. They had almost no agents of their own in Eastern Europe and had a desperate need for information about the Soviet Union, its forces in Europe, and the communist regimes east of the river Elbe. Gehlen's group was one of the few agencies which seemed capable of providing that. So began a manoeuvring for position between Gehlen and the Americans, first in the guise of G-2 army intelligence and later the Central Intelligence Agency (CIA). It had been US policy, laid down in the White House, not to spy on its Soviet allies during the war, which left Gehlen as one of the few specialists on the subject. Even then his role had been primarily in analysis rather than intelligence gathering. He had little experience of running espionage operations.

Sibert had, during the final months of the war and with the approval of US Secret Service officer Allen W. Dulles, been involved with an operation to encourage German frontline commanders to surrender and assist the Allies with information. Dulles was now head of the Office of Strategic Services (OSS) in Germany and had tried to convert his wartime group of German officials, politicians, academics and businessmen into a post-war intelligence network but most of them were keen to get back to their professional life and few had any interest in spying for the Americans now that the war was over. The OSS had, in fact, lost the battle against the US Army for control of occupied Germany. It was G-2 and US Army Counterintelligence Corps (CIC) who took on the security role.

Both Sibert and Dulles were accused of harbouring an 'American Gestapo' and Sibert especially had been unable to get US War Department approval to continue recruiting former Wehrmacht officers leaving him sidelined but now that the fighting was over, he saw Gehlen as a means of updating his plan to utilise German officers in an intelligence role. Sibert would later say that he had a 'most excellent impression' of Gehlen despite having to converse through an interpreter.[16] Gehlen's exposition of a Soviet Union determined to deny independence to any of its occupied regions and with the ambition to occupy the whole of Germany coincided with Sibert's own opinions. He then told Sibert that he had a vast resource of intelligence that would help the United States to combat Soviet moves but to fully exploit it he would need his erstwhile staff of FHO to be allowed to join him. Under direct orders from Sibert, Philp authorised Boker to trawl the PoW camps for ex-members of Gehlen's FHO staff and have them brought to Wiesbaden. Crucially, he also had their names removed from allied PoW lists to protect them from Soviet demands for their extradition.

While the general mood among the Allies was still one of cooperation with the Soviets and emphasis was still on seeking out war criminals, the Americans had to be cautious when dealing with German prisoners and could not move too quickly. They were still a long way from thinking that the animosity towards the Germans in official circles was sufficiently ameliorated to allow one of their generals to work with US intelligence. Furthermore, to advertise the fact that they were holding the former head of FHO would have led to an immediate demand by the Soviets to have him handed over to them. The Yalta Treaty stipulated that the United States was to hand over to the Soviets all captured German officers who had been involved in what were called 'eastern area activities'.

Reinhard Gehlen in 1918

Reinhard Gehlen in Muhrau 1924

Wedding of Herta von Seydlitz-Kurzbach and Reinhard Gehlen, 10 September 1931

Heinz Danko Herre, Gehlen's senior staff officer in FHO

Hermann Baun, head of Walli I

Adolf Heusinger and Hans Speidel; FHO officers who both played prominent parts in the FDR

Misery Meadow where Gehlen hid in 1945 before surrendering to US forces

General Vlasov inspecting ranks of his Russian Army of Liberation

Gehlen employee and Soviet spy Hans Clemens

FHO files

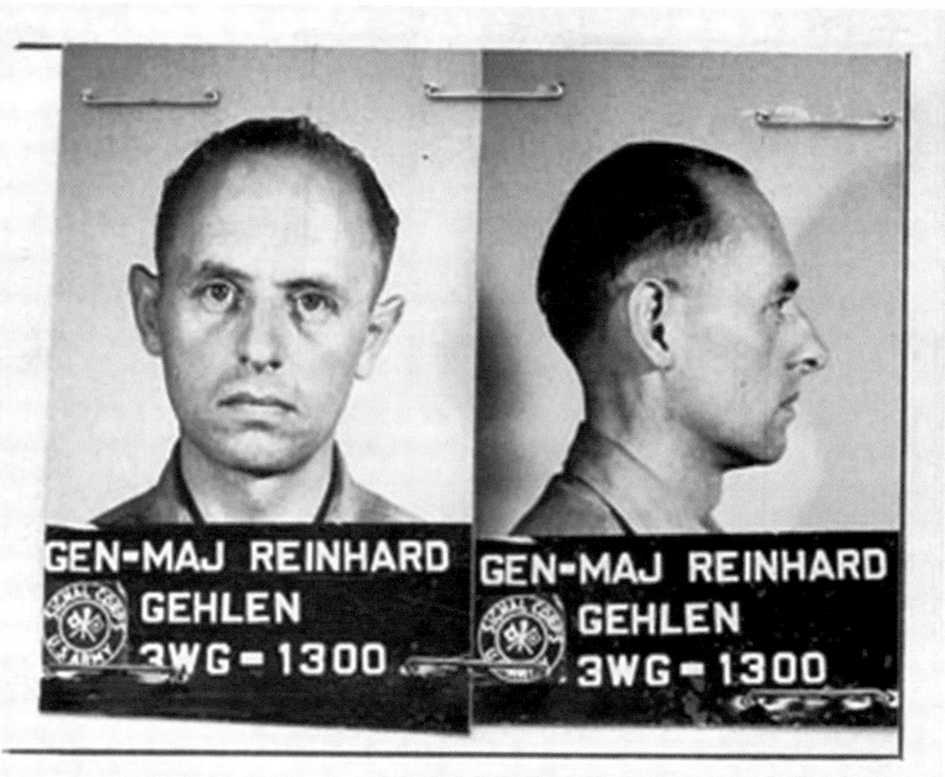

Reinhard Gehlen in US captivity 1945

Eric Waldman who did more than anyone to rehabilitate Gehlen

Pullach, the headquarters of the Gehlan Organisation after the war

Otto John, Gehlen's rival for post of head of the BfV

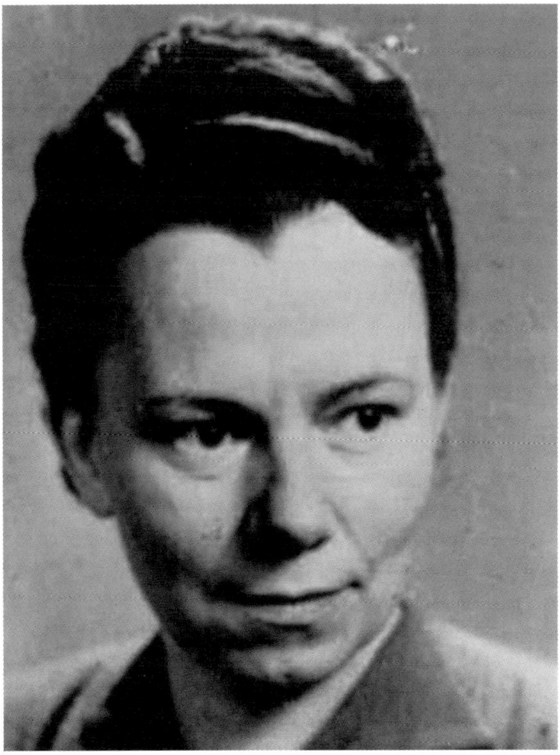

Gehlen spy Elli Barczatis who was executed by the Statis in 1954

Reinhard Gehlen in Zurich 1949

Gehlen now judged that it was time to apprise his captors of the locations of the buried files. Units were despatched to retrieve them, but Boker hit a snag when it transpired that one of the caches of documents had been recovered by the British and held at Höchst Document Repository but had not yet been evaluated by them. The last thing Boker wanted was for the British to know about Gehlen and his files so he rushed to Höchst with hastily prepared false documentation authorising transfer of the files to Wiesbaden in the US sector.

Using these files, Gehlen was allowed to bring together a group of eight ex-FHO officers in order to show what special knowledge and skills his former department possessed. Working inside 7th Army Historical Research Section in Wiesbaden, they produced a number of reports, *Arbeitsweise und Methoden des deutschen Ic-Dienstes im Osten während des Krieges* (methods of operation and methods of the German Ic service in the East during the war), *Kurzer Überblick über russische Maßnahmen zur Tarnung und Verschleierung von Aufmärschen und Truppenbewegungen* (brief overview of Russian measures for camouflage and concealment of marches and troop movements), *Aufgaben und Arbeitsweise des Armee-Ic* (tasks and working methods of the Army Ic) and *Auswertemethoden des deutschen Ic-Dienstes im Osten* (evaluation methods of the German Ic service in the east).

The Pentagon was busy arranging for the demobilisation of millions of US soldiers and bringing them home but became somewhat nervous when it was obvious that the Soviets were not going to follow suit. They retained a standing army of some 6 million men on east European soil. There were ominous signs that the wartime coalition would fracture very quickly. In this atmosphere Gehlen's reports were welcomed and the files on which they were based considered to be of strategic importance. Director of the US Military Intelligence Division Major General Clayton L. Bissell and the Intelligence Section of the Supreme Allied Headquarters agreed that the FHO files should probably be transported straight away to the United States, for evaluation but the fate of Gehlen and his staff remained temporarily unresolved.

Boker argued strongly for keeping Gehlen's staff and the files together, but Gehlen had no bargaining power left. He offered to bring Baun's network of agents into the discussion, emphasising their importance in any future US-Soviet stand-off but he did not know that Baun had already been recruited by Sibert. He had been arrested on 29 July 1945 and interned, with Wessel, as a 'mandatory arrestee' in the US Detention and Interrogation Centre (USDIC) at Camp King in Oberursel where officers of the disbanded German General Staff and the intelligence services were housed. Sibert was trying to keep them out of the hands of the Soviets as well.

Baun had convinced Sibert that his agent networks east of the river Elbe were still intact and functioning. He was deemed to be of much greater value than Gehlen because it had been he who actually ran the *Walli* espionage networks behind Soviet lines. He submitted two detailed proposals for the resumption of his group's activities but Sibert had yet another putative espionage organisation. Quite unaware that it had been exposed as suspicious, he was hoping to reactivate the Klatt network under Kauder and Turkul.

Arnold M. Silver, who was assigned to investigate Kauder and Turkul, both of whom were held at Oberursel and were showing a strong desire to make themselves useful to the Americans, found Turkul to be 'a useless oaf' who had lent his name to the Klatt network but never recruited a single source, although Klauder had managed to convince the Abwehr that he had been one of his principal agents. Silver's opinion of Longin was no better.

> An intelligent liar who could spin off 60 cover stories in as many minutes

was how he described him. Longin claimed to have been in Istanbul during most of the war and had communicated his reports on the Soviet military to Klatt in Sofia by telephone. Only Kauder was of any real interest but Silver had already interviewed Wagner, who had been head of the Abwehr station in Sofia and was being held by the French at Bad Wildungen, and knew of Wagner's suspicions about Kauder.[17]

Eventually Kauder admitted that he had suspected, as early as 1941, that he was being used by the Soviets but had seen no advantage to himself by sharing his doubts with the Abwehr. Right at the end of the war, Kauder said, Schultz had confessed to being a Soviet agent. Turkul and Longin had been mere figureheads to give the scheme authenticity and knew nothing about the subterfuge. Given the level of support Turkul, and especially Kauder were getting, Baun saw that there was a real danger that he was being sidelined so he began a whispering campaign to undermine Turkul. Both the British and US were obliged to investigate Baun's accusation that the wartime Kauder ring had been a Soviet subterfuge, but reported that they could find no evidence to support it. There were enough suspicions aroused, however, to persuade Sibert to abandon any idea of using Kauder.

Before he had been apprehended by the Americans in 1946, Kauder had been living in Salzburg where he had been approached by his old friend Schultz and invited to go to Vienna to set up an import-export business. To Kauder that sounded like a plot to lure him into Soviet hands and he was not too unhappy to be swept up into US custody soon afterwards. Silver came across Kauder again in 1952 in Salzburg when Kauder unsuccessfully tried to interest him in a 'real' network he had now set up in the Soviet Union. Kauder's name cropped up again in 1962 when a CIA agent in Austria reported that he also had been approached by him with an offer of a Soviet network of spies. Both Baun and Gehlen would later play down FHO reliance on the Klatt network and claimed that most of its intelligence he provided had been derived from newspapers and radio reports and was not secret material at all.

In US Custody

> We were led out of the airport building and loaded into a van with no windows and just one barely adequate ventilating slot.
>
> Reinhard Gehlen[18]

A tug-of-war had developed between the Bissell and Sibert for control of both Gehlen and his FHO files. Bissell had previously reached an agreement with British Major Kenneth Strong to have all German PoWs with special knowledge of the Soviet Union to be handed over to British intelligence (MI6). With General Dwight D. Eisenhower's agreement, Bissell instructed Sibert to hand over all the intelligence he had gathered concerning the Soviet Union and scale down his activities in that department. All FHO files were to be sent to London before being handed over to Washington but Sibert was anxious to keep both Gehlen and his files in Germany 'for necessary local exploitation'.[19] Sibert was in no position to deny Bissell and Eisenhower, however, and he was not even apprised of the fact that Gehlen had been flown to the United States in the official aircraft of General Bedell Smith, the future US ambassador in Moscow and later head of the CIA, until after the event. With Gehlen had gone six of his staff, Colonel (retired) Konrad Stephanus (Ic of Army Group A), Major (retired) Albert Schoeller (deputy head of the Command Group FHO, responsible for the daily assessment of the enemy situation), Major (retired) Horst Hiemenz (Group Leader II – Overall Situation Russia-Balkans), Major (retired) Hans Hinrichs (head of Division IIe, evaluation of Soviet command and operational principles), Major (retired) Karl Freiherr von Lütgendorf (Ic of the 8th Army), and Captain Herbert Füner. After a thirty-three-hour journey with stopovers in the Azores and Newfoundland, they arrived in Washington DC on 22 August 1945.

Silbert flew to Washington DC for a 'frank and open' discussion with Bissell who was forced to admit that Silbert should have been informed before Gehlen left German soil. A compromise was reached. The files would go to Washington where Gehlen's people would have access to them and produce reports for Bissell while Bissell was given authority to build another group from the inmates of Camp King in Germany. This became known as Operation X.

Gehlen's welcome was not exactly warm, however. Boker, who had accompanied him on the flight, was no longer allowed to stay with his group and experienced significant hostility from the Pentagon to working with Germans in any way. He was officially denied access to Operation X but he found ways to keep in touch. After a lengthy medical examination, the Germans were put in a windowless prison van and taken for intensive interrogation at the classified military base of Fort Hunt, near Alexandria in Virginia. The twenty cases of documents, however, went to Fort Ritchie in Maryland. Gehlen's compound, surrounded by barbed wire and guarded by four watchtowers, was part of a military intelligence unit established in 1942 to house and interrogate high-ranking German PoWs. Contrary to what had been the case during the Second World War when it had been the British who had typically taken the lead in interrogating high-ranking Wehrmacht officers, they now relinquished that responsibility to the Americans and relied on them to share their findings.

Fort Hunt was quite independent of all other US intelligence agencies who had no idea that Gehlen was in the country, or even in US custody. Here, the men were treated well but essentially kept in isolation in rooms that were 'bugged' and were refused permission to send letters. It was very different from the conditions at the Villa Pagenstecher and it was by no means clear to Gehlen that his strategy was working out as he hoped. The Americans seemed to want to make use of him, but they couldn't quite work out how and meanwhile showed little enthusiasm or urgency. There was no interest in Gehlen's ideas for a future German intelligence service. He could only hope that Boker and Sibert were taking a more positive approach and were working for his rehabilitation.

Some of Vlasov's veterans found themselves at Camp King telling interrogators all they knew about the Soviet Union while others were smuggled out of Germany to avoid repatriation to the Soviet Union and taken to Fort Hunt. US intelligence considered these men to be 'prized' sources of intelligence about the Soviets and some were eventually recruited by the CIA as agents for covert operations inside the Soviet Union.

Eric Waldman was a Jewish émigré from Vienna who had lost members of his family in the Holocaust. Technically he was not part of Fort Hunt staff, but he worked there as part of G-2 military intelligence. As a student of German military and political history, he had, for some time, been collecting information about German and Soviet military tactics gathered from interrogation of PoWs and was given an early warning that Gehlen's group would be on his agenda. While Gehlen was languishing in a sort of 'limbo', it was Boker who saw an opportunity to advance Gehlen's cause. He contacted his friend Waldman and told him about the idea of recycling Gehlen's FHO as part of an anti-Soviet intelligence organisation. Waldman was, on the face of it, an unlikely ally in Boker's scheme but he had been impressed by Gehlen's updating of the *Handbook on the Red Army* he had written and interviewed him at length. The two men were somewhat different in character but were well matched intellectually and, amazingly, given their backgrounds, the two men warmed to each other almost at once and became firm friends.[20] Waldman urged Gehlen not to lose heart and irked the camp commander by using his G-2 authority to keep Gehlen and his companions out of the clutches of the Fort Hunt interrogators. As an indication of the way their relationship developed, Waldman made arrangements for Gehlen's family to be picked up from their quarters in Cham and taken to the much safer Hotel zur Krone in Oberstaufen in the Allgäu. It was the beginning of what would become a much closer friendship.

By mid-November 1945, Gehlen's group had been augmented by another fourteen personnel, some of whom had been members of Vlasov's army, and produced 716 typewriter pages and 68 maps and appendices which encouraged their captors to grant improvements in their circumstances with better accommodation and facilities to send (censored) letters and cigarettes to their families in Germany.

Waldman was now instrumental also in getting the War Department to ask for Gehlen's comments on its assessments of Soviet military deployment. When he saw the material the US Army had, Gehlen's confidence was considerably boosted by his realisation of just how much US military intelligence was in its infancy compared with FHO and he used this to demonstrate to them just how useful he could be when it came down to analysing Soviet warfare capabilities and strategy. There was still too much residual hostility towards Germany to allow any talk of setting up a purely German intelligence service under his leadership, however. With the Nuremberg war trials only just opening, it was impossible to make public any suggestion that there was even one operational unit of the Wehrmacht working in the service of the US Army.

The War Department commissioned him to produce another batch of reports over the coming six months covering the Red Army order of battle in Europe and a study of how to acquire political and military intelligence about the Soviet Union. This was no easy task given the extent to which Gehlen had relied on Baun for much of the intelligence upon which such reports were made during the war. Gehlen was slowly resigning himself to remaining in the United States permanently and investigated the possibility of taking out American citizenship and bringing his family over from Germany.

At first, only the documents had been of real interest to the Americans with Gehlen's people brought as a compromise measure and were of secondary importance. By early September 1945, however, Gehlen, with his six assistants, was commissioned by Colonel John Raymond Lovell, the former military attaché in Berlin, to write a number of reports for the Historical Branch of the War Department on various aspects of Soviet military capabilities. These included *Methods of the German Intelligence Service in Russia, Development of the Russian High Command and Its Conception of Strategy during the Eastern Campaign, Fighting Methods of the Russian Armies Based on Experience Gained from the Large-Scale Russian Offensives in the Summer of 1944 and the Winter of 1945* and *Development and Establishment of the Russian Political Commissars within the Red Army*, as well as studies of the Russian army order of battle, surveys of Russian army units and equipment and the organisation of Russian commands and troop leadership.[21] Other work included a study of *Mobilization and Deployment of the Red Army, Desertion and Defection in the Red Army during the Second World War* and *Influence of Terrain and Climate on motorized warfare in the European part of the USSR.*[22]

In addition, what became known as the Bolero Group produced 42 assessments of senior Soviet leaders and numerous projects of various kinds, such as the evaluation of 2,000 paybooks with discharge certificates from Soviet captivity and a list of the Red Army's field post numbers and their vehicle registration numbers. The FHO files that had come to the United States with Gehlen had been taken and stored in the Pentagon and also made available to the German Military Documents Centre Project (GMDS), which had been set up by Colonel Lovell at Camp Ritchie, where a number of former senior Wehrmacht officers had been brought to in September 1945. The 'Hill Project', as it was called, was set up jointly by G-2 and the British War Office military intelligence. The task of this group, who became known colloquially as the 'hillbillies', was to create a comprehensive history of German army experiences on the Eastern Front including studies of combat under all types of circumstances and conditions. The GMDS and Gehlen's staff worked independently and quite unaware of each other's existence until the bulk of the German component of GMDS was repatriated in April 1946 and the remaining eleven officers, including three generals, transferred to Bolero at which time all the documents at GMDS were transferred to be stored in the Pentagon. Particular attention was now given to Panzer warfare and logistical issues associated with the eastern campaign. There was a palpable shift in emphasis on research to focus on aspects of a potential war against the Soviets.

Despite the obvious interest in the research conducted by Bolero, there is no evidence that these documents had any impact on American strategic or operational planning in the immediate postwar world in the way that later studies carried out in the 1950s had. Neither is there any evidence that any of these documents ever appeared as part of the curriculum for the training of Western Allied military officers.[23]

During his time at Fort Hunt, Gehlen had contact with a number of high-ranking Americans including Admiral William D. Leahy, chief of staff and President Truman's national security advisor and Allen Dulles. Leahy was close to the president, but there is no evidence that he ever discussed Gehlen or the implications of hiring a Nazi spy network with him.

Meanwhile, Bissell and Sibert had started work on their 'other group'. Wessel and Baun had been taken out of detention and recruited to resurrect the *Walli I* network but they were getting a lot of opposition from the SSU, who wanted nothing to do with it, calling the idea 'rather grandiose and vague', and objected on the basis of cost and poor security. They had discovered Schmalschläger in a PoW camp and believed that his *Einsatzkommando* experience was a much better basis upon which to build a counterespionage operation. Their opinion was that Baun and his FHO associates be dismissed and the whole idea dropped.[24] Sibert ignored the advice and sent officers round PoW camps in the US zone in Germany to look for useful former members of the Gestapo, *Bundesnachrichtendienst* and *Die Geheime Feldpolize* (GFP – Nazi Secret Field Police), and at the same time for former counterintelligence officers who might be able to work against the Soviet intelligence service.

Baun had impressed Sibert with his initial concept for setting up an intelligence service but he had not been able to get authorisation to operate within the entire Soviet-controlled area in Europe, the Middle East and the Far East, which is what he proposed. G-2 USFET would only countenance a much smaller operation. He would only be given permission to collect information about spies in the American occupied zone of Germany, but he did not let that constrain him. He managed to hoodwink Sibert's people to provide enough money and black-market goods to expand his enterprise from 150 employees in May 1946 to over 2,000 twelve months later. G-2 didn't seem to have given too much thought about the fact that their supervision of Baun was quite inadequate and he was able to build his espionage apparatus very much according to his own ideas and staffed with people he knew personally and who, if possible, had already served in a similar role during the war. These would ideally be former officers of the mobile front-line reconnaissance units who would be able to revive their old contacts and establish new ones. They were provided with enough American goods and money to establish stable connections as thus qualify for permanent funding. His objective was to revive and rapidly expand his espionage activities as quickly as possible to impress the army.

While Gehlen was hard at work writing his reports at Fort Hunt, Sibert had authorised Baun to establish contacts with his old Abwehr crew and get his new operation up and running within six months. Gehlen's authorisation for this was requested and given but Baun had no idea that Gehlen was in the US and believed that he was being allowed to reactivate his networks as a result of his own initiative. He initially recruited circles of friends and comrades who would be occasionally visited in the eastern zones when information would be passed on in a way that did seem particularly to have any subversive connotations. Many were not professional spies and they certainly had no idea that it had anything to do with the Americans. These were outdated methods quite unsuited to post-war circumstances and many agents were quickly identified by Soviet security particularly after the East German *Ministerium für Staatssicherheit* (MfS, better known as the Stasi – Ministry of State Security) was formed in 1950.

Baun was nothing if not ambitious and he grasped the opportunity. He planned an extensive espionage operation under the general cover of an economic venture, with headquarters in Argentina and bases in China, Afghanistan, Iran, Turkey, Yugoslavia, Italy, Spain, France, Germany, Austria, England and Sweden. Baun had a particular disdain for fiscal restraint and caused eyebrows to be raised in Washington when an estimate of the cost of all this was put at around $40 million.

Undaunted, he eagerly started planning but waited in vain for funds beyond what would keep his current agents in place. This amounted to a monthly allowance of 300 kilograms of coffee, 25,000 cigarettes, and 10,000 matchboxes.[25]

The most important branch position was set up at Karlsruhe and became an important gateway for former Nazis. It was in the 'Blue House' separated from the main Camp King and run by 26-year-old West Point graduate, Lieutenant Colonel John R. Deane Jr. It was an indication of how US intelligence viewed these remnants of FHO that they appointed an officer who had no intelligence background and did not even speak German. Deane reported directly to Sibert but Philp had too much on his agenda to take much notice leaving, what Deane had christened Operation Rusty, in the care of USFET. Baun wrote to Gehlen informing him of developments in Oberursel but omitted to tell him what he had already told Wessel; that he, and not Gehlen, should be 'head of the network of the secret intelligence service in the East'.[26] He was clearly stealing a march on Gehlen but Gehlen was a little more aware of the disinterest G-2 was showing in the whole idea and had some hope that Baun would not get far with his 'grandiose' plans.

He countered Baun's move with a report *Current Possibilities of Gaining Political and Military Knowledge and List of Possible Questions of Enlightenment with Regard to the Soviet Occupation Zone, Poland and the Baltic Sea Region* that, on the face of it, was much less ambitious than anything Baun was offering but, crucially, much more in line with War Department budgets. He followed it up with *Russian Operations to the West in Central Europe* in which he concluded that the Red Army was sufficiently strong to take on the current occupying forces of the Western Powers with every prospect of a quick success but he doubted that, the Soviets would seek a direct conflict with the US and Britain in the near future while tensions were boiling over in the Caucasus.

Gehlen also secretly asked Wessel to personally scrutinise all recruits to Baun's organisation to ensure that as many as possible were from FHO and not the Abwehr, the clear implication being that the organisation would then be much more likely to accept Gehlen if he could turn his fortunes around and force the issue of leadership. Baun was having his own problems by now. There was very little interest in his over-ambitious plans for an intelligence network to cover the whole Soviet-controlled territories in Europe and the Middle East. Having taken some time to work out which way they wanted to play the spying game, the US had opted for counterintelligence to be the focus of their efforts and Baun could bring no relevant experience to that table but the Americans were willing to consider a scaled-down operation of intelligence gathering with him in charge. There was still time for Gehlen to stake his claim if he bent a little towards US expectations.

He had urgently requested Waldman to locate Herre, the man upon whom he had come to rely for so much. Herre had been made aware of Gehlen's post-war plans as early as February 1945 before going to Czechoslovakia to work with Vlasov so he was well primed to study how Vlasov's men might become useful in that context. He had narrowly avoided capture by Soviet forces and interned at Marquandstein PoW camp where he was the senior German officer until his release in December 1945. From his home in Krün in the Bavarian Alps, he had been called to Oberursel to meet up with Wessel and Baun who encouraged him to reestablish contact with as many of Vlasov's 'army' as he could. Then in March, at Gehlen's request, he was taken to the US to him at Fort Hunt where he was appointed deputy leader of the Bolero Group. It was entirely in keeping with Herre's character and professional competence that he immediately set about immersing himself in American culture, learning as much as he could about all aspects so that he could perform a useful role as intermediary between Bolero and their hosts.

As an influence on Gehlen's career, there were few who rivalled Herre's contribution. When meeting others, Gehlen was rarely seen without him and relied on him to smooth any negotiations. Herre's competence ranged from assisting Gehlen with personal decisions to a later facility in handling sensitive issues with Bonn when the German government was formed. He was not so much a superlative personal assistant as an alter ego.

Gustav Hilger, an experienced German diplomat and expert on Soviet matters, was also located and recruited. To further promote his case to be recognised as the expert on counterintelligence against the Soviets, Gehlen came up with a report entitled *The Problems of Germany's Western Occupation Zones in the Light of Russian Aims*, which predicted that communist reconstruction and re-education in the Soviet controlled part of Germany would draw on ideas developed under National Socialism and could be much more rapidly implemented than the complicated process of democratisation in the west.

Events beyond Oberursel and Fort Hunt now impacted on the way that the United States would move forward in its dealings with the Soviet Union and with Gehlen. Soviet intransigence in Persia had thrown into sharp focus the altered relationship between the Soviet Union and its erstwhile Western allies. Nobody in the Truman administration really knew what it wanted of any new intelligence agency but there was certainly going to be a requirement for the US to step up its vigilance. Essential functions were identified and brought together in a permanent, if incomplete, intelligence structure incorporating the most important capabilities of the wartime OSS into a firmer institutional framework. On 22 January 1946, the National Intelligence Authority (NIA) under William Leahy and the Central Intelligence Group (CIG) under Rear Admiral Sidney W. Souers were created as the primary agencies for strategic warning and management of clandestine activities abroad. US President Harry S. Truman called the CIG his 'Cloak and Dagger Group of Snoopers'.[27] Then just a few weeks later, instead of withdrawing its forces from Iran (northern Persia) as agreed, the Soviets sent more troops into the region and shattered the illusion of peaceful post-war coexistence between east and west. Baun, Wessel and Gehlen would be among the first beneficiaries of this breakdown of trust. The Americans found they had a sudden need for a counterintelligence capability to monitor Soviet activities in the US-occupied zone but had no experience in the field.

As a stop-gap measure, on 1 April 1946, while Gehlen was still in the US, Baun got official authorisation to set up the *Dienststelle 114* counterintelligence units as part of Rusty but the Americans did not put in place any adequate means of supervising recruitment into Baun's networks which expanded in an uncontrolled fashion. Meanwhile, arrangements were made to return Gehlen's Bolero Group to German soil. One of Gehlen's first priorities was to discover which of his FHO staff had been taken into Soviet captivity and try to get them back through exchange of prisoners.

The Germany to which Gehlen would return was little changed from the one he had left a year previously. It was a world of

> craters, caves [and] mountains of rubble [where] life was a daily struggle for a handful of potatoes, a loaf of bread, a few lumps of coal [or] some cigarettes.[28]

The country was staring famine in the face and the threat of disease hung over the smashed cities. All across the country, more than 10 million displaced persons and ex-slave labourers from every nation that had been occupied by the Nazis joined those released from concentration camps, many requiring some form of medical care. The US Army had lived with this for a year, and it was clear to them that the United States was really the only country with the resources to pick up the pieces of the broken country but it was only the Germans themselves who could fit them back together. This meant that those who knew what was required, the ones who knew how German ran and the ones who had the knowledge and experience were the same ones who had run the country under the Nazis. How this could be squared with the stated policy of de-Nazification and demobilisation of US forces was a political conundrum, however. Even as Nazi leaders were facing the hangman at Nuremberg, the victors were forging a necessary alliance with the German people to rebuild their nation but, at best, it would be no more than half a nation. At Versailles in 1919, Germany had lost its empire and only just avoided a communist revolution. Now in 1945, 5 million communist soldiers were camped on half of its homeland and in no hurry to leave.

Churchill warned that unless matters were resolved with the Soviets quickly, the continent would once again be engulfed by war. As US soldiers were being repatriated in their millions, the Soviets were relentlessly pursuing their own hostile agenda with constant provocation and harassment. Even Italy looked as if it might fall to the communists. Allied aircraft that flew too close to the demarcation lines were shot down. Now more than ever, intelligence about Soviet capabilities and intentions was every bit as urgent to the Western Allied nations as they had been to the Wehrmacht on the Russian steppes.

The questions revolved around whether the Soviets would pursue their agenda by political or military means. Specifically, intelligence was urgently needed on the structure of the Red Army and the political leadership, possible radical groupings in the Soviet leadership under General Georgy Zhukov and Soviet Foreign Minister Vyacheslav Molotov and the question of whether Zhukov believed that militarily occupation of Central and Eastern Europe, even the whole of Germany, was more important than the question of the Mediterranean and the Near East. On a practical level, the US required information about how Soviet troops in eastern Europe were to be accommodated, whether the occupying army would be reduced or strengthened, the whereabouts of the tank armies, the nature of any camouflage measures employed, what training priorities will be set, what bridge reinforcements, road construction and stockpiles were being organised. Other issues involved assessing the public mood, understanding what propaganda measures were being employed to influence it, how were the police to be organised and which German generals and general staff officers in Soviet captivity were getting preferential treatment.

There was also the issue of Western press speculation about the persistence of fascist influences in post-war Germany, much of it fuelled by Soviet propaganda, but still influential, which would find new impetus if it was widely known that Gehlen and FHO officers were returning to Germany as official members of Western intelligence agencies. It was vital to keep Gehlen's people at arm's length and make clear that while they might be working alongside US agencies, they were certainly not working for them. These were the questions facing the Western Powers and their dilemma was to what extent they were willing to allow Gehlen, Baun and Wessel to help resolve them. While Baun and Wessel had remained in Germany, Gehlen had grasped the opportunity to impress his hosts with his expert knowledge and believed that he was making progress towards his ultimate goal but Baun had not been wasting his time either.

In June 1946, the US State Department demanded that all German PoWs in the US be repatriated and that included all Bolero personnel. G-2 protested but to no avail. Waldman was concerned that some of those returnees might face de-Nazification courts risking exposure of where they had been and what they had been doing at Fort Hunt for the past few months. His warnings resulted in Deputy Governor of Germany General Lucius D. Clay granting blanket amnesty to them all. It was a clear indication that the Americans were much more relaxed about the de-Nazification programme than the German courts were in 1946. When Gehlen was told that Bolero was being sent to German, he found it prudent to 'one hundred percent' agree to 'spend a few years' work under Baun's leadership but once there he had no intention of doing so.[29]

Oberursel

> I felt that the common defence interests of the western powers must inevitably lead them to recognise that without Germany all Europe was lost.
>
> Reinhard Gehlen[30]

Waldman had championed Gehlen's cause in negotiations with an advisory committee set up by the War Department over exactly how the Gehlen Group might work within US intelligence. A 'gentlemen's agreement' was reached between Gehlen and Sibert the details of which were never written down so we only have the version Gehlen, who set great store by it, gave in his autobiography *The Service*.

1. A clandestine German intelligence organisation was to be set up, using the existing potential to continue information gathering in the East just as we have been doing before. The basis for this was our common interest in a defence against communism.
2. The German organisation was to work not 'for' or 'under' the Americans, but 'jointly with the Americans'.
3. The organisation would operate exclusively under German leadership, which would receive its directives and assignments from the Americans until a new government was established in Germany.
4. The organisation was to be financed by the Americans with funds which were not to be part of the occupation costs, and in return the organisation would supply all its intelligence reports to the Americans.
5. As soon as a sovereign German government was established, that government should decide whether the organisation should continue to function or not, but that until such time the care and control of the organisation should remain in American hands.
6. Should the organisation at any time find itself in a position where American and German interests diverge it was accepted that the organisation would consider the interests of Germany first.

Gehlen claimed that Sibert made the agreement without the knowledge of the US War Department and he acknowledged the political risks he took. He heaped praise on Sibert for his 'great vision' in taking such a 'bold step' in the face of anti-German feelings.[31] It was a very open-ended commitment that the CIA was never able to renegotiate and, over the following years, allowed the strong-willed Gehlen to resist US control over his activities.[32] Gehlen also claimed that the Americans agreed that it would be he and not Baun who would head the new organisation but in reality, in the early stages at least, it was Baun who made all the running and he had every expectation that it would be he who was in charge. His *Walli* operation had essentially been independent of the FHO during the war and he was not inclined to submit to Gehlen's dominance now. It was unfortunate for him, however, that Gehlen was a much more sophisticated negotiator.

When he stepped onto the MS *Seaflier* that was taking him home on 8 July 1946, Gehlen was confident that his time was coming but when it docked at Le Havre instead of Bremerhaven, the French authorities were waiting to board it and search for any Germans who they wanted to interrogate as part of their own post-war investigations. It was touch and go whether Waldman, who had been waiting in Bremerhaven and had only learned of the new arrangements at the last minute, would arrive in time to prevent Gehlen ending up in a French prison and possibly a French court of law. Fortunately, he made it and whisked Gehlen and his team away to Orly for a flight to Frankfurt am Main before the French authorities knew he was ever in the country. Once there Gehlen was assigned a cover identity as Richard Garner, residential address: c/o Dr. Erhardt, Günthersburgallee 10, Frankfurt am Main and later became Hans Holbein. Arrangements were made to have all the close families of Gehlen's group to be brought to the Blue House.

Gehlen assumed that he would be the pivotal figure in whatever intelligence strategy the US had worked out and he was shocked to see just how far Baun, who had remained in Germany working closely with Sibert, had progressed in taking on that role for himself. Baun had been informed of Gehlen's impending return and, when asked for his reaction, was quick to make it known to Sibert that he would be pleased to 'make use' of Gehlen's group.[33] With little bargaining power and uncertain just how much backing he had in Washington, Gehlen met Baun and, somewhat disingenuously, agreed to Deane's proposal to have Rusty and the Bolero to work side-by-side but with separate leadership and under the overall supervision of Colonel Philp. Wessel had remained in Germany working with Baun but had remained loyal to Gehlen and had spent much of his time recruiting into Rusty ex-FHO officers and operatives whose loyalty would ultimately be to Gehlen.

It was going to be Deane's job to pull all these strands together and create a functioning intelligence service as quickly as possible before the FHO intelligence files became outdated and obsolete. This was not going to be made any easier by his lack of experience in intelligence and his barely adequate mastery of the German language, but he was a seasoned veteran who had commanded a battalion during the war and he had no qualms about working with his former enemies. Crucially for Gehlen, Deane had been working with Baun for some months and had not formed a favourable opinion of him. Despite Baun's considerable links with agent networks, Deane found him and his 'cooked-up' schemes 'unsavoury'.[34] It was hard to keep track of his comings and goings and very little was known about who he was actually meeting on his frequent clandestine trips. He was building his network almost entirely according to his own ideas and avoiding scrutiny of the recruitment of his old wartime agents.

Firstly, he searched for former officers of his *Walli* reconnaissance units by trawling through the lists of prisoners held in the many PoW camps but later, through them, it would mean reactivating sources that had remained in what was now Soviet-occupied territory. The consequences of a hastily put together organisation were largely independent and isolated networks that operated way beyond any sort of central control. The only stabilising factor was Baun himself to whom all agents owed their allegiance. Many agents had little idea of who their ultimate controllers were. They had no contact with anyone except their immediate handler who needed well-developed personal skill and a fair amount of psychological awareness. Both agents and handlers required local knowledge, an ability to move around unobtrusively and a keen sense of self-preservation. Since 1942 when he took over FHO, Gehlen had shown no understanding of this aspect of intelligence and showed no inclination to learn about it. For agent-running, he had been totally reliant on Baun.

Considering the level of investment Baun had requested for his post-war schemes, it was also a serious concern for his US backers that his financial accounting was a shambles. He had no fixed budget since his operations were funded with money and barter goods on a success-related basis. This encouraged quantity over quality resulting in some overlapping of operations and duplication of intelligence. Evidence of success often rested entirely on the basis Baun's own self-assessment reports, which proliferated. During the time that Baun had been the leading figure in post-war intelligence in Germany, the ramshackle way in which he operated at such a critical time when the country was broken and at the mercy of competing forces had exposed its security in ways that would have far-reaching consequences.

Gehlen was comforted by the fact that his wife and children had been brought to 'Basket', the name the Americans had given to the Oberursel compound, but his Bolero Group was back on home soil on a strictly limited and experimental basis. Their exact role had yet to be defined beyond historical research but in preparation for a more significant role, Gehlen immediately resorted to military discipline with his former staff and left them in no doubt that even if the war was over any new organisation led by him would run on lines familiar to them from the war years. Especially, since he had not been impressed by US security during his time there, he began to impose upon his new organisation his customary cloak of secrecy but, significantly, this increasingly excluded the Americans.

Bolero was beginning to evolve, uncertainly and with small steps, into what would become the Gehlen Organisation (OG). In it, Schoeller managed the card index, Hinrichs monitored the radio and newspapers, Hiemenz liaised with Baun, Hilger evaluated the Soviet economic and political environment while Füner did something similar on the military questions. Von Lütgendorf, one of the original Gehlen evacuees had been quietly shipped back to Austria having disgraced himself in the US by calling Waldman a 'Viennese pig Jew'.[35] He later became the Austrian minister of defence and died in mysterious circumstances in 1981. Richard Helms remarked that, for all his professed admiration for the British approach to official secrets where the identity of the British intelligence chief was never publicly acknowledged, Gehlen was the only intelligence chief who never discouraged the linking of his own name to that of his service.

At this time, Baun's Rusty was being expanded with former officers of frontline Abwehr reconnaissance units who had been quietly recruited from PoW camps. Recruitment of one erstwhile Abwehr, SS or SD intelligence specialist led to the recruitment of their old comrades as word spread. They would not have to present a curriculum vitae. There would be no interview. Word of mouth recommendations made sure that nothing was committed to paper, identities could be shielded from scrutiny. Baun knew that these were the very people who could do the work. There was no time to train others and when it was obvious to Gehlen what was happening, he accepted that employing ex-Nazis was a political risk worth taking and did his best to avoid addressing the issue and where that was not possible, play down its significance. These officers were then instructed to revive their old informants and agents who were infiltrated into the Soviet zone. They went in carrying false papers identifying them as released US PoWs and once there used those documents to acquire official documents. They were the free to circulate and eventually to return to the Western zone without hindrance. In this way, Baun was building a decentralised organisation very much according to his own ideas with little oversight by Sibert. Up to this point, he had only a vague idea of what the Americans had agreed with Gehlen and he showed little interest in finding out.

Networks were created with subordinate services made up of staff described as *bunt und uneinheitlich* (colourful and inconsistent) that were allowed to operate very much according to their own preferences.[36] By mid-1946, Baun had six networks up and running. *Leitstelle I Ost*, under Arthur Moos looked after the training of agents especially in the Baltics. Herre was in charge of what was left of Vlasov's army in Germany while one of Herre's colleagues, Roman Hönlinger, was brought in alongside Alfred Bentzinger, who recruited a number of ex-SS men and whose responsibilities were in counterespionage. Hoping to impress Sibert, Baun instructed his staff to come up with as much intelligence as they could and not worry too much about its quality and relevance. Left to operate with lose control, it was inevitable that there would be duplication of efforts where agents would interfere with each other's activities. Some agents worked for more than one section and some ended up inadvertently spying on members of other sections. Rusty was fast becoming

> a mixture of independent, control-resistant and isolated personal network.[37]

Gehlen and Baun were fortunate that they were not working with the British who took one look at their output and concluded that they contributed little to understanding of current Soviet capabilities or intentions. They had not been impressed by Gehlen and Baun's manifesto *Gedanken zu den ideologischen Grundlagen unserer Arbeit im Dienst der USA* (thoughts on the ideological foundations of our work in the service of the United States of America), which, to them, was little more than a 'pompous and pathetic apology' for their part in the Nazi war machine.[38] As for domestic political analysis, this had been the responsibility of the Gestapo during the war, they said, and Gehlen had no experience of it, only 'newspaper knowledge'. They thought Baun a little more informed about the local situation, but believed his vision lacked a 'global' perspective. They obviously did not know just how far and wide were the ideas Baun had been pestering Sibert with. Perspective might also be required when looking more closely at this British response to Gehlen and Baun. It was actually drawn up by one Harold Adrian Russell 'Kim' Philby who was later exposed in 1963 as one of the 'Cambridge Five' Soviet double agents in the British MI6.

When it dawned on Baun that Gehlen was planning to take over the Rusty network, he was unsure just how much support he could count on from Sibert. He reacted angrily accusing Gehlen of going back on his word. Gehlen replied that he had Sibert's backing as the senior officer, a claim that Baun disputed but he was reluctant to take his case directly to the Americans. In any case, Sibert was on the cusp of a recall to the US and he had always been susceptible to Gehlen's persuasive, subtle and cleverly constructed style of argument. During the months spent in the United States, Gehlen had developed a keen understanding of American attitudes and sensibilities and held a distinct advantage over Baun when dealing with Waldman and Sibert. Baun, he knew would try to retain as much independence as possible, which did not play well with the Americans. Baun's character had been forged as a German with strong Russian influences. He was completely bilingual and according to Gehlen, 'had absorbed the Russian mentality', which 'put a natural barrier between him and the Americans'.[39]

Gehlen appealed directly to G-2 USFET with a report on his ideas of the sort of framework required for an intelligence organisation. It was not uncommon for the two men to slant their recommendations according to which Washington department they were dealing with, but this report was superficially amended by Deane and Waldman in such a way as to make it even more appealing to Sibert's own views.[40] It fundamentally challenged the idea of Bolero and Rusty operating side by side, as they had during the war, with Baun sourcing the intelligence and Gehlen evaluating it. At that time Baun had, strictly speaking, worked under Gehlen whose pride, as much as anything, meant that he baulked at giving Baun a joint leadership role now. Sibert's plan would have meant that Baun controlled the flow of intelligence and Gehlen would only see it after Baun's people had summarised it, translated it and passed in on to G-2. Indeed, a great deal of intelligence would not reach the Bolero at all.[41] If G-2 had any questions, however, they were to go straight to Gehlen's people who did not even have access to the raw intelligence and would be forced to go to Rusty for clarification. Gehlen would resist such an approach with all his guile and energy. It was not only extremely inefficient and cumbersome but threatened to enhance Baun's position at Gehlen's expense. To reinforce his claim to leadership, Gehlen encouraged his people to refer to Rusty as the Gehlen Organisation or simply the Org.

This led to a crunch meeting on 30 August 1946 between Gehlen, Baun and Sibert. Sibert was scheduled to return to the US and transfer to the new CIG and he planned to take Rusty back with him keeping it out of the hands of CIC. He was anxious to ensure that there were no upheavals or embarrassments before he was relieved of his responsibilities in Germany. Gehlen had no problem with that, but Baun resisted it. He had no illusions about what it would mean if his immediate superiors were sitting in Washington and not Oberursel. While Gehlen would later boast of his great patriotism and resistance to American control, it was Baun who was the one who most stoutly defended the independence of Rusty. He lost control of the narrative, however, primarily because his barely concealed hostility and slipshod manners put him in a poor light compared to the calm, respectful and efficient impression that Gehlen projected. He obviously lacked Gehlen's ability to make a good impression. He had little understanding of American sensibilities in the way that Gehlen and Herre had and, in all that he did, seemed to show mild contempt for the Americans and then, of course, his early death also prevented him from giving his side of the story.

During most of the war in the east, Baun had worked for the Abwehr and had only latterly come under Gehlen's control but now he had got used to working independently of Gehlen again and he was in no hurry to give up his freedom of action. He suspected, rightly, that in the immediate aftermath of the war, he had been of significantly greater interest to the Americans than Gehlen and with his hands firmly on the purse strings, Baun channelled the bulk of his funding into building his networks and kept Gehlen continually short of the means of expanding the evaluation side. The pattern of uncontrolled growth of Baun's networks, lack of US control and simmering animosity between Gehlen and Baun was established and it would be a constant burden for Gehlen and the Americans in the years to come.

The new arrangements would mean much greater US intrusion into Baun's operations and threatened to restrict his control. Neither was he particularly happy about giving the Americans a window through which they could observe his methods of working. They were hardly likely to approve of the liberal way he allowed his agents to spend their money any way they saw fit and recruit whomsoever they chose. He thought that he was sufficiently important to oppose would force a rethink, but Gehlen saw that, if Baun persisted with his obstructive tactics the Americans would simply cut Rusty loose and leave Baun and Gehlen to go their own way and that would be the end of his own ambitions also. It was a pivotal moment not only in Gehlen's career but for the way that German intelligence would evolve and grow through the following decade.

Gehlen and Wessel now plotted Baun's downfall. Wessel took on the day-to-day running of the Bolero side of operations while Gehlen spent his time working on ways to modify the relationship between that and Baun's outfit and bring them closer together in such a way that Sibert's concept of a joint agency could be realised. Gehlen needed to do that because without Baun's network, he was essentially 'blind'. It was a clear break with the way that FHO and the Abwehr had operated during the war and one that was brought about not out of conviction but of necessity. At the same time, Gehlen retained the hope that he might persuade Sibert not to relocate the operation to the US. For him, it was not a matter of principle rather an issue of control. He knew that Sibert's longer term ambition was to integrate the whole of his organisation into existing US intelligence agencies on US soil and by keeping it in Germany he would be able to maintain the momentum towards a purely German organisation.

Deane and Gehlen together formulated a proposal for a combined Rusty-Bolero organisation that left Rusty as the procurement service outside the overall management structure as Baun's *Walli I* service had been during the war. Despite having been almost irrelevant since his return to Germany, Gehlen was now touted as more compliant than the troublesome Baun and the natural choice to take over the leadership. Deane allowed him to expand his staff and set up two new departments, 'economic evaluation' under Helmut Kloche and 'political evaluation' under Hilger, both of which carried English titles in recognition of US sensibilities. Deane's submission to G-2 also stressed the extent to which any intelligence operation aimed at the Soviet Union would be much better served by officers who had long experience and knowledge of the Soviet mentality. He played on the fact that Baun was lower in rank than Gehlen and had never really been trusted by the US Army.

For his part, Baun asked for and got a relocation of his staff to the *Jagdhaus*, a remote hunting lodge, in the Taunus mountains north of Frankfurt. He had never been comfortable working amongst the Americans and, especially, Gehlen's former Wehrmacht officers and was much happier away from them all but it tended to leave Gehlen a free hand to promote himself with the Americans. Out of sight, Baun continued to bring back into his fold many Russian experts who had served with him in *Walli I* during the war. People like Kurt Kohler and Hans von Lossow who were more than happy to turn their backs on their miserable circumstances in PoW camps. With limited support and virtually no control from Oberursel, Baun set up a network of bases in the US zone of occupation under the umbrella of the Technical Intelligence Branch (TIB). From there, agents were dispatched into the Soviet zone to recruit informants particularly to gather information about the Soviet order of battle.

Attention was now focused on the Soviet occupied zone where, on 21 April 1946 two political parties had united, creating a single, dominant party, the *Sozialistische Einheitspartei Deutschlands* (SED – Socialist Unity Party of Germany) in what would become East Germany. It was an amalgamation of the *Sozialdemokratische Partei Deutschlands* (SPD –Social Democratic Party of Germany), a mass organisation of the political left, and *Kommunistische Partei Deutschlands* (KPD – Germany's small Communist Party). It was a clear statement that the Soviets were staying put and were poised to take advantage of any political unrest. This gave Gehlen a clear target to aim at. There was no shortage of Germans who were only too willing to sign up to 'give the Ivans and the SED a smack in the eye'.[42]

On 6 September 1946, SSU informed Sibert that they were willing to take over the running of Bolero and Rusty on the condition that Deane,

Waldman and Philp remained in Germany to oversee the operation and take responsibility for it. SSU referred to the two outfits as 'Keystone' but it continued in everyday operations to be called simply Rusty. Sibert had been recalled to Washington a few days earlier to join the staff of new CIS and was replaced by Major General Withers A. 'Pinky' Burress who, on 1 October 1946, recommended to Director of Central Intelligence Lieutenant General Hoyt S. Vandenberg that SSU take over Rusty's estimated 600 agents operating inside the Soviet-controlled part of Germany and run them from US soil.[43] Rusty was still very much on trial as far as its US backers were concerned and the disruption caused by the changeover from Sibert to Burress came at a time when Gehlen still had no real idea about what the Americans hoped to do with his organisation. Support for it was slipping away as the US's own nascent intelligence agencies, such as the CIG, were beginning to make their presence felt and were threatening to swallow it up. The army still considered that Rusty was 'one of the most prolific and dependable sources' but it should be remembered that they were trying to persuade the SSU to take it over. Some in the SSU were not convinced and argued that Gehlen's product was

> comparatively low-level [and produced] little new or particularly valuable information.

An oft-quoted study contending that the OG provided 70 per cent of all American intelligence at this time was probably conducted by Gehlen himself.[44]

One of the SSU staff, Colonel Donald H. Galloway, conducted a review on behalf of Vandenberg. He criticised the cost of the operation and lamented its lack of US control. In his view, the Germans produced only low-level intelligence and strongly suspected that the group had been penetrated by the Soviets. He had no hesitation in recommended that the CIG leave it well alone. By December, the amalgamation of the Bolero and Rusty within the SSU was still very much on the G-2 agenda but there was a reluctance to progress the idea until CIG approved it.

A CIG response to Burress's letter on 16 October showed a distinct nervousness about the risk of Rusty employing ex-Nazi war criminals when it stated,

> It is considered highly undesirable that any large-scale US-sponsored intelligence unit be permitted to operate under even semi-autonomous conditions. Unless responsible US personnel are fully acquainted not only with the details of each operation carried out but also with the

> identities and backgrounds of all individuals concerned, no high degree of reliability can be placed from an American point of view upon the intelligence produced.[45]

This was far from a ringing endorsement and Deane feared that Rusty could lose US backing completely if he did not act. He went to New York for a meeting with Allen Dulles, head of the OSS in December to persuade him to give Gehlen his backing. Sibert was also in New York at the same time and he had also gone to see Dulles but his message was quite different. Gehlen and Baun were out of control, he told Dulles. They had hundreds of agents in the Soviet zone and the US Army knew almost nothing about any of them. He was speaking for the whole army when he begged Dulles to take over responsibility for it. From the start, Dulles had been intrigued by the prospect of utilising Gehlen. He understood the issue of infiltration but strongly supported the idea that Gehlen was a force to be harnessed and utilised to the full. As a compromise, he agreed to take a closer look at Rusty. He asked CIG officer Samuel Bossard to undertake a study of reports from Gehlen and check them for credibility against intelligence from other sources. Bossard then went to Oberursel in early 1947 for an in-depth on-site investigation.

Baun, who spoke no English, had made few friends among the Americans and was usually treated with suspicion by them meaning that he was relatively powerless to oppose Gehlen, Deane and Waldman's combined attack on his leadership of Rusty but he still controlled the majority of the US Army funds coming their way and so retained an important hold over Gehlen. At first, he would not even sanction the purchase of a car for Gehlen and when he eventually was forced to do so he, childishly, provided one with no battery.[46] Having very little money and struggling to make it relevant, Gehlen's plans for his organisation were stalled. Money was the key to fund operations. Without it they would simply fade away but, at this time, Germany was a place where a great deal of money could be made on the black market. Deane, whose commitment to Gehlen never faltered, was only too willing to turn a blind eye when Gehlen's people resorted to black market economics, which they did with great frequency, skill and ruthlessness, but it just further increased the animosity towards them from other sections of the US Army of occupation. What little money the organisation got from the army it used to buy supplies, such as cigarettes, which it proceeded to sell on to black market dealers sometimes for ten times what they cost. They would then tip off members of the US Army Criminal Affairs Division who would confiscate them and sell them back to Gehlen who would sell them back to the market. Agents in the field were paid in US dollars, which, again, could be exchanged for local currency increasing spending power manyfold. Trade with the Soviet zone in penicillin was also very lucrative. Occasionally, Gehlen's agents were picked up by the CIC whose remit included arresting former German intelligence officers but that was of little concern to them. With an arrogance that infuriated and frustrated the CIC, detainees would put in a call to headquarters, which quickly saw them back on the street again.

On a broader front, Gehlen looked to the renewal of the German state. His experience of US Army intelligence had shown him just how naïve and ignorant they were of the subtleties of European political dynamics. His experience of dealing with OKH and, in particular Hitler, on an active battlefront left him with a keen instinct for survival and a great deal of experience of navigating a career through difficult circumstances. His feeling now was that he was in a situation ripe for exploitation. He was one of the few Germans to whom the Americans could turn for advice in their dealings with the Soviets and his distinct impression was that they were going to need an awful lot of it. His sense was that his previous military rank would give him the advantage over his main rival, Baun, when it came down to the rehabilitation of the post-war German state but Baun would not be easily outmanoeuvred. Baun's had bold ambitions of leading a combined Western intelligence alliance in an anti-communist crusade, but he had an unrealistic view of just how much his new American paymasters shared this vision. Gehlen, whilst in no doubt that the Americans were becoming more willing to face up to the communist threat, was more realistic about the length to which they would go, however. He was not entirely convinced that the Americans yet fully appreciated what they were up against and he knew that the width of the Atlantic Ocean would persuade many US leaders to consider the threat to Europe as something for Europe to worry about. In the long term, and maybe even in the short term, he believed that the German people were going to have to grow strong again to take responsibility for their fate and they would need leaders.

It became one of Gehlen's first priorities to make contact with officers who had served on the General Staff. These were the natural leaders he revered who understood duty and discipline and had experience of command. Who else could be the backbone of the new state? This did not go down at all well with sections of the US occupation forces who started referring disparagingly to Rusty as 'that bunch of Nazis'.[47] This was not entirely unwarranted. As early as summer 1946, CIC had picked up a number of Germans who claimed to work for US intelligence. Investigations showed them to be ex-Nazis with unsavoury war records who turned out to be working for Baun. At this time, Waldman leapt to Gehlen's defence saying he was quite sure that Gehlen was not recruiting Nazis. The two of them went together when interviewing recruits, Waldman said, and he made it clear from the start that he would have nothing to do with any SD men. Apart from his personal antipathy, ex-Nazis would be very susceptible to blackmail and pose a serious security risk. Walter Schellenberg was one of those who was eager to offer his services but Waldman vetoed it.

It must be concluded that Waldman's obvious admiration for Gehlen had clouded his judgement because there were a great many former Nazis who had scrambled into Gehlen's 'lifeboat' to later become the core of the German intelligence service.[48] In fact, it would later be the case that some former Wehrmacht General Staff officers who had been working within the Operational History (German) Section of the US Army Historical Division were, themselves, integrated into Rusty from 1947 onwards. It was not politically convenient to advertise the fact, but there was considerable collusion between Gehlen and the US Army in the early stages of planning and implementation of German rearmament. A significant impediment to this strategy was the difficulty that would arise when trying to bind both actors and sympathisers of the military resistance against Hitler as well as former soldiers of the Waffen-SS under a unified leadership.[49]

The pressure was on Deane to show that Gehlen was worth all the trouble, so he set Gehlen a target date of July 1947 by which time he had to show evidence of a network of agents within the Soviet Zone of Germany, Poland and the Soviet Union. Baun's radio operators had tried to make contact with agents who had worked for *Walli I* during the Second World War but most had ditched their radio sets and given up after Germany's defeat. This was no surprise to Gehlen who used it to undermine Baun's position with the Americans. In January, Wessel had written a report entitled *über die Notwendigkeit neuer Führungsmaßnahmen in der Rusty* (On the Need for New Leadership Measures in Rusty), which had impressed Deane who was now persuaded to install ex-Colonel Hans-Jürgen Dingler, a cousin of Gehlen, as Baun's second-in-command, which was a serious blow to Baun's prestige. Dingler had no intelligence experience but had been Chief of Staff of the LVII Panzerkorps.

Naturally, placing agents in positions where they could have access to useful information was extremely difficult and Gehlen had little success in doing so but he did institute a system that produced important intelligence. During the Second World War, interrogation of Soviet

PoWs had proved productive and the Abwehr had developed great expertise in amalgamating large quantities of seemingly unimportant information and from it building a comprehensive picture of Soviet resources, deployment, order of battle, military production and, on rare occasions, objectives. In a modification of that system, called *Aktion Hermes*, Gehlen now interrogated German soldiers who were returning from Soviet captivity. During their time there, these men, probably as many as 3 million, had been moved around from place to place all across Soviet-controlled territory building roads, mining, laying railway tracks even working in factories. Each saw only a tiny fragment of the Soviet world but together they painted a picture from which Gehlen's Evaluation Group, under Herre, could learn much about what was going on.

He turned now to a complete assessment of Soviet intentions and in this he was very much reliant on Baun's sources and Wessel's opinions. From Baun, he wanted intelligence about the current ideas being discussed by Soviet leaders and he wanted to know who were, currently, the leading influential figures in the Kremlin. At the same time, he subtly tried to persuade Baun to scale down his ambitions and adopt a longer-term acquisition strategy and one less reliant on the Americans. Baun responded with some bitterness at the way his people in Oberursel were being treated by the German authorities. The local police, he said, were too much under the influence of the Western Powers, whose priorities were de-Nazification, and who took little interest in communist infiltration, Soviet-sponsored provocations and personal attacks on him and his staff. Gehlen was not unsympathetic to his concerns. An intelligence agency can only be effective if its security is watertight and he too worried about his staff being recognised. Strict protocols were instituted to safeguard their identities. Gehlen assumed the pseudonym Dr Schneider.

Baun's authority, already diminished by Deane's championing of Gehlen, was further weakened when he was found to be hoarding foreign currency in anticipation of funding his own independent espionage outfit. Increasingly Baun's 'personal leadership style' was found to be incompatible with his responsibilities and he was replaced as head of Rusty by Dingler in April 1947.[50] It was a risky move. Despite Baun's 'web of vanities and financial machinations' Gehlen had to avoid the risk that he might look for another client and take his agents with him.[51]

At this point, Gehlen also brought in his brother-in-law Joachim von Seydlitz-Kurzbach even thought, like Dingler, he had no intelligence experience. In, also, came Adolf Heusinger as head of evaluation, a move that was initially resented by Wessel who was increasingly prone to criticise Gehlen's leadership decisions although he would later come to see Heusinger as a viable option to replace Gehlen. Heusinger always denied any involvement in war crimes but his position as head of operations on the Eastern Front would have placed him right at the heart of the fight against partisans which was conducted with ruthless brutality.

He had surrendered to the Americans in the Harz mountains and placed in a PoW camp where he was recruited to assist the US Army Historical Division that was compiling a history of Operation Barbarossa. He had been frustrated by having to stay working for the Americans for more than two years so it was with some relief and great enthusiasm that he responded to Gehlen's call in September 1947. Working under a former subordinate was a small price to pay for the opportunity to make a contribution to the rehabilitation of his country. Heusinger, however, would not make a significant contribution to OG intelligence capabilities, preferring to spend his time with other former Wehrmacht leaders such as Hermann Foertsch, Horst von bn and August Winter discussing military and political matters. Mellenthin, a sophisticated and intelligent man, was particularly useful as a political ally having headed a department running military attachés before the Second World War and he would prove adept as a lobbyist for the OG with the Americans and later with Bonn. He assiduously canvassed all OG staff inquiring about old friends and acquaintances to locate his former attachés.

Both Wessel and Dingler, especially, were uncomfortable with Gehlen's recruitment of these men whose presence was changing the whole character of the organisation. This was, in part, because Gehlen had his eye on the log-term objective of reforming the German armed forces but also to give sustenance to ex-Wehrmacht officers and their families who were suffering post-war deprivations. Such attention, quite naturally, bound these recruits to Gehlen in ways that the Americans were slow to appreciate. Gehlen was basing his judgements more and more on the candidate's background in the Wehrmacht, family connections and what his own instincts told him about their reliability. Deane was supposed to vet all applicants for top jobs but, in practice, he lacked the experience to set his judgement against Gehlen's. Sibert would look back on this as a failure of US management. It was inevitably because even when Bolero and Rusty were combined and their staff increased to around 2,000, there were essentially still only two US Army officers monitoring them. Gehlen, himself, was later to say that

> it was fortunate that initially we had to deal with two Americans who had no idea about the business.[52]

Even with its increase in personnel, however, and its reputation as the 'most dependable and prolific source of information on Russian military intentions and strength', Rusty constituted a worryingly small agency with which to confront the immense Soviet machine.[53]

When Bossard had arrived at the end of March 1947 to carry out his investigation into Rusty, Waldman, in particular, found his presence onerous as he peered and probed into every nook and cranny over a two-month period during which he interviewed all the leading OG members at length and finally submitted his report to Washington on 29 May 1947. It was the first time that Gehlen had been subjected to scrutiny by anyone who had any real knowledge of Germany's wartime intelligence networks. Bossard commended Rusty for the 'strength and nature of German personnel employed' and its productivity due to

> the wide scope ... and relative freedom [afforded them by the United States] in their planning and actions.

However, he also warned that because of the low ranks of Deane and Waldman, that very lack of tight control and the obvious inclusion of former Nazis and SS personnel could

> constitute a source of political embarrassment to the US Government and a security menace to American overt as well as covert activities in Germany.[54]

His view, however, was that employment of former Gestapo, SS or SD personnel was restricted to the agent level and there were none in top management positions. It can only be assumed that Gehlen had, on a personal level, made such a positive impression on Bossard that he was willing to take Gehlen's word for much that went into his report. Gehlen had given his 'word of honour' that any responsibility placed in him would not be betrayed and Bossard thought Gehlen to be a Prussian officer of the highest standing. It helped that Gehlen was able to persuade Bossard that responsibility for any shortcomings in agent recruitment and deployment were the responsibility of Baun who had just been demoted.[55] That, however, did not prevent Gehlen from utilising Baun's networks to maximum effect and with little or no modification as control over them was transferred to him. It would prove to be a decision that would have financial, political and professional costs for the future government and intelligence services of the FRG.[56]

The real danger for the Americans was that the OG was evolving from an instrument of the army to a semi-independent German intelligence agency that assisted the Americans on its own terms. The staff numbers had ballooned to around 3,000 and the current monthly bill was around $47,000.[57] Despite noting that there were 700 Georgian, Ukrainian, Polish and White Russian agents in one operational group and another 800 White Russians in another. Brossard said

> There is no evidence to show that any section of the operation has suffered penetration, defection or compromise from a hostile agency.

Just how confident he thought he could have been about that is hard to fathom.[58] To emphasise just how wrong Bossard was, the organisations susceptibility to Soviet penetration was illuminated in November 1947 when the Soviets arrested a Rusty agent, Rudolf Harnisch, in Leipzig and 'turned' him leading to the arrest of some thirty of Gehlen's Soviet Zone agents.

At around the same time, a Russian émigré named Alexander F. Chikalov-Almazov came under suspicion also. He had been a member of Soviet intelligence before the Second World War and had become one of Vlasov's men after he was captured in 1943. After the war, he offered his services to Western intelligence agencies 'offering excellent information about Soviet arms'.[59] He was taken up by the OG and settled in Munich building up a network of Russian émigrés telling them they were working for American intelligence agencies. He came under scrutiny along with another Rusty agent V.P. Tukhol'nikov-Sokolov when the CIC launched Operation Hagberry to root out Soviet agents. They could find no single report ever having been filed by either man but neither could they prove that they were Soviet penetration agents. Chikalov disappeared from Germany in 1949 and declassified Soviet documents show that he was condemned to death by a Soviet military court. Although Operation Hagberry did not succeed in identifying Chikalov as a spy one way or the other, the illuminated the real problems surrounding the employment of émigrés, which was that there could never be any confidence about their allegiances.

Bossard did not propose that CIG liquidate Rusty but did recommend a serious restructuring. He said,

> The magnitude of responsibility either to continue or liquidate [cannot be] exaggerated.[60]

Its more valuable elements should be identified and 'brought into control for long-term production', preferably leaving Gehlen in charge since he was 'more amenable' and 'the only one who could get the *Monstrum* of Rusty under control.'[61] All personnel, contacts and future plans of the organisation should be recorded to prevent it becoming an underground organisation using US funding to prosecute a covert guerilla war against the Soviet forces in occupied become the German Democratic Republic (GDR East Germany). On a positive note, Bossard suggested that the organisation offers talented and skilful personnel who may form the nucleus of a future German intelligence service.[62] In essence what he was saying was that the OG could potentially be a very useful adjunct to US intelligence but its ultimate goals might not coincide with the best interest of the US and it was unlikely that the US could influence the course of its evolution without much tighter controls. Bossard concluded his report by saying that

> Every effort should be made … to allow Gehlen to dominate the organization at the expense of Baun [who] should be reduced to the status of a high-level operator with little, if any, executive power,[63]

Wessel warned that political events often moved at an alarmingly faster pace than they had been used to in the military. The Soviets, he told Gehlen, would try to expand their influence all across the European continent first by supporting socialist parties in fragile political environments such as Italy and Germany, and then by expanding their influence over trade unions. Using anti-fascist propaganda, they would try to undermine the social structure with a kind of cultural Bolshevism aimed at the broad masses. All this would be in the shadow cast by a huge and ominous Soviet military presence all across eastern Europe from the Baltic to Albania. Wessel doubted US commitment to Europe and saw another war as an inevitable consequence of their withdrawal but Gehlen thought this assessment over-pessimistic and expected the Soviet Union to concentrate on economic exploitation and consolidation of occupied territories He did, however, qualify this with his customary caveat by saying that 'surprises … should not be completely excluded'.[64] It was also indicative of his cautious approach that he had gone with Waldman to Spain to make secret arrangements for the evacuation of the whole OG staff there in the event of a surprise Soviet attack.

For Gehlen and his people, security and secrecy were second nature. Most of the US personnel Gehlen had to deal with in Germany were military men who were up to their eyes in administering a country still ravaged by the effects of war. Their intelligence operatives were rank amateurs by comparison and virtually nobody in the occupying administration understood the population they were dealing with. Well accustomed to US working methods, Gehlen found it relatively easy to outmanoeuvre them. After all, he had cut his teeth militarily in a Reichswehr that operated for years illegally under the noses of occupying forces. All the US Army wanted from him were results, it cared little about how he got them. Waldman was later to say that the army did not have the experience or time to control, or even try to control, Gehlen's operations.

Washington's wily political warriors were not quite so ready to turn a blind eye to Gehlen, however. Vandenberg's successor, Rear Admiral Roscoe H. Hillenkoetter had read Bossard's report and strongly recommended that 'Rusty be liquidated' and that CIG absolve itself from any further responsibility for it. Others saw only former Wehrmacht officers and SD people and were willing to see its destroyed as they circled to pick up any valuable debris. The army, however, had invested a great deal in Rusty and, while they were not overly confident in it, they felt the need to offer support. Director of Military Intelligence Major General Stephen J. Chamberlin went as far as to give his 'unqualified backing' to Gehlen and rejected Hillenkoetter's criticism but he was forced to acknowledged that there was an issue around the perception of a resurgence of the German General Staff and intelligence service which looked to some like reactivation of the Abwehr.

One of the crucial issues was that of minimal American oversight of Rusty. Beyond Deane and Waldman there were few US personnel involved in supervisory roles. At least that was how it worked until Deane was called back to the US in September 1947 and replaced by Colonel Willard Koehler Liebel, a tough combat veteran who was keen to remind Gehlen who had won the war and delighted in lecturing him on how German stupidity had lost it. How much Gehlen understood is doubtful since Liebel, spoke no German, did not like Germans and was not shy about letting them know. Obviously, he gained neither the respect of Gehlen or Waldman and fortunately for Gehlen, the brash, authoritarian Liebel had few admirers in Washington either. The more he tried to impose his authority on the organisation, the more Gehlen closed ranks on him and made it extremely difficult for Liebel to keep track of what he was up to and Liebel soon realised that he was losing what little control he had over Gehlen. Liebel's position was undermined by his wife's proclivity for taking advantage of the many temptations all around to make a little money for herself by illegal currency exchange. When the wife of a fellow officer threatened to testify against her, Liebel had her sent back to the United States as an 'undesirable dependent'.[65]

Chapter 4

THE GEHLEN ORGANISATION

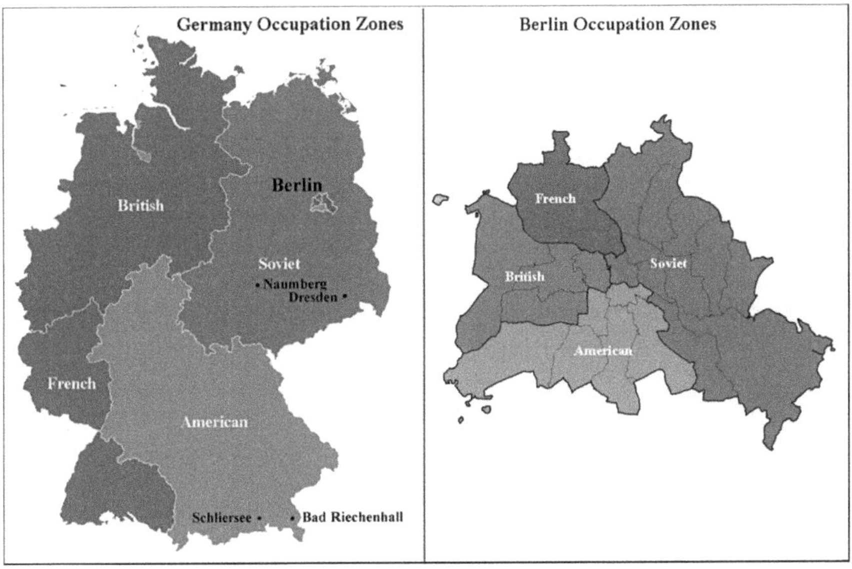

Zones of Occupation of Germany 1945.

Structure and Methods

> *Der Gehlen wird größenwahnsinnig. Der will doch wahrhaftig Gestapo für die Amis spielen. Da machen wir nicht mit.* [Gehlen is becoming megalomaniacal. He really wants to play Gestapo for the Americans. We're not going to take part in that.]
>
> Hermann Baun[1]

The post-war peace was fragile and uncomfortable. Germany was occupied in zones run by the United States, Britain, France and the Soviet Union with Berlin, in the Soviet zone, split into four zones also. The intelligence war had taken on huge importance almost as soon as the fighting war ended. Over the following years, intelligence forces on both sides of the political divide waged 'the largest, most concentrated and intense intelligence warfare in history',[2] competing for the services of former German intelligence officers. For Germany itself, after its unconditional surrender, during the occupation period and up to the founding of the Federal Republic in 1949, many government structures had to be rebuilt, especially in the field of internal and external security.

At the end of the Second World War, Germany had lost as much as half of its housing stock, food production was halved, and industrial output was no more than one third of 1938 levels. Factories were closed, credit institutions had ceased to function and to all intents and purposes, conventional economic life had come to an end. North German harbours and the river Rhine waterways were choked with wreckage and the railways were crippled by the destruction of tracks and thousands of bridges. Coal production was 40 per cent of 1938 levels. Inflation had risen by only 31 per cent in the ten years before 1948 but the amount of money in the German economy was now five times greater. Price controls had held down food production and much business was done in a highly sophisticate form of barter. After Soviet withdrawal from the Allied Control Authority, the three remaining powers undertook a currency reform on 20 June 1948, which substituted a much smaller number of Deutschmarks (DM), the new legal currency, for Reichsmarks the net result of which was to contract the money supply by 90 per cent and price controls, that had been introduced in 1936, were relaxed. The result for the German economy was immediate and electric. Shops were suddenly filled with merchandise and industrial output soared. Whilst good for the country, this was catastrophic for Gehlen. The US dollars that were financing his operation suddenly lost much of their premium exchange value. The resulting funding gap had to be made up by extending black market operations.

Gehlen responded to the German 'economic miracle' by formulating the OG more along the lines of industry and away from the previous military model. He was not going to turn it completely into a business, however. While it might take on the structure of a commercial enterprise, he was careful to retain a military style of administration. He became *Generaldirektor* (director general) at the head of the *Generaldirektion* (directorate general) headquarters. This was divided into *Hauptabteilungen* (departments), *Abteilungen* (sections), Gruppen (groups) and *Referate* (desks). Beneath that came *Generalvertretungen*

(GV – general agencies), *Bezirksvertretungen* (BV – district agencies), *Untervertretungen* (UV – sub-agencies) and *Filialen* (local branches). Of all those working in the field, only heads of *Generalvertretungen* were allowed into OG headquarters and even then, by invitation only.

Hauptabteilungen I collected and evaluated foreign intelligence. *Hauptabteilungen II* concerned itself with psychological warfare both aggressive and defensive, and *Hauptabteilungen III* was charged with counterintelligence. All heads of *Hauptabteilungen* and their top aides were ex-General Staff officers or ex-Abwehr men. Gehlen's cousin Dingler was responsible for evaluation, Abwehr counterespionage officer, ex-Lieutenant Colonel Oscar Reille ran *Hauptabteilungen III* and ex-Lieutenant Colonel Horst Wendland took on administration. Wessel and Herre ran Baun's old section of intelligence-gathering between them.

The *Generalvertretungen* had a full-time staff who enjoyed a great deal of independence with their own budgets. The Karlsruhe *Bezirksvertretungen* was run by Gehlen's personal friend Alfred Bentzinger, nicknamed *der Dicke* (the fat man), a former sergeant with GFP. The agency was located in a back courtyard on Gerwigstrasse behind a doorplate advertising Zimmerle & Co., a company supposedly specialising in roller blinds. In Darmstadt, ex-Military attaché General Kretschmer was in charge, in Munich it was ex-Colonel Joachim Rohleder and in Bremen ex-Lieutenant Colonel Hermann Giskes.

There were *Bezirksvertretungen* in almost all major German cities in the west. Their small staffs were mostly involved with the recruitment, training and supervision of new agents and acted as cut-outs between the *Generalvertretungen* and the *Untervertretungen*. It was at this third level of administration in medium-size towns where many ex-SS officers were to be found. Often, premises occupied by *Untervertretungen* and *Filialen* would be short-term with personnel moving from one location to another. Some premises were just 'fronts' with no staff at all and some were established for a purpose known only to Gehlen.

All these agencies masqueraded as business enterprises ranging from insurance companies and employment agencies to champagne dealers and booksellers. The level of secrecy was such that these 'businesses' would not be aware of the identity of others. Once recruited, informers and agents in the field would leave their material in 'dead-letterboxes', a place where messages can be left and collected without the sender and recipient meeting and collect their remuneration in similar fashion. They generally would not know the identity of the person who serviced the letterbox from the other side.

Informers came in many shapes and sizes. Some had worked their way into important civil service posts or roles in industry in the Soviet-occupied regions. Others lived near important military establishments. Some had occupations that meant they had to travel frequently across the country who could report on rail and road infrastructure. Some actually worked for rival espionage agencies. The bulk of Org informants, however, came from among the 'dispossessed, the unemployed or the down-and outs'.[3] Many were former Nazi Party members who had served short sentences and lost everything. They would often be approached by a member of the OG who, themselves, might have a Nazi past and with whom they could strike some sort of bond. Others might be facing criminal proceedings for their Nazi past and might be persuaded by a promise to have proceedings against them quashed. People who had suffered badly at the hands of marauding Red Army soldiers needed little encouragement to 'sign up' to the cause.

Women were particularly valuable as go-betweens in cities such as Vienna where there were large numbers of Soviet troops. They would make initial contact with officers in a bar or club and might draw them into a relationship or just promise black market goods such as watches, which were highly prized by the Soviets. The Soviets, thus compromised, would then be introduced to an agent of the OG who would ascertain whether or not they could be persuaded to trade merchandise for information. It was mostly low-grade intelligence and low-risk for those involved. It was this intricate web of agents and informants in place that the US agencies simply could not replicate.

As US demands for more and more intelligence increased so Gehlen's army of agents grew. There were far too many recruits now for the old system of vetting to suffice and a rigorous method of selection was laid out in writing. If a likely candidate was suggested by someone already in the OG, an officer from one of the *Generalvertretungen* would investigate their background, personality, way of life etc., according to specific criteria. First of all the proposer would be questioned about the circumstances under which they encountered the prospect, what they knew about them and what their relationship, if any, with them was. The candidate would then be interviewed to ensure that they were well-grounded with a keen sense of reality but also that they had what the document called a 'conspiratorial turn of mind'.[4] When the assessment went to headquarters neither the proposer or the investigator would be informed whether or not the recruitment was approved.

Whilst many new recruits had seen active service during the war, few had any experience of espionage and so a rigorous programme of training was established. The first lesson for organisers, officers of the OG, was the code of secrecy especially in relation to their agents in the field who must be kept in ignorance about any details of who and what they were dealing with beyond the organiser who was running them and the fact that they were working, in some capacity, for an anti-communist organisation.

If a person was taken on as an agent or informer the relationship between them and their organiser would be based strictly on a business foundation and have no personal dimension but that regulation would be frequently flouted in the murky and perilous world of espionage where the only person to whom an agent might turn to talk and relieve the stress was the only other person who knew what risks they took. This might be particularly relevant where agents, couriers or *Schleusenders* (handlers) were not particularly efficient and suffered opprobrium raining down on them from on high.

Rules were also laid down for communications. Sometimes there might be as many as four 'dead-letterboxes' between source and *Filialen*. These dead letterboxes were only as secure as the people who used them and, naturally, not all agents were as security conscious as their handlers would have liked. Both depositor and retriever had to be absolutely sure that they were not observed while accessing them. Agents travelling through Soviet-occupied regions were instructed to have credible cover-stories and make several passes along their designated route making sure they carried no incriminating material and only when they were quite familiar with the environment should they initiate contact with the source. The risks were many and the consequences of being caught by the enemy could turn out to be extreme.

The OG scored its first major successes in the Soviet zone of Germany. An agent whose cover name was Dieter Keuner (real name unknown) ran a group of agents from his house in Berlin-Wilmersdorf. He had been a frontline officer in the war and joined the OG in 1947 running some twenty handlers with about ten agents each, all in the Soviet zone of Germany. One of the agent runners was Keuner's ex-commander Kurt Tölle (real name unknown) who had recruited Walter Zentner (real name unknown) to report on Soviet military activity. Zentner was paid in cigarettes, chocolate and coffee, which he used to pay his informants that included a baker from Döberitz who reported on the number of loaves going into the local Red Army barracks, a washerwoman in Eberswalde who reported on the number of Soviet shirts she washed, a man who counted the number of windows lit at night in nearby barracks and another who went round rubbish bins at night picking out anything written in Russian script.

By far the most important of Zentner's informants turned out to be a young building worker, Klaus Imhoff (real name unknown), whose father had been killed by the Soviets during the Second World War. Inhoff heard from an old school friend who was in the *Kaisernieste Volkspolitzei* in the Soviet zone that he had been receiving military training with machine guns and mortars and had heard that T34 tanks were coming soon. Training was by former Wehrmacht personnel under Soviet command. Tölle thought this unlikely and was inclined to disregard it as gossip but eventually passed the intelligence on to Keuner. Keuner, too, was used to being hustled with dubious 'intelligence' but thought the source sufficiently worthy to warrant allowing the report to go further up the line. He arranged a meeting outside the monkey house at the Berlin Zoo. Wordlessly, his contact took from him a sealed envelope in exchange for a copy of the *Telegraf* and whisked it way to Templehof airport where he took it on board the regular US Dakota shuttle to Frankfurt. There, he exchanged codewords with the driver of a German car who took him to a house in Bad Nauheim. Another courier took it from there by US military train to OG headquarters where it landed on Dingler's desk. He took it direct to Gehlen and a lively debate ensued about the veracity of the information. Gehlen thought it highly likely that the Soviets would arm the security forces in their occupied zone and, long before the politicians had contemplated such a move, he was putting together a special staff to use all OG resources to investigate. Soon he had the information. By early 1949, he was informing the Americans that the *Volkspolitzei* were planning to have twenty-four infantry regiments, seven artillery regiments, and three tank regiments in place by the end of that year. Months later, a senior *Volkspolitzei* defector confirmed that Gehlen's estimates were accurate.

An equally momentous intelligence coup followed in spring 1949 when reports came in of aircraft 'without wings or propellors' having been sighted near Schönwalde airfield north of Berlin.[5] An ex-fighter pilot working for the OG, agent Horst, at Bad Nauheim was given a Leica camera and told to go 'mushroom picking' in the vicinity of the airfield and take photographs of any strange craft. In Munich, US Air Force officers and former Luftwaffe personnel examined the photographs. The craft were indeed aircraft but ones resembling the Luftwaffe's own *Wundervögel* jet-propelled Me262 and He172 developed in the final years of the Second World War. The Americans had their own F86 Sabre, first flown in 1947, that had been developed in part from the Me262.

Gehlen went to his archive to came up with names of returned PoWs who had at one time worked in Soviet aircraft factories. One who emerged was a man who had worked at a metal-pressing workshop at Tbilisi, Georgia and made himself a small pot out of waste material which he had brought back as a souvenir. Metallurgists examined the material and concluded that it was similar to that use in the F86. Other agents were now sent to temporarily block the railway line near Chemnitz, the GDR as a fuel train approached. When it stopped to clear the line, an agent climbed onto one of the fuel trucks, opened the cover and filled a beer bottle with a sample of the contents. Now the Americans not only knew what the mysterious aircraft, which turned out to be a Yakovlev Yak-17, was made of, they also knew what fuel it was using.

Gehlen's stock was rising and with it came a renewed freedom to act. He expanded OG activities to include domestic and economic intelligence as well as military. Herbert Richter was an ex-Wehrmacht officer now employed by the State Railways of the Soviet zone. He had worked his way up to head the construction and production staff in Berlin and made regular monthly reports to his handler. Ewald Misera, head of the traffic and service department, reported regularly on troop movements. He copied reports and timetables and wrote character studies of leading headquarters staff.

Karli Bandelow was a senior engineer with the State Secretariat for Motor Traffic and Roads who supplied information about bridge construction in particular. Walter Schneider, an officer with the Ministry for Reconstruction, provided information about building projects. From 'Agent 9980' there was requested prospectuses and catalogues of new electronic products, especially those involved with long-wave signalling, on show at the Leipzig Fair. Others were asked to investigate why trains had suddenly stopped bringing in uranium ore from Czechoslovakia through Bad Schandau and Frankfurt am Oder on their way to the Soviet Union.

While running agents in the Soviet-occupied zone of Germany and eastern Europe, the main prize for Gehlen, however, was penetration of the Soviet Union, itself. *Operation Pfiffikus* (Operation Cunning Devil) involved agents in the FRG contacting any professional or academic planning a trip to the Soviet Union whom they think might be persuaded to carry out small tasks. It might be just surreptitiously taking a few photographs or it might involve bringing back the name of someone they met who showed interest in earning a little money. The most important category of agents infiltrated were those who had been specially trained for espionage work such as radio operators and couriers. Of necessity, these people had to be native Russians who would not be conspicuous by looks or speech but who harboured a deep hatred for the communists. Fortunately, Germany was not short of Russian, Ukrainian or Baltic fugitives and émigrés, the remnants of Vlasov's 'army' and Red Army deserters. The problem, of course, was that these were also the very sort of people that the Smersh might have 'planted' in the west hoping to be picked up by Western intelligence agencies.

Amongst the more successful networks of agents run by the OG were the Baltic émigrés who spoke Russian most of whom were German Balts who had fled the region after the Soviet annexation of June 1940. A trawl of the thousands now living in refugee camps found many willing to believe that the OG was working with the US to liberate their homeland. What they needed right now were agents who would move in to prepare the ground for this liberation by collecting military intelligence about the Soviet occupation. Volunteers were given a written contract guaranteeing them $100 for each day spent in Soviet territory and a $1,000 bonus at the end of their mission all financed directly by the Americans. If they were killed during the mission, their families would receive $5,000.

Those selected were taken to a US training camp in Bavaria then flown to Fort Bragg in North Carolina, United States for three months' special training, which included parachuting. When the training was complete, they were handed over to the OG for deployment. They were given authentic Russian clothing into the lining of which was sewn money and, in some cases, watches for bribes, identity papers, work permits and ration coupons.

They then became part of Operation Jungle, an MI6 programme for the clandestine insertion of intelligence and resistance agents into Poland and the Baltic states. The agents were mostly Polish, Estonian, Latvian and Lithuanian exiles who had been trained in a special centre in Chelsea, London and Sweden. The naval operation of the programme used former German navy E-boats crewed by Gehlen's people posing as the German Mine Sweeping Administration under the control of the Royal Navy. Agents were transported to the Baltic states by sea under the cover of fictitious maritime transport company British Baltic Fishery Protection Service. The operation was led by Henry Carr, director of the north European department of MI6, and the head of the Baltic branch, Alexander McKibbin. The actual transport of agents across the Baltic was under the control of a man who was very much at home on the Baltic Sea, Rear Admiral Hans-Helmut Klose who had commanded No. 2 Fast Patrol Boat Training Flotilla against the Russian navy during the war. Klose had hand-picked his crews from old comrades who had previously served with him.

The Soviet navy soon became aware of Klose's missions but were unable to catch the E-boats, stripped of all cumbersome equipment for maximum speed, even when they were detected. Operations were initially very successful prompting Gehlen to consider a similar initiative to land agents in the Crimea.

Operation Jungle would not stand the test of time, however. Two factors brought it down. The Latvian State Security Service knew about Klose's missions but could not intercept the boats so commissioned Colonel Albert Janovich Balodis of the counterespionage division to infiltrate the anti-communist partisan groups with whom Gehlen's agents were working. The second reason for the collapse of Operation Jungle was that information about the operation was passed to the Soviets by their MI6 'mole', Kim Philby. By 1953, almost all of the forty-two agents infiltrated into the Baltics had been captured or killed. There were other operations whose early catastrophic curtailment should have made it glaringly obvious that the OG was compromised. The Russian émigré organisation, NTS, sent Gehlen-trained parachutists to be dropped close to Moscow but all were immediately rounded up.

While Gehlen and Baun had been fighting for control in 1947, they frequently and vehemently espoused opposing strategies, which exposed significant areas of discord. Gehlen, for instance, at the behest of the US or so he claimed, argued that the OG should create a state security agency to track down communist infiltrators and dismantle red agent networks in the FRG. This was the moment that Baun accused him of playing at 'Gestapo' and acting as footpad for his American masters. In this, he was a little more attuned than Gehlen to German public opinion that would not take kindly to being spied on by other Germans after their wartime experiences and swore that he would never countenance interference in German internal politics. Instead of snooping in their own back yard, Baun proposed that the OG could expand the existing counterintelligence apparatus to find out about infiltrators by penetrating enemy intelligence agencies and then simply handing over the names of Soviet agents to their US paymasters to deal with. To make his point, Baun recruited a 19-year-old Czech philosophy student called Bozena Hajek who had turned up at Regensburg refugee camp. She applied to immigrate to America but when she filled out the customary forms it was discovered that her sister, Slavka, was married to Captain Vojtech Jerabek head of the Czech military secret service in Karlsbad. At first Bozena was suspected of trying to enter the United

States as a Czech agent but enquiries convinced Baun that she was a genuine political refugee.

Operation Bohemia was launched, which turned out to be one of the OG's major successes. A young Czech working for Baun, under the codename 'Ondrej' befriended Bozena and learned about her family. He then went to Prague where he introduced himself to the family as a friend of their daughter. After several weeks, he had inveigled himself into their confidence and learned enough about Vojtech to know that he held anti-communist views. Ondrej judged that it was worth the risk and offered him money in exchange for information. Jerabek did not reject the idea but while he was considering whether to accept, rumours emerged that the communists were planning a purge of the Czech officer corps. It was enough for Vojtech and some of his close friends to signal Ondrej to get them out. He came over the border into Bavaria with Staff Captain Fejfar, Major Tyr of the Prague Ministry of Defence, five family members and lists of Czech agents in the FRG and the code key for the Prague secret service radio. Within days, the CIC had arrested eighteen agents of the Czechoslovak intelligence service, and an American military court sentenced the Czech main agent Jaromir Koska to twenty years in prison.

A year or so later, the OG had another major success when the French Sûreté uncovered a Yugoslav spy network was in Friedrichshafen, the FRG. Among the arrestees was Yugoslav called Levec, who had been working as a Yugoslav agent in the French occupied zone of Germany. Named the head of the network in Germany as Topa alias Mimara, plus other agents of the Belgrade secret service, such as First Lieutenant Doran, agent Blagojevic, Lieutenant Colonel Podkonjak, Major Franjo Ozbolt, and Captain Dusan Padjan. Gehlen's agents tracked the Yugoslavs for six months to gain information about their contacts before handing them over to the US liaison officers after which all the Yugoslavs were expelled.

Pullach

> Ever since Hitler's invasion of the Soviet Union many of Gehlen's staff had been in the front rank of the anti-Soviet crusade and they regarded the Cold War as merely the logical continuation of the war begun in 1941.[6]

Towards the end of 1947, Rusty had grown to such an extent that it desperately needed bigger premises. Intelligence that Gehlen was forwarding to the Americans was also having a galvanising effect.

While the US was mothballing its navy and bomber fleets and sending its GIs back home, Gehlen's PoW interrogation reports were indicating Soviet tank and aircraft production continuing to rise. Not only could the Americans not afford to ignore these facts, but they also needed to know more. Gehlen was starting to become indispensable and his organisation needed space in which to expand its services and, importantly, a more secure location than the one at Oberursel. In one of his more cooperative moods, Liebel took Herre on a scouting trip to locate new premises and they found exactly what they wanted at Pullach near Munich. On 6 December 1947, he moved the group, now officially codenamed the 7821st Composite Group, from Camp King to a place the Germans called Camp Nikolaus, (Camp Santa Claus) 200 miles to the south between the villages of Pullach and Grosshesselohe.

Here, the German intelligence personnel and their families lived in two-storey houses each with a small garden all within a 2-metre-high wall topped off with an electric fence closing it off from public access. The compound included a hospital, a school, a shop stocked with American supplies, a swimming pool, and a kindergarten making it essentially independent of the outside world. OG staff and family members were strongly advised not to venture outside the walls. The shop ensured that they were well supplied with butter, coffee, tinned food and cigarettes, the sort of luxuries undreamed of by the vast majority of German citizens elsewhere in the country. With their families around them, and everyone else kept out, officers were reassured about their safety and anonymity and when wives took on secretarial roles it significantly increased OG efficiency without compromising security.

Right from the start, the whole compound was subjected to strict security protocols with Washington calling for very limited access by other operational staff and a total blackout of information. Up to this point, there was no certain public knowledge of what was going on. There were rumours about shadowy intelligence outfits, but they were just some of the many stories that were circulating about Nazis in South America organising a Fourth Reich with looted gold, and German scientists building rockets and bombs for the Americans and Soviets. Gehlen employed the device of letting it be known that the compound was indeed secret but was a very small and boring secret. He had a sign erected at the gates indicating that the compound was run by Süddeutsche Industrie-Verwertungs GmbH. A corporation involved with scientific research. This allowed Gehlen to establish a cover for local offices throughout the country by opening subsidiaries or other independent commercial enterprises each of which was under the control of a director. These men had no rank within the OG but included lowly former sergeants, ex-SS men and even in the case of west Berlin, a major general, Rudolf Kleinkamp who, according to the name on his door, ran a publicity firm called Reklame & Werbe Zentrale.

Gehlen took steps to safeguard his own security. Very few of his staff knew him personally and most, if they came across him at all, were not aware who he was. There were no ranks inside Pullach, no saluting, and everyone was given pseudonyms by which they referred to each other at all times. None of the agents in the field ever passed through the gates of Pullach and most would not even have known anything about it. If the OG was to become an integral part of the state, as Gehlen hoped it would, he would have to take extreme precautions to maintain his personal cloak of secrecy. The anonymity of the head of British intelligence was one of its features of MI6 that Gehlen most approved of. As a precaution for himself, he considered having a Lichtenstein passport made showing his Dutch mother's maiden name as von Vaernewyck. This would effectively 'de-Nazified' him and it even opened up the possibility of creating a Swiss bank account for him and the organisation. He rejected the idea, however, thinking it might cause resentment among his staff if it became known that he was giving himself special treatment.

The compound had been built in 1936 by Hitler's deputy, Rudolf Hess, and afterwards was the headquarters of another, later deputy Führer Martin Bormann. The move was another important milestone along the path to realising Gehlen's ultimate ambitions. At Oberursel, the American presence dominated his enterprise but at Pullach the Germans were in the majority and became even more self-confident as the organisation grew into a self-contained community moving away from US control. Many Western intelligence agencies had not shied away from recruiting ex-Nazis into their ranks and Liebel had insisted on vetting all of Gehlen's recruits to ensure that he was not doing the same but Waldman objected. It could hardly have been to protect Gehlen, whom he believed was not guilty of recruiting Nazis, and was more to do with the general hostility towards Liebel. This championing of Gehlen's autonomy would have serious consequences when Waldman returned to the United States.

The move to Pullach with its enhanced facilities indicated that the Americans had finally decided to take Gehlen seriously and he responded with a flurry of intelligence about Soviet troop concentrations and movements. This was all well and good but what the Americans really wanted was strategic intelligence. They wanted to read the Soviet mind, they wanted insight into Kremlin ambitions and it was precisely this kind of intelligence that Baun's networks had been unable to provide and nothing had improved in that regard since he was forced out of a leadership role.

Alongside these demands from the Americans, Gehlen had continued to anticipate future trends at home. The more he could prove his worth to the Americans, the more likely his organisation was to be adopted by a future German state. His policy of giving 'dignified employment' to ex-Wehrmacht personnel within the OG was crucial and through these people, he established links to political and industry elites. The Pentagon had little interest in political developments, but Washington recognised the importance of what Gehlen was doing even though some US political leaders were still seriously concerned about the number of ex-Nazis he was employing.

This newfound confidence now emboldened Gehlen to confront the criticisms he was facing and to challenge Liebel's authority over the OG. It had always been a feature of Gehlen's character, no doubt developed in part through his many torrid audiences with Hitler, that he was able to dismiss unpleasant encounters and emerge from them with a positive attitude. In March 1948, irked by the rising number of security lapses, Liebel had issued a memorandum calling for 'drastic action to reduce the number of bad agents' and later in August 1948 speculated over dismantling the OG altogether. Even Dingler had waded in with criticism of Gehlen who was thought to be going too far too quick and suggested that Heusinger, a wartime subordinate of Gehlen, might be a better fit as leader.[7] Facing charges of a 'lack of intellectual and ideological leadership', Gehlen responded by suggesting that Dingler might be shuffled off as liaison to the Swiss Intelligence Service. Dingler, in turn, accused Gehlen of being authoritarian, immune to criticism, too subservient to US control and not making enough effort to represent German interests. He went so far as to suggest that Halder be brought in to assume control of the OG and dictate overall strategy in place of Gehlen. Faced with such a challenge, Gehlen remained polite and friendly towards his cousin but completely rejected his criticisms. He had, at one time, contemplated making Dingler his chief of staff but that was no longer possible. He commended Dingler for his contribution but, pointedly, said that he would not stand in his way if he chose to leave.

Gehlen understood perfectly that his organisation could only flourish if a Cold War existed between the United States and the Soviet Union. As a distraction from criticism from Washington, he ramped up the anti-Soviet paranoia by convincing General Clay, the military governor of the US zone of occupation in Germany, that a major Soviet war mobilisation had begun in eastern Europe. Clay responded by dashing off a frantic, top-secret telegram to Washington warning that war 'may come with dramatic suddenness'.[8]

Baun was still posing problems. Despite his technical skills. neither Gehlen nor Wissel wanted him in any position of control but could not afford to lose him and his web of agents to another organisation. Neither could they agree what to do about him. He might be retained as a special advisor but could not be allowed to be in a position where he issued orders and he definitely had to be kept on a tight rein. For his part, Baun, encouraged by his new wife, harboured a deep resentment of the way that Gehlen had treated him and there was a distinct impression that, given the chance, he would bring down the whole organisation or abandon it taking all his networks with him.

Gehlen made it known that he was considered resignation. Whether or not he meant it is open to conjecture but, in the end, he stayed his hand and chose to challenge Liebel. He complained to Director of Intelligence at European Command (EUCOM) General Robert L. Walsh about Liebel's reluctance to take the Germans seriously again insinuating that he might resign unless Liebel was recalled but Walsh assured him that Washington recognised how important his organisation was. He subtly implied, however, that good as the OG was, it was not the only US intelligence asset and refused to replace Liebel. Gehlen took these remarks to be a counter threat to break up the OG and take what the Americans considered the most important sections for themselves. Gehlen suggested that as a compromise, Waldman might act as liaison in Liebel's place.

Before that, however, the Soviets were turning the screw. Ostensibly, in response to the currency reforms that introduced the Deutschmark, on 24 June 1948 their forces blockaded rail, road, and water access to Allied-controlled areas of Berlin. Coming soon after the setting up of the State of Israel, this new Soviet provocation together with the takeover of power in Prague, the rising up of Greek communists and the formation of the People's Republic in North Korea all signalled a significant rise in tensions worldwide. Gehlen took this to mean that he would become indispensable to the American cause but it was evident that the Americans were more interested in Heusinger's assessments of the military situation and Gehlen had played down the threat because of no evidence of significant movement of Soviet land forces in eastern Europe.

Then, on 1 September 1948, the *Parlamentarischer Rat* (Parliamentary Council) in Bonn drafted and adopted the constitution of the FRG. The tantalising prospect now was the formation of a new German state to which Gehlen could migrate his organisation away from US dominance but that was still something for the future. Wessel was still unhappy about Gehlen's leadership but Heusinger argued that Gehlen was the only man who could keep American support for the OG which would collapse overnight if American financial support, now set at $125,000 a month, ended.

By now the US Army had grown tired of seeing more than $1 million of its budget being swallowed up every year by Gehlen and wanted to hive his organisation off to the newly formed CIA. The National Security Act of 26 July 1947 had restructured the US military and intelligence agencies. When it was signed off by President Truman in September 1947, the CIA was born as an independent, civilian intelligence agency. Its stated task was to coordinate the nation's intelligence activities and, among other duties, collect, evaluate and disseminate intelligence affecting national security. The army hoped that in its youthful enthusiasm and the administrative upheaval of its inauguration, the agency would be tempted to take on the OG without checking it out too closely. They advertised it as 'one of its most prolific and dependable sources' but the CIA head of Berlin station, Peter M.F. Sichel, objected on the grounds that it would be 'a danger to our security [and] a waste of time'.[9]

The danger for the Americans of rejecting the OG in its entirety was that it had become essentially too big to fail. Disbanding the thousands of its staff would be a gift to the Soviets who would not be slow to recruit them into their own ranks. For this reason alone, there was pressure in Washington to try to make good use of the OG but if they were going to go down this road, they would have to accept that they were giving support to a semi-autonomous, intrinsically insecure, German espionage organisation whose staff was little changed from the one that had served the Nazis. Some in Washington were willing to pay that price anticipating that Gehlen would become a pivotal figure in the intelligence and military affairs of any future West German state, while others saw him as someone whose ultimate goal was to

> offer shelter and support [to ex-Nazis] for a future German General Staff.[10]

At a time when CIC were still on the lookout for war criminals there was a lot of residual hostility towards the OG, which was suspected of harbouring some and rival intelligence agencies were fishing in the same pond for ex-Abwehr staff. Hans-Heinrich Worgitzky, who had been Gehlen's adjutant in the FHO, was lucky to escape from the clutches of the British, who were thinking about setting up their own version of the OG under Adolf Wicht. For all their inducements, however, Wicht refused to cooperate and waited for a call from Gehlen which he was confident would come soon. Given the chance, most ex-FHO and Abwehr staff preferred to work for a German organisation being bound by a common wartime experience and a deep hatred for the Soviets after the ravaging of German civilians by the Red Army in 1945.

Few realised that Gehlen's ambition was greater even than that. The critical issue was the extent to which the US was willing to champion a Western Europe free of communist control. Whichever way that turned out, Germany was the key to European security. It was in the interests of the Western Powers to stabilise the West German state and fortify it against communism. Despite its wrecked state, Germany still had the potential and resources to regenerate its economy and whilst reinstatement of its military services was a political hot potato Gehlen envisaged Germany becoming the major ally of the US in Europe. An essential prerequisite for that was the rapid integration of wartime leaders, political and military, into a new democratic structure and Gehlen saw his organisation as the principal agency through which this could be brought about.

He now actively recruited people such as Heina Paul Johannes, who served in SS units and joined the organisation under the name Karl Schuetz, SS-Obersturmführers Frans Göring and Hans Sommer, and SS-Sturmführer Herbert Stein. Gehlen also took in Lieutenant General Friedrich Wilhelm von Mellenthin, former commander of the 4th Panzer Army, Major General Nichtke, who commanded divisions in Poland and Russia, Major General Rudolf Kleinkamp, who headed the personnel service of the Wehrmacht High Command, Lieutenant Colonel Heinz Guderian, Colonel von Kretschmer, former military attaché in Tokyo, and other former Wehrmacht officers. Leading positions at the head of the groups were occupied by former SS officers whom Gehlen knew personally. Colonel Ulrich Noack headed the research group on the Soviet economy; Captain Blossfeldt led the interrogations and Herre became the chief analyst. Herre later said that the important thing at that time was to get as many officers as possible 'off the street'. It is worth noting that the US sponsorship of Gehlen at this time meant that war criminals on his payroll were technically employed by the US government.

Sommer is an example of how these people were integrated into the OG. On the night of 2/3 October 1941, seven synagogues in Paris were destroyed by the fascist *Mouvement social révolutionnaire*

(MSR) using explosives supplied by Sommer who, at that time, was an Untersturmführer in the SS. After the war he worked for French intelligence before being tried and given a ten-year sentence by a French court for war crimes. He served only one year before returning to Germany where he was recruited by Gehlen. In 1953, he changed sides and began working for the Stasi as a double agent.

The OG could not be a strictly military agency because there were now too many members who did not have a military background. Whilst military ranks still counted for something with many, they were not openly recognised within the headquarters staff where Gehlen tried to create a certain equality of status. In the place of military discipline, however, came the bonding of members through an 'oath-bound brotherhood of secrecy'.[11] New recruits were asked to sign a declaration giving 'their word of honour as an officer [of OG]' to maintain strict secrecy with a clear warning that breaking such an oath would render them liable to punishment even after they had retired from active duty. They became members of a virtual secret society, whose role within it was to be kept secret from anyone not bound by the same oath. Even the Americans had no idea who was a member and who was not. While considering its options, the CIA thought it prudent to find out and agreed with the Army to make a joint study of OG workings and its evaluate its potential.

Critchfield

> Life was not a bed of roses with the CIA.
>
> Reinhard Gehlen[12]

There had been a growing sense of crisis in Germany towards the end of 1947 with US Secretary of State George C. Marshall exposing Soviet sabotage of the rehabilitation process for Germany, which would manifest itself as the Berlin blockade a few months later. The need for a more robust response from the US was becoming acute but Hillenkoetter's CIA was slow to get up to speed. Dulles had called in Frank Wisner and put him in charge of the Office of Policy Coordination (OPC), which had been created as the covert action arm of the CIA alongside the Office of Special Operations (OSO). It operated under the aegis of a special directorate and had responsibility directly to the National Security Council but, in practice, Wisner had been given almost total personal control of the OPC, which was soon to earn a reputation for 'dirty tricks'. At least three former SS men – Friedrich

Carstenn, Karl Otto Jobke and Eberhard Tellkamp – were recruited and used extensively by Wisner.[13]

Wisner arrived in Berlin in summer 1948 and met Gehlen to discuss the Berlin crisis. Gehlen warned him that the East Germans were planning to formalise their zone of occupation as an independent republic with its own security and political police organisations. Wisner was suitably impressed with Gehlen's organisation and Gehlen learned much about the darker side of intelligence from Wisner. The two men formed a close working relationship and Wisner was able to divert part of his budget to the OG. Gehlen was at one of the low point of his early struggle for acceptance by the Americans and toyed with the idea of offering his services to Wisner. It could mean a different and possibly more generous financial backer that might allow him to rely less on black market dealings to pay his staff. He was tempted to angle for a closer working relationship with Wisner who saw the benefit of using Gehlen's war-hardened veterans in his new organisation but nothing came of it.

Liebel's position had weakened to the point where Gehlen felt sufficiently confident to officially complained about 'the disparity between resources available and tasks allotted'[14] and refused to work with him at all. The conflict reached crisis point in November 1948, when Liebel was recalled and replaced by the commander of Camp King, Colonel Philp, an easy-going man who was already an admirer of Gehlen and unlikely to give him a hard time. His other duties left him little time to spend supervising Rusty and his appointment effectively marked the end of the army's effort to reintegrate it into its intelligence apparatus.

Bossard's report had left many issues unresolved, and the Americans still could not make up their minds what to do about Rusty. It was accepted that Germany would have to be allowed to realise its economic potential and regain sovereignty, which would once again make it a major player in European politics, and it would necessarily need an intelligence service. Nobody was sure if Rusty was the right foundation for that, but things could not go on as they were, and decisions had to be made. The army had just about washed its hands of Gehlen but the CIA had not yet agreed to take it over.

Exploratory talks with the OPC might have resulted in a new trajectory for Gehlen's career had the CIA not sent their own man to take a look at Gehlen's group. The Director of the Central European Desk of the Office of Special Operations (OSO), Richard Helms described Rusty as 'at best a controversial intelligence package about which the CIA did not know a lot' but he hoped that, if handled correctly, it might become 'a great intelligence producer.'[15] He chose the 31-year-old Colonel James H. Critchfield who had served as a tank commander in North Africa, Italy, France and Germany and had, coincidentally, led a column of tanks through the valley of the river Vallep at the very time when Gehlen was in hiding just above him at Misery Meadow in May 1945. He had been part of the team taking the surrender of the German 1st Army at Kufstein where he faced, across the table General Hermann Foertsch, whom he would later come to know better as a member of the OG and who he would later describe as a 'reserved taciturn man, tall with an angular build'.[16] Posted to Europe in 1946, Critchfield was employed in occupation administration and had training in counterintelligence as head of US intelligence in Austria. Two years later he was attracted to working for the CIA which he thought might give him a 'wide horizon against which to examine the future.'[17] He was assigned to Munich with a brief to focus on the Soviet Union, which he described as a 'nation about which Americans were almost totally uninformed'.[18] At his first CIA monthly meeting, the agenda included a request from Galloway for a report on Rusty to see if the CIA should accede to the army's request to take it over. None present showed much interest in an assignment that 'would not enhance anyone's career' so it was with no great pleasure that Critchfield received an instruction a few days later to undertake a four-week investigation of the Pullach operation about which he 'had been given virtually no background information'.[19]

Despite the general apathy displayed whenever Rusty was mentioned, Critchfield was intrigued by his assignment and obviously wanted to make a success of it, but he waited in vain for any information or guidance from Helms. When he enquired why not, he was dismayed to hear that G-2 had no files on Rusty beyond anything that was held at Pullach. Undaunted, he turned his ignorance into an asset and decided to approach the assignment with a completely open mind but with four key issues to address. Were any former Nazi Party members in the organisation? Were any of them war criminals? Did it include any of the former German General Staff and High Command, and, if so, how did they fit into the organisation? The army sent Colonel Charles Bromley with him to make it look as if they were interested. Bromley, however, stayed for only a short time and left as soon he could.

With a bare minimum of directive from Washington, Critchfield arrived at Pullach on 18 November 1948, dressed in an army uniform and introduced himself as Colonel Kent James Marshall. He described the man who met him as

> of average stature, lean and trim in appearance with a small, neatly trimmed moustache and closely cut brown hair … a clear, almost translucent complexion with the skin below his noticeably blue eyes stretched tightly over moderately high cheekbones.[20]

Wearing a dark business suit, Gehlen, calling himself Doktor Schneider, offered Critchfield a cigar, which he declined, and when coffee was served, they sat down to talk. Critchfield had only a smattering of German and Gehlen's English was not good either but, as ever, Herre, whose English was fluent, was on hand to help when needed. Critchfield was vague about who had sent him, but Gehlen knew straightaway that he was a CIA man and was determined to make a good impression on him. The CIA would be a much more comfortable fit for Gehlen than the US Army had been.

It was a crucial meeting for both men. After coffee and polite exchanges, Critchfield wasted no time in getting down to business. He requested the identities of every member of Gehlen's organisation. Gehlen paused before answering and took a sip of coffee. After a couple of puffs on his thin cigar, he explained that his own priority was to safeguard the integrity and essentially German character of his organisation in order that it might, at some point in the future, be accepted as part of a new German government. Although he was aware of the importance of maintain a good relationship with the Americans, Gehlen was not going open his organisation up to the scrutiny of this man who was clearly not who he said he was and whose status and importance were yet to be determined. A few more exchanges convinced Critchfield that he would get nowhere at this point, so he abruptly closed his briefcase, stood up and offered his hand. Here was a man who had been part of a military regime that had surrendered unconditionally facing a representative of an occupying power but whose pride was preventing him from making rational decisions. Before Critchfield made a move towards the door, however, Gehlen softened although it was obviously difficult for him to do so. He made a gesture for Critchfield to pause and, looking him in the eye, took a long puff of his cigar, leaned back in his chair and raised his hands, palm upwards in a gesture of agreement. It was a gesture that Critchfield would become familiar with. There were no war criminals on his staff, Gehlen told Critchfield but little progress was made beyond that and the meeting ended without rancour. The next day Critchfield met Heusinger, whom he described as

> soft-spoken and quite articulate in a nearly unaccentuated English … relaxed and self-confident

and Wessel, both assuming pseudonyms.[21] Waldman was frequently on hand to accompany Critchfield on his visits to the various sections at Pullach and was able to fill him in with background. He backed up Gehlen's assertion that there were no Nazi Party members or war criminals in the compound. It might be argued that Critchfield's failure to pursue the matter was the most damaging mistake that the Americans made. Whilst the numbers of actual former SS and SD members in the OG was small at this time, the precedent set in terms of scrutiny of personnel was to come back and haunt them a few years later when the numbers were significantly higher.

At that point, Critchfield had no way of verifying what Gehlen told him but it was apparent to him, by their demeanour, that most of the people he came across and talked to had been in the military but few seemed to have any background in intelligence. It was during conversations with Heusinger that he realised Gehlen had a parallel agenda and Heusinger was fundamental to that. Within the security and politically isolated environment of Pullach, he, along with former Lieutenant General Hans Speidel, Horst von Mellenthin and Foertsch, were theorising about how an entirely new German defence force might be created as part of a Western response to the challenge of communism. The group, which included the Free Democratic Party politician Eberhard Wildermuth, aimed to promote rearmament and secure key positions of influence within the new state bureaucracy for those from within their circle or approved by them. Hans Speidel and Wildermuth were old friends and held strong views about how to combat the prevailing 'pacifist illusions' in light of the Soviet threat.[22] Throughout the late 1940s, rearmament was not popular with the war-weary German public, however, and veterans were unwilling to express any positive views on remilitarisation while the purging of Nazi war criminals went on.

Critchfield's four-weeks of intense meetings, interviews and briefings found that while there were many former German General Staff and Abwehr people, none were in the 'automatic arrest categories' and as far as Critchfield could see, posed no risk to the security of the US. Gehlen wrote a report for Critchfield entitled *Thoughts on the Future Development of the Organisation* in which he suggested that the OG might take a role alongside, but not within, the German police to combat the black market and investigate exchange control violations, about which Gehlen knew a great deal. It was, in part, a preparation in case the Americans pulled out and he would have to align himself directly with the German state.

When Critchfield submitted his final report, two months later, it was a wake-up call for Washington. He had been impressed with Gehlen's '*Thoughts*' document with all its ten appendices and had included it in full when he submitted his report. Clearly Gehlen had made a good impression on Critchfield; it was the sort of thing he was very good at doing, especially when he had told Critchfield that he had a total

> conviction that the time of nationalism [was] past and [that the] only hope [lay] in [a] Western European and Atlantic Union.[23]

The OG, Critchfield said, now employed some 4,000 people but he could not say exactly how far its influence extended within the political landscape inside Germany. What he did say, in no uncertain terms, was that, in his opinion, a decision had to be made quickly before it got out of hand. Helms said it was like having 'an outsized and ravenous bear by the tail'.[24] Critchfield advised that the OG had to be broken up or taken under strict US control. On a positive note, he stressed the importance of the OG as a political entity that had so many experienced and influential members in its ranks who would inevitably play an important part in any future independent Germany. It was in the US interest to take a hand in shaping its character. The option of disbanding it was to open Germany up to influences over which the US would rapidly lose control. His report went to the highest levels of the US government. Essentially it was greeted with muted enthusiasm but, as the CIA's Donald Galloway pointed out, there was still far too little known about the inner workings of the OG. It could well turn out to be a vehicle for the complete penetration of US intelligence by the Soviets. What was required now was an in-depth analysis of the OG to find out exactly what it was about. Little did Critchfield know that he had just inadvertently volunteered himself for a job that would last for the next seven years.

One of the problems he faced was the lack of resources at his disposal for the kind of wide-ranging reconnaissance work the Americans were starting to demand. There was also the question of the way that Baun had allowed his networks to expand during the months that Gehlen was in the US creating unsustainable financial pressures especially after the currency reforms. With one eye on the developing political moves towards a new West German state and the other on the nascent CIA, Gehlen could see no clear way forward, but he was determined not to lower his ambitions. Baun had responded to Critchfield by making a move towards rehabilitation of his career and writing a report for him entitled *Thoughts for the Establishment of Strategic Intelligence against the USSR* but Critchfield was not impressed by it. Baun had tried to interest the Americans with new, somewhat unorthodox, ideas such as creating escape routes for downed US airmen in the event of war, but the CIA requirement was for more immediate results from his networks. Critchfield found Baun and those around him, to be contemptuous of Gehlen's former General Staff personnel. It was the natural attitude of those who actually did all the dangerous work in the field towards those who sat around at head office getting friendly with the Americans and soaking up all the glory. Many thought Baun to be more Russian in character than German and he was certainly never comfortable in the company of Americans, whose language he did not speak or understand.

Over the next few months, Critchfield gathered together a staff of German-speaking officers who had experience in intelligence. In came Andre Rittner, Fred Stalder and Toivo Rosvall from OSS. Tom Lucid, Bill Graver and Henry Pleasants joined later. Along the way, Gehlen was to lose his friend Waldman. It was felt that he had been altogether too lenient with Gehlen and had allowed him to get away with far too much. His Austrian birth was cited by some as having influenced him towards being too sympathetic to German sensibilities and not sufficiently objective in his dealings with Gehlen. With control now having passed to the CIA, he had effectively been sidelined, anyway, and returned to the US. Turning down the chance to transfer to the CIA, he left the army to join the Department of Political Science at Marquette University.

In May 1949, Critchfield was ready to start. First of all, he called for information about strategic sources such as emigrant organisations the OG was dealing with and its contacts in other countries such as Spain, Switzerland and France where the risk of double agents was particularly acute. On the one hand, Gehlen was anxious to please Critchfield because army money was drying up and he would have to negotiate with the CIA for future funding but on the other hand, he wanted to avoid the US learning too much about his organisation. As for the funding gap, it was driving Gehlen to distraction. He held meetings with US generals about increasing his budget, but they were looking forward to getting the OG off the army payroll as soon as possible. Critchfield laid down new ground rules, which did not entirely go down well with Gehlen. He wanted full disclosure of budgets, operations and sources.

Discussions between Critchfield's staff and Gehlen, whom they now routinely referred to as 'the doctor' or occasionally 'old blue eyes', were long and sometimes heated.[25] Both sides knew that success lay in cooperation not confrontation, but Gehlen feared, at times, that he was losing the battle. While Critchfield clearly understood that the ultimate goal was to see the OG become part of the German government, he was determined that, in the meantime, Gehlen would know who was calling the shots. Becoming so much under US control after the freewheeling days of Deane and Waldman was a bitter blow to Gehlen's pride and ambition. Even when the Americans relaxed their grip, as they surely would in time, the danger for Gehlen was that he might then be seen as having been an American 'puppet', which would tarnish his image to such an extent that he would have no hope of playing a leading role in the new Germany. The constraints, especially financial ones, placed on his organisation caused him, at one time, to confided to Herre, who along with Gehlen's long-time secretary, Annelore, were constantly at his side, that he was 'ready to throw the whole thing away'.[26] He never made such a claim to Critchfield but he was sure that word of his outburst would find its way to him and hopefully have the desired effect.

Over the weeks, Critchfield had many conversations with Gehlen, whom he found to be a difficult personality, pragmatic and intelligent but by no means intellectual. He showed little interest in conventional politics believing that counterespionage was the most effective way of dealing with international political issues. The war had encouraged him to think in geopolitical terms and he had clear ideas about how his organisation, with its essential German character should retain its integrity and play a part in the future of Germany, and indeed the whole of the Western world. While he was not given to delegating responsibilities, he often procrastinated and skirted around difficult decisions. A secretive and quite insecure man, Gehlen seemed to Critchfield to shy away from contact with all but a few close associates unless it was absolutely necessary, but he seemed also to be a man who quietly enjoyed notoriety.

Critchfield was not willing to suggest that his superiors reach a written agreement with Gehlen. What he did instead was approve a new 'gentlemen's agreement' and when Gehlen bridled at that, the relationship between the two men started to show signs of fracture. It was not helped when Critchfield told him that the budget proposed by the CIA was exactly the same as the army had provided. For Gehlen that meant a slimming down of the organisation, something that Critchfield probably thought was no bad thing.

From a CIA perspective, there seemed to be scope for budget cuts by reducing operations in areas that were already well covered by other agencies. Counterespionage would continue to be funded but as soon as possible that was to be handed over to the German government. That would leave Gehlen at the head of a CIA auxiliary force that would be stripped of 'unsuitable' characters and at the mercy of a progressive government that would find working with former Wehrmacht officers in the pay of the US too much of an embarrassment. These were conditions so far away from what he had in mind for the future of the organisation that it was simply unthinkable. His ambition was to be at the heart of, and fundamentally indispensable to, whatever government came to power in Germany. Not only would he continue to welcome ex-Nazis, but he also considered their administrative contribution fundamental to the success of his ambitions as long as they kept a low profile and did not try to bring their politics into play. Three weeks before the OG was due to be taken over by the CIA, Gehlen laid down guidelines for restructuring it as an interim measure to navigate the handover by creating fictional business fronts for OG operations and establishments throughout the country to disguise their true purpose and obscure any connections to the Americans.

Critchfield was prepared to supply Gehlen with 40,000 cartons of cigarettes a month to cover costs, which was an insult to the Germans for the Americans to treat them like criminals surviving on black market deals. There was still the question of Baun, who had been held at bay for a couple of years but whose agents were still of vital importance to the organisation.

On 1 July 1949, the OG was officially taken over by the CIA. For them, the advantage of taking it on was that it now had control of the very organisation that might well be at the heart of a remilitarised the FRG. The takeover was a very low-key affair with no contract and no guarantees only an accumulation of understandings between Critchfield and Gehlen hammered out with Herre acting as 'marriage counsellor'.[27] Two of the CIA's fundamental reservations about the OG were to what extent its ranks were filled with ex-Nazis and the question of possible infiltration by the Soviets. To allay the fears of his masters in Washington, it was vital that Critchfield be given the identities of all agents in the field but this was the one area in which Gehlen would not compromise. There was no central register of employees, he said. The logic being that this would avoid a single security breach compromising the whole organisation but it only heightened Critchfield's suspicions that Gehlen was shielding the identities of former Nazis. The more Nazis Gehlen employed the more likely the OG would be to follow its own, possibly revanchist, strategies against the Soviets that were very unlikely to serve US interests.

Critchfield, however, was as wily and manipulative as Gehlen. He did not meet the issue head-on but took a more measured approach. He utilised the resources of the CIA to spy on Gehlen's organisation. Critchfield's people scrutinised all operations from finance to travel permits and by checks and cross-checks winkled out information that allowed them to compose a personnel dossier of all operatives. Only about a dozen names they uncovered gave Critchfield any concerns about Gehlen's use of Nazis, but future events would show that he had been less than successful in identifying the true number.

Critchfield consulted with Helms, whom he had persuaded to take responsibility for the OG in preference to Wisner's OPC, which, having a more aggressive pro-active anti-Soviet policy, appeared actually to have been a better fit. Helms and his boss Galloway together decided to treat the OG as a subordinate agency of the CIA. That meant closer control of its operations. He had concluded that the OG was far from the high-functioning intelligence outfit the army had led the CIA to believe. Critchfield even called it a 'second-rate organisation' to Gehlen's face, but Gehlen was now in a position to resist such criticism. Germany was on the cusp of becoming a sovereign state and many of those who would be in charge of it were people who owed something to Gehlen or people with whom Gehlen had developed a friendship. The time was coming when he could free himself from US control and become a wholly German organisation as part of the German government.

Nazis in the OG

> From the summer of 1950 he accepted numerous recruits from the ruins of the old SS empire.[28]

While there was so little known about the people Gehlen was employing, there persisted the strong suspicion that the group had been penetrated by the Soviets which meant keeping it at arm's length from all other CIA operations. There was also a significant body of opinion in Washington that believed

> Rusty [represented] a tightly knit organization of former German officers, a good number of which formerly belonged to the German general staff [and was] in a position to provide safe haven for a good many undesirable elements from the standpoint of a future democratic Germany.[29]

Control might best be achieved through the level of funding the CIA was giving. Critchfield explained to Gehlen that the CIA was anxious that he curtail his operations outside the Soviet zone of occupation in Germany. Specifically, he was told to close down operations in Austria, Hungary, Bulgaria and Yugoslavia. All others would be funded strictly on a project-by-project basis.

This hardly came as a surprise to Gehlen but it showed him that the CIA was not going to relax its drive to take total control of the OG. He resented the intervention and came out fighting. Gambling that the Soviet blockade of Berlin had raised tensions in Washington, he played a strong hand by simply refusing to comply with Critchfield's demands. They would hardly be likely to cut him adrift in the midst of a crisis. He made no effort to trim his operations and started making excuses as to why it was impossible to open up his personnel files. A compromise was arrived at which gave Critchfield limited access to operations and personnel and what he found disturbed him.

His analysts found the OG 'amateurish and wasteful' and 'incapable of handling serious intelligence operations'.[30] Gehlen responded in a very high-handed way by insinuating that the CIA really had no understanding of intelligence in the field where decisions had to be made quickly on the basis of imperfect information. He told Critchfield that he would hire whomsoever he chose to hire and continue to run operations the way he wanted. He couldn't be expected to get US approval for every little thing. Their naïve attitude was an indication of inexperience. Mechanical application of American principles with red tape and regulations, he said, was inimicable to efficiency and crushed the initiative instincts of agents. Sometimes decisions had to be made on the spur of the moment and, of course, mistakes were made, he conceded, but it was better to act wrongly than not act at all. Gehlen was enjoying lecturing Critchfield but again the American chose a subtle response.

Bonn sent two accountants to Pullach to examine the books of the OG in preparation for the possibility of its employees formally joining the West German civil service. This required a complete list of the real names of all OG employees, Unbeknown to Gehlen, Critchfield became privy to this information and so using travel receipts and salary payments, he was able painstakingly to piece together a roster of all personnel. Amongst those uncovered were Heinz Felfe, Carl Schuetz and the war criminals Erich Deppner, Konrad Fiebig and Emil Augsburg whom Gehlen had selected to be his chief specialist on the structure and tactics of the Soviet intelligence services.[31] More than 100 names of former SS, SD and Gestapo personnel was a revelation for Critchfield but it was still a conservative estimate.

While this number is a small proportion of the more than 4,000 people in the OG some of those, such as Alois Brunner, chief deputy to Adolf Eichmann, and Klaus Barbie, the 'Butcher of Lyons' had participated in the most heinous crimes. Barbie would go on to assist a succession of military regimes in Bolivia. At least eleven former SD and Gestapo officers were the backbone of a counterintelligence service *Dienststelle 114*, which had been set up by Baun in Karlsruhe. In 2011, the magazine *Der Spiegel* was to call it

> the main gateway into the West German secret service for Nazi war criminals.[32]

Former SS-Oberführer Wilhelm 'Willi' Krichbaum had been a close associate of Reinhard Heydrich, the 'Butcher of Prague', former SS-Sturmbannführer Fritz Schmidt was the former head of the Gestapo in Kiel, Paul Hodosy-Strobl had been chief of the Hungarian State Police under the Nazis, Herbert Boehrsch had been with the SD in Prague, Walter Otten had been an SS-Sturmbannführer in Bremen, and ex-SS-Oberführer Otto Somann, had served with the SD and *Sicherheitspolizei* (Sipo) before being seconded to the Gestapo. Emil Augsburg had joined *Dienststelle 114* in October 1948. He had been involved in *spezialle Aufgaben*, the killing of Jews and suspected communists, in Poland between 1939 and 1940. Much of the SD's Balkan network had been retained, including the leader of the Romanian Fascist 'Iron Guard', Otto von Bolschwing, whom Gehlen would later reject for incompetence but who went on to work for Dulles in the OSS. After relocating to the US in February 1954, he became closely associated with Richard Nixon's political career and ended up as president of Trans-International Computer Investment Corporation in Sacramento, California, a company that held classified US Department of Defence contracts.[33] Others from the Iron Guard were Horia Sima, Kurt Auner, Ernst Schlandt and Joachim Vacarescu.[34]

Another section, *Dienststelle 12*, that organized penetrations of the Soviet zone through Berlin, had on its payroll Erich Deppner, a deputy to SS-Brigadeführer Wilhelm Harster, the SD and Sipo commander who organised the deportation of more than 100,000 Dutch Jews to extermination camps. Ernst Makowski had been a Gestapo officer in southwestern Germany while SS-Obersturmbannführer Karl Guse had been chief of the Gestapo in Rome and SS-Hauptsturmführer Werner Krassowski had served first as a concentration camp guard and then with an SS unit in the Baltics. Former SS-Hauptsturmführer Caspar ran Gehlen's sub-agency 1600, ex-Gestapo man Max Staudinger worked at Pullach headquarters and former SS-Sturmbannführer Josef Adolf Urban, who had been head of the SD in Budapest, headed up the OG network in Austria.

The *Einstazkommando* units were the main German agencies of the Holocaust in the occupied regions during the Second World War. Konrad Fiebig had served with the *Einsatzkommando 9* of *Einsatzgruppe B* that murdered 11,000 Jews in the Belorussian town of Vitebsk and later acted as judge in the *Sondergericht* judicial system, which was used by the SS to kill political enemies. In 1948, he was acting as a Rusty courier in Stuttgart, and would go on to work for West German intelligence into the early 1960s. Walter Kurreck had been in *Einsatzgruppe D* in 1942 where he had been involved in assassinations behind Soviet lines and the executions of political commissars in Russian PoW camps.[35]

It was not only the former officers who posed serious security threats. Many of the lower functionaries who had worked behind enemy lines and were still there along with agents whose locations had been overrun by the Soviet advance had been Nazis and, again their identities were kept from US scrutiny. In his biography, Helms would say

> There is no principle in the espionage canon more important than that an intelligence service must know, or at the least continuously strive to know, exactly with whom it is dealing

but that is exactly what the CIA did not do.[36] They failed to insist in the strongest possible terms to be given the names of and biographic data on all Rusty staff personnel or the agents and sources employed in the field. Gehlen had assured G-2 that no he employed no former SS, Gestapo, or SD personnel G-2 could not check its own files or the captured Nazi Party, SS, Gestapo, SD and Wehrmacht records for war criminals or other compromised Nazis. All they had to go on was Rusty's own security and background checks on new employees which were minimal.

The confusion of the immediate postwar years, when the demand for military and political intelligence was increasing daily, he said, was no excuse for breaking one of the fundamental rules of secret intelligence, and thereby sowing the seeds of the security disasters to follow. Failure to keep Rusty clean of former Nazis proved to be a costly mistake by providing the East Germans and Soviets with a potent tool of propaganda. The threat to expose someone's Nazi background also offered the various communist espionage services a potentially useful blackmail tool.

Of the Germans, some would go on to play leading roles in European neofascist organisations establishing a Nazi lineage that stretched right through into the twenty-first century. The *Frankfurter Rundschau* newspaper would describe them as 'Himmler's elite … having happy reunion ceremonies'.[37] What all these men had in common was a deep hatred of communists, the Soviets in particular. They had been conditioned over many years to view the Slavic races as 'sub-human' and resented any criticism of Nazi extermination policies in the eastern regions during the German occupation. This loathing of 'all things Russian', Gehlen believed, was what made these men so reliable. He went so far as to call SS-Rottenführer Hans Brachmüller 'politically completely impeccable'.[38]

Gehlen claimed that because of the decentralised system of recording details of personnel, he was unaware of the extent to which former Nazis populated his organisation, but it is hard to believe that he did not know that the head of his organization's Combined Reports, Translation and Editing Office, Erich Ulich Kayser-Eichberg, had worked as an SS-Sturmbannführer with the Race and Settlement unit in the Waffen-SS Alpenland and in Bohemia, Czechoslovakia. He certainly knew about Emil Augsburg, whom he had worked with before and who he had promoted to a high rank as an advisor on Soviet intelligence. While there was so little known outside the OG about the people Gehlen was employing, there also persisted the strong suspicion that the group had been penetrated by the Soviets, which meant keeping it at arm's length from all other US intelligence operations.

When the CIA officially took over the OG, they began referring to the Rusty Operation as 'Zipper' (other names they gave it were Odeum and Offspring) presumably on the assumption that they were going to open it up. There was no official contract, just an understanding which the CIA intended to interpret as meaning that Gehlen would do what he was told to do. Critchfield established a counterintelligence group called the Pullach Operations Base (POB) adjacent to Zipper and run by the former CIC officer Tom Lucid whose cover name was Herr Lucas. Lucid was a 'tall, handsome extrovert' to whom Gehlen warmed immediately. He got on well with Germans leading one observer to remark that the guests at the christening of his daughter looked like 'a gathering of the General Staff'.[39]

By 1949, de-Nazification was much less of an issue for the Americans and the CIA had no official policy about employing former Nazi war criminals, SD or Gestapo. If they were deemed to have useful skills or information they could use, the CIA was happy to ignore their war record, provided that it was not too colourful, and focus on what contribution they could make to the Cold War with the Soviet Union. This did not go as far as hiring anyone whose crimes were well known because of the difficulty in maintaining a covert status for them. Allowing Gehlen to employ such people was a different matter. Apart from the lack of control over them, the CIA was clearly concerned that if it became known, the US government would be held to account for sponsoring a criminal organisation in the FRG. They went to some lengths to conceal the very existence of the OG. Gehlen, himself, appeared on official US Army 'wanted' lists right up until 1949. In reality, because they could not control recruitment inro the OG themselves, the Americans began to place responsibility for monitoring the credentials of OG employees more onto the German government and began the process of erecting a security screen between the OG and all US agencies.

By the mid-1949, Gehlen was frustrated by the cuts in CIA funding for the OG and wrote to his American controllers,

> I [have] the impression that [you lack] ... a complete picture about the significance of our work for the United States, not only concerning Intelligence matters but also for the political future ... For the common US and German future interest, I ask ... for your help and support for the continuation of our work.[40]

Critchfield, under instructions from Washington, confirmed the financial cuts and again suggested that operations should be curtailed in all regions except the Soviet-controlled parts of Germany. Counterintelligence and counterespionage, he said, should be handed over to the government of the new FRG, which had been founded on 23 May 1949, and funded by Bonn.

The FRG emerged at the end of a process that had started on 2 December 1946 when the British and Americans decided to merge their respective occupation zones. The French zone was added in 1948. On 1 September 1948, the Parliamentary Council started work in Bonn by electing a Christian Democrat, Konrad Adenauer, to lead it and formulated the Basic Law, which was promulgated on 23 May 1949. This law became the provisional Constitution of FRG and gave rise to the first legislative elections. Bonn was chosen ahead of Frankfurt to be the provisional capital and West Berlin was incorporated as part of the FRG in spite of its special status.

Although not yet fully independent, the FRG was permitted by the French, British and US authorities to establish its own government.

Gehlen saw this as a ploy to force him to strip his organisation of lower-rank former SD members who were the ones who had been more active in the very areas that Critchfield wanted to close down. Naturally, Gehlen resisted such a move. In order to realise his own ambition of leading the whole German intelligence community, it was essential to keep all sections of the OG together. It was also clear to him that putting these former Nazis out into the cold would simply hand them over to the Soviets. Gehlen would later tell Crichfield that, in percentage terms, he employed fewer former SS and SD members 'than most [Federal German] ministries.'

Enemies of the State

> Bolshevik Trojan Horses undermining West Germany in preparation for an assault by the Russians or a communist seizure of power by subversive means[41]

Gehlen was becoming more and more focused on internal threats to Germany and with Baun out of the way, he had more freedom to pursue this agenda. Considering the make-up of OG leadership it is no surprise that many viewed its historic mission as a continuation of the wartime crusade against communism. The feverish Nazi propaganda that had engulfed the nation during the previous decade which, itself, had built on a history of anti-communist prejudice going back to the early Weimar days of the *Freikorps* street battles, had been absorbed deep into the psyche of the Wehrmacht, SS and SD. Now, with half of their country occupied by the hated 'reds', there would be no diminution of hostility towards Moscow. The OG's trend towards internal surveillance of suspected communist activists in the FRG was only to be expected.

Anyone who had family connections in the DDR and travelled there to visit them automatically came under suspicion of subversive activity. This encouraged a culture not unlike that which had existed under the Nazis in the 1930s where neighbours informed on anyone who seemed to them to be somehow different from the norm in habit or demeanour. OG files from 1950 show significant intrusion into the lives of the many people living in the country who had foreign connections. It is hardly surprising that there were many such people given the huge movements of populations during and immediately after the war with returnees from captivity in the east and displaced persons of many different east European nationalities. Anyone uttering the most innocuous pro-communist sympathies could easily find themselves on an OG card index.

Not only was the search for Soviet agents ramped up but the German Communist Party was kept under close surveillance. The list grew longer to include left-wing pacifists and Gehlen needed to recruit more agents to meet the demand he had created. The obvious choice were the ex-employees of the Nazi police force. He excused this decision by saying that by employing these people he was denying their services to the East Germans.

The outbreak of the Korean War on 25 June 1950, in which the Soviet Union and China supported the military invasion of South Korea, heightened fears that the Soviets might flex their muscles in Europe also. Gehlen thought it prudent to make available to the German government a list of all those who should be taken into preventive custody if an emergency arose. Naturally, the former-SD men who now worked for the OG were familiar with the locations and organisations where communist sympathies lay. In places they enjoyed full cooperation from the civilian police who gave them access to files of the Resident's Registration Office. In this way the OG card index included all members of the KPD and many Social Democrats including Erich Ollenhauer and Herbert Wehner who was listed as 'a most dangerous enemy of the state'.[42] Secretaries and cleaners, many of whom were the widows of Wehrmacht or SS personnel killed during the Second World War, were placed in positions where they could spy on people of interest. Organisations were also listed as potential threats to the state. The Study Group for Economic Advancement in Hamburg, came under suspicion for planning an exhibition in Moscow. Any groups who showed interest in peace initiatives with the DDR, such as the East Prussian Nationals Society were infiltrated with informants. Gehlen's man who headed up the surveillance section lamented that he did not have executive powers to implement *lückenlose Überwachung* (complete surveillance).[43] Nevertheless, the result of this close cooperation between the OG and the political elite was ruthlessly exploited by Gehlen on the road to his realising his ambitions.

As early as 1948, Gehlen had identified Adenauer as one who would play a leading role in West German politics and during the following years, he assiduously worked towards an understanding with him through intermediaries such as Hans Ritter von Lex to emphasise the counterintelligence role played by the OG in the fight against communist infiltration of Adenauer's government. Lex was sympathetic to Gehlen's approach but when he sought approval from Germany's allies it was the British, in particular, who saw any concentration of power in Gehlen's hands as politically dangerous and the British viewpoint, at that time, was still held in some regard by Washington. MI6 feared that if Germany became part of the newly created mutual defence force called the North Atlantic Treaty Organisation (NATO), its intelligence services would be integrated with those of other member countries and, given that there were grave misgivings about Soviet infiltration of the OG, that was a risk not worth taking. It was not helpful either that so many powerful interests that Gehlen would have to persuade or defeat still referred to the OG as 'Gehlen and his Nazis' who were perceived as competing with the *Bundesamt für Verfassungsschutz* (BfV – Federal Office for the Protection of the Constitution).[44]

Gehlen, however, was energised by being within sight of his ultimate goal of transforming the OG into the official secret service organisation of the FRG but the moral and political ambiguity of combining external, internal and police functions would be a stumbling block in the short term. Adenauer was the key and Adenauer was greatly exercised by fear of the Soviet menace now that the Korean situation had erupted from an east-west exchange of vitriol into a full-blown war. His paranoia was fuelled by Gehlen's reporting of the DDR and its KVP internal police force. The issue of German remilitarisation was very much on Adenauer's agenda, which brought Gehlen to his attention as someone whom he perceived as having years of experience in combatting Soviet infiltration and espionage. When it was suggested to Gehlen that Adenauer was worried about communist agitation in the Ruhr, he expanded the OG's presence in Bochum and Essen, then when a similar fear was expressed about Soviet propaganda radicalising the Hamburg dockers, extra agents were sent there.

Gehlen's contacts in foreign intelligence agencies was another bonus. Colonel Max Waibel of the Swiss Secret Service had been in contact with Gehlen since 1948 when the OG had identified and exposed Soviet agents moving into Switzerland from the French zone and the two agencies had subsequently developed a good working relationship. From that had developed a relationship, brokered by Waibel, between the OG and the *Service de Documentation Extérieure et de Contre-Espionage* (SDECE – French Intelligence Service). Gehlen had a low opinion of SDECE but was assured that their stables were being cleansed of what he thought were unsuitable agents and replaced by men trained by General Charles de Gaulle. The main impediment was still Gehlen's relationship with the Americans, which would be politically embarrassing if Adenauer's government embraced the OG so an agreement was hatched with the SPD's Schumacher for the OG to continue its work under American trusteeship even though Schumacher had openly accused the OG of being 'riddled with' former war criminals who had been 'deliberately placed in low-ranking positions, to disguise them'.[45]

The relationship was enshrined in the Allied High Commission Law No. 62 which gave Gehlen's men legal authority to share intelligence with the CIA. Hans Globke, Ministerial Director for Internal Affairs, arranged for special Federal funding which allowed Gehlen to increase surveillance measures, but which also gave Globke a hold over Gehlen. For Gehlen, this was a small price to pay for an important step towards full integration into the Federal government and leveraged his position vis-à-vis the CIA. At a meeting with Adenauer in December 1950, an understanding was arrived at whereby Globke would undertake 'concrete measures' to prepare for legalisation of the OG within the Federal government.[46] It was little more than a verbal agreement but one that Gehlen would place great store by over the next few difficult years. It seemed to be a matter of honour for Gehlen that he had such a high regard for verbal agreements but it was rather naïve of him to think that others, whose character had not been forged in the German High Command, would honour them to the last syllable.

Through all this, Critchfield, for all his many reservations about the OG, proved to be one of Gehlen's most prominent advocates. As the bridge between Gehlen and Washington, Critchfield was able to emphasise the advantages of working with Gehlen and strove to project an image of the OG that was not altogether unfavourable. There would need to be changes, however, if he was to prevent Gehlen slipping into obscurity. In order to make the OG more resistant to opposing forces and more relevant to both Washington and the FRG, he urged Gehlen to focus on CIA priorities, which meant delivering greater operational competence in the area of military intelligence. As an inducement, he promised that if that could be done the CIA would provide an additional DM 100,000 per month and he would do all he could to expedite OG's transition into becoming the legal intelligence agency of the FRG despite opposition from Britain who felt that such a move would fortify a US-German intelligence relationship and leave them devoid of influence. Remilitarisation of the FRG was now right at the top of Washington's European agenda. Whatever Gehlen could do to make his organisation more central to that agenda could only be to his advantage, but it was Heusinger who had been the true advocate of German militarisation and Gehlen would have to face that challenge first. It was Heusinger who had protected the better-known former Wehrmacht generals from public scrutiny and given them the freedom within the OG to develop plans for what would become the Bundeswehr.

The British and French, fearing that the OG was too much under US influence, continued to resist the formation of a purely German secret service until the FRG had achieved full sovereignty and could make its own decisions about the way to proceed with its intelligence services. Gehlen was getting backed into a corner but managed to arrange a meeting with Adenauer on 20 September 1950. Adenauer, Gehlen said, received him with 'a warmth and open-mindedness that immediately dispelled all concerns'.[47] Following the meeting, Gehlen sent the Chancellor a 'simple and pointed' memorandum entitled *Gedanken zur Frage eines deutschen Nachrichtendienstes* (Thoughts on the Question of a German Intelligence Service).[48] He outlined a possible new structure and estimated the annual cost to in the region of DM 40 million.

The BfV

> [Otto John] had interrogated many prominent German officers as prisoners, including several under me at Pullach, who would now be expected to work with him.
>
> Reinhard Gehlen[49]

Federal Elections to the *Bundeshaus* on 14 August 1949 saw the two main parties, the SPD and the *Christlich Demokratische Union Deutschlands* (CDU – Christian Democratic Union of Germany) battling for control. Gehlen feared an SPD victory that would be antagonistic towards the OG both for its General Staff connections and its association with the Americans. Under its leader, the stridently anti-communist, Konrad Adenauer, the CDU had canvassed in cooperation with the *Christlich-Soziale Union in Bayern* (CSU – Christian Social Union in Bavaria) and, fortuitously for Gehlen narrowly defeated the SPD forming a coalition government with the *Freie Demokratische Partei* (FDP – Free Democratic Party) and the *Deutsche Partei* (DP – German Party). The Soviet zone of Germany responded by presented itself to the world on 7 October 1949 as the *Deutsche Demokratische Republik* (DDR – German Democratic Republic), a satellite state of the Soviet Union with a state military police force, the KVP.

Gehlen looked to the new government for a pathway towards achieving some sort of legal status for the OG and he hoped that the Americans would support him but knew that, in the long term, Bonn would demand that he sever all ties with the US. This could not be done overnight, and any transition from one to the other would demand every ounce of Gehlen's guile and tenacity. It was not going to be easy for the Prussian Protestant Gehlen to find common ground with the Catholic fundamentalist Bavarian Adenauer or the CSU leader and avowed anti-Nazi Alois Hundhammer. At this time, it is doubtful if either Adenauer or Hundhammer knew much about the OG or its connections to the CIA.[50] At the same time, Gehlen was having to resist continuing pressure from Critchfield for total control of the OG. The CIA man was demanding daily written reports and was not slow to lecture Gehlen about the importance of complying. Gehlen worked all his frustration and anger into a paper concerning 'fundamental considerations'. He began by thanking Critchfield for his help and in working through the difficulties they both faced and reiterated his commitment to German-US cooperation. However, he made clear that he considered it his duty to make a strong argument when their views diverge but hoped that the personal relationship that had developed between them would ensure that problems were solved through discussion. The question of Germany's place in the new Europe and its relationship with the US was fundamental to how the CIA and the OG would work with each other but there was a distinct difference between the German and the Anglo-American mentality and methodology. The US system of regulating down to the finest detail was not how the Germans had been trained. The fact that the Red Army is camped on the doorstep of the FRG gave Gehlen a much sharper perspective and required his organisation to react much quicker to Soviet provocations even at the risk of making mistakes. He would not agree to always waiting for authority from Washington before acting.

Gehlen had gone to Switzerland in December 1948 to have discussions with Max Ulrich of the Swiss Federal Police, the Marquis de Villalobar of the Spanish secret Service and Colonel Marcel-André Mercier of the French Secret Service. Ostensibly this was to lay down agreements for evacuation of the OG in the event of war but also touched on the future creation of a closer European political union. Critchfield suspected that Gehlen was 'spinning secret threads'.[51]

Towards Adenauer, Gehlen took a very cautious line. The two men had met around 20 September 1948 in a private meeting at which no notes were taken. It is not known what the two men discussed but days earlier, Adenauer had complained about the lack of knowledge about what was happening in the Soviet zone, which is what precipitated the meeting. Both of Adenauer's main opponents in the coming elections, Jakob Kaiser of the CDU and Kurt Schumacher of the SPD were both particularly well-informed about the Soviet zone. It is probable that Adenauer and Gehlen discussed ways and means of advancing both their agendas.

To Adenauer's representatives Gehlen subsequently emphasised the role that the FHO had played during the war during which, he said, they had developed *zur höchsten Perfektion* (to the highest perfection), and, somewhat disingenuously, claimed that by 1944 when the Abwehr was disbanded, all German intelligence had been subordinated to him. He went on to say that during his time as head of FHO, he had provided accurate intelligence well in advance of events to the Chiefs of Staff and Canaris but it had been rejected by Hitler because it contradicted the Führer's own assessments. He defended his dalliance with the Americans as an urgent need to perpetuate a German 'concept' and culture and emphasised that he had, in fact, been working alongside the Americans and not under or for them.

The issue with Baun had still not been resolved and it threatened to weaken Gehlen's case to be taken seriously by the Bonn government. Baun had been fatally wounded by the embezzlement claims, which he had not denied, but Gehlen had continued to work with him, despite moves by the Americans and his own acolyte Herre, to have him removed. Gehlen knew full well that had it not been for Baun's *Walli* networks, he would have had a much weaker case to be taken on by G-2 in the first place and it had only been by presenting himself as a more reliable and trustworthy contact that he had been able, eventually, to acquire the dominant role in Rusty. He used his personal connections with Deane and Waldman to subjugate Baun but never lost sight of the fact that he needed him because of his personal control of the networks in the Soviet zone of influence. Now Critchfield wanted Baun out and the pressure was building on Gehlen who found it difficult to cope with. Herre was concerned about his mood swings and occasional outbursts of frustration against the Americans, which he attributed to Gehlen's defensive mindset. Eventually, Gehlen relented and informed Critchfield on 26 October 1949 that he would dismiss Baun. His final repudiation of Baun was bitter. He had too much of a Russian mentality that made it difficult for Westerners to understand his methods, Gehlen now said, not to mention a debilitating inferiority complex resulting from his lowly background. His psychology made him a particularly efficient agent runner, but his organisational skills were sadly lacking and his management abilities virtually non-existent. It would still be another four months before Baun left the service and was pensioned off with a very generous allowance, however and only a year beyond that before he was dead from lung cancer.

With the Baun question off the agenda, Gehlen went to Bonn on 15 November 1949 to meet Adenauer's personal advisor Herbert

Blankenhorn, Interior Minister Gustav Heinemann and Vice Chancellor Franz Blücher none of whom had even heard of the OG and thought Gehlen was the head of some sort of defence organisation set up by the Americans. Gehlen wanted to make his case for leading a combined domestic and foreign secret service. Gehlen had tried to keep his contacts with Bonn a secret, but the CIA had good contacts in the government there and knew what was going on. They told Critchfield to let Gehlen know that they knew and to discourage further negotiations, but he was struggling to keep a rein on Gehlen who was planning to speak to Adenauer before the Americans could properly brief him. The Americans wanted to play a part in the formulation of a purely German intelligence service but Gehlen, while still reliant on the CIA, was obviously trying to inch his organisation away from American influence. In November, Critchfield made it clear to Gehlen that he was not to enter any further discussions with representatives of the Bonn government.

On 20 March 1950, Gordon M. Stewart, the CIA man in Karsruhe who also had responsibility for Pullach wrote to Director of Intelligence for the US Army Benjamin Slute with a comprehensive assessment of Gehlen at this time. Gehlen, he said, was an intense and self-confident person primarily motivated by a desire for personal success. His hatred of communism, which he held in common with many of his associates, was well-documented and beyond doubt but he was also driven by a keen sense of duty and patriotism. His main flaw was a lack of critical judgement, which Stewart attributed to his lack of academic training, leaving him unable to fully appreciate the nuanced arguments around issues of democracy and the legacy of Nazism. Working closely with the Americans had allowed him to take, what for him was a natural position; a strong ideological stance against left-wing movements but that was not necessarily going to play well in the context of German domestic politics. Although Stewart believed that Gehlen's cautious, even indifferent, approach to party politics meant that he would be a loyal servant to Adenauer, there was an open question about whether he would serve the interests of the German government, regardless of its political stripe.

In March 1950, Adenauer officially proposed Gehlen to the office of President of the BfV which would have duties equivalent to those of the American FBI. Specifically, it would be tasked with

> acquisition and evaluation of information and intelligence … concerning tendencies aiming at suspension, alteration or disturbance of the constitutional order in the Federal Republic.[52]

Despite having no experience in police work, Gehlen saw himself as the leading candidate, but any appointment would have to be sanctioned by Britain, France and the United States. British codebreakers had known much better than the Americans just how woefully the FHO had performed during the war and had a low opinion of Gehlen, who apparently had not been aware of the extent to which the British had penetrated his communications at that time. Based on their wartime assessment, the British thought there was every chance that Gehlen would bring a 'cavalier attitude' to Cold War operational security.[53] Gehlen was already making preparations for an orderly handover of his organisation to the BfV against a background of more severe cuts in CIA funding when the British vetoed his nomination. The CIA were not particularly enthusiastic about having Gehlen running the BfV either believing that it was merely a step towards his known ambition to head up a combined foreign and domestic intelligence agency, which they considered to be a potential threat to German democracy.

When they realised that Gehlen might get the post, the British were quick, once again, to block his elevation and put forward their own candidate, Otto John, which as it turned out, was far from being a good choice either. Gehlen was bitterly disappointed and critical thinking that the Americans were abandoning him which was true to some extent given that the intelligence provided by the OG was becoming less and less pertinent to their overall intelligence requirements. The Americans were demanding more at the same time as cutting the budget and funding only those operations that Critchfield approved, which mostly involved intelligence gathering in the eastern zone thereby hoping once and for all to rein in the sprawling networks over which even Gehlen did not seem to have complete understanding or control. There seemed to be no way of circumventing the budgetary constraints that caused Gehlen extreme frustration but neither was there a clear path to transfer the OG over to the Bonn government, that was looking elsewhere for development of its military and security services. Gehlen's candidacy had triggered another crisis for the OG. He was in danger of falling between two stools and could quite easily find himself with no role to play at all.

Gehlen was getting quite desperate to see the OG dissolved and recreated in a different form, but Heusinger warned that, in order to do that successfully, the framework of a new organisation had to be in place before dissolving the OG. Neither was it comfortable for the Americans to contemplate the loss of control of OG resources to another agency. A CIA memorandum of May 1950, in which for the first time the OG was referred to as 'Utility', said, Bonn's recognition of Gehlen 'before the proper counterintelligence controls were firmly established' left the possibility that the West German government

> would find itself able to rob us of our intelligence assets and with serious strategic or political consequences turn them against us.[54]

Critchfield, whom his CIA masters had given pretty much all control of Gehlen's operations, wanted to identify those aspects of the OG that were most important from a US perspective and make sure that the CIA held onto them if the OG was broken up, which may or may not have been his hidden agenda all along. What might have been crucial intelligence in 1945 was no longer quite so valuable. Much of the intelligence that Gehlen was giving the CIA was of little interest to them. The goldrush was over, Critchfield said, it was now a buyer's market and Gehlen would have to tailor his organisation's product to the marketplace. Contact with intelligence agencies of other countries should cease. Gehlen should stop acting as if he was already head of an independent German agency. For Gehlen, that was precisely the point, however. He was acting in this way because that is exactly what he was working towards.

All this was playing out as Western European governments were staring at 6,000 Soviet tanks, 1,500 aircraft and 32 Red Army divisions and all effort to bind France and the FRG into a political alliance were being vetoed by Britain. There was a growing feeling in Bonn that the European situation was viewed very differently from a Washington perspective where the fears of a revival of German right-wing nationalism seemed to outweigh the fear of communism. Anti-American feeling was growing and the demand for increased autonomy and freedom for the West German government to choose its own brand of democracy was becoming strident. Inside the OG, also, there was increasing resentment at the way American methods were taking over and Gehlen had to respond to that. He was being eased out of the frame in Bonn, also, with ex-Panzer General Gerhard Graf von Schwerin, with British support, taking up his appointment as security advisor to Adenauer, and Major Achim Oster, the son of Canaris's second in command, Hans Oster, coming in as Schwerin's advisor and organiser. Von Schwerin's appointment included external affairs under Blankenhorn, which saw the emergence of yet another intelligence agency, a military secret service that, crucially for Bonn, was not under any obligation to the Americans.

Born into Prussian aristocracy, von Schwerin had become a staff officer in the OKH and claimed to have risked high treason by making approaches to the British government in 1939 to persuade them to take a firm stand against Hitler's expansionist policies. Although known to a number of private individuals in England as anti-Nazi, there is no independent evidence to corroborate his involvement in any anti-Hitler plots.

Von Schwerin had adopted an obstructive approach to Gehlen threatening to '*die Schotten dicht zu machen* [close the doors]' to the OG on questions of homeland defence and external security.[55] He was particularly disliked by OG personnel for his close ties to the British who, they believed, used him to undermine Gehlen's position. Critchfield suggested that Gehlen go straight to Adenauer and complain but Gehlen was afraid that, for political expediency, Adenauer might take von Schwerin's side, which would make Gehlen look weak. He wanted to challenge von Schwerin but found little incriminating evidence with which to attack him.

He did, however, make a trip to England in mid-April 1950 to meet leading Conservative politicians and military figures to discuss German rearmament. During his visit, which had the blessing of the federal government, he met the influential intelligence figure, Kenneth Strong, also the distinguished British diplomat, Sir Ivone Kirkpatrick. By April 1950, von Schwerin had already been earmarked for the post of Adenauer's security adviser and was, in fact, the preferred choice of the British to head up any independent German security service but Adenauer was prepared to go only so far to accommodate the British and, in the end, would not countenance von Schwerin's appointment.

Oster, no doubt with von Schwerin's blessing, had suggested that Gehlen could be assigned as a *Morgengabe* (morning gift) liaison to the various NATO committees that were springing up in Fontainebleau, which would see him comfortably nudged out of the picture. It was with some difficulty that Herre persuaded Gehlen to give it some thought and not reject the idea out of hand, but it didn't go much farther than that. Gehlen considered applying to become an advisor to Adenauer to acquire more influence in Bonn and counter von Schwerin's aggression, but Critchfield thought he carried too much baggage as head of the OG to be taken seriously as someone so close to levers of power.

Von Schwerin had not given his attacks up on Gehlen. On 22 July, he had complained to Deputy US High Commissioner for Germany General George P. Hays that there were 'unreliable individuals' working for Gehlen and since Gehlen could not be trusted to carry out his own investigation into the claims, he would be happy to do it for him. He had also been able to get the agreement of the American High Commissioner in Germany John Jay McCloy for access to official information and US military intelligence about the OG on the understanding that he was receiving it on behalf of the federal chancellor.[56]

Gehlen's main rival for leadership of all German intelligence services, however, emerged when Adenauer created the *Zentrale für Heimatdienst* (ZfH), an umbrella organisation of four detachments charged with national defence, one of which, the *Friedrich-Wilhelm-Heinz-Amt* (FWHA), under another former Abwehr officer, Friedrich Wilhelm Heinz (CIA codename Capote), which enjoyed very close ties to the Americans and was charged with gathering intelligence from the GDR and the other Soviet satellites working under the tightest security. In October 1950, the entire ZfH, was placed under the so-called *Amt Blank*, which would later become the official West German Ministry of Defence.[57]

Heinz had been politically active from a very early age in the right-wing nationalist *Deutschen Vaterlandspartei* (German Fatherland Party) before serving in the First World War where he survived serious injuries. After the First World War, he took part in the failed Kapp Putsch against the Weimar government and then went on to join the right-wing radical *Schwartze Reichswehr* (Black Reichswehr) an illegal paramilitary organisation. He also worked in the illegal *Deutscher Überseedienst* (intelligence service carrying out espionage against the French during the occupation of the Ruhr). He joined the Wehrmacht in 1936 where he came into contact with 'resistance martyr'[58] Hans Oster whose planned coup against Hitler was aborted after the Hitler-Chamberlain Munich Agreement of September 1938.[59] Peripherally involved in the 20 July Stauffenberg Plot, he went into hiding until the end of the Second World War. Working as a journalist in Berlin in 1946, Heinz made contact with British and French intelligence services, where he was known by the codename 'Tulip', eventually setting up a network of agents working with the Americans. Under the guise of a journalist working for *Time* and *Life* magazines, he set up the FWHA specialising in the sale of information about the location and strength of Soviet forces in Soviet controlled Berlin.

Oster and Heinz, with their historic family connection through the 1938 anti-Hitler plot, carried on military espionage in the GDR under the guise of the *Institut für Zeitgeschichte* (IfZ – Institute for Contemporary Research). With their anti-Hitler credentials, they shored up their position in government by accusing Gehlen's organisation of harbouring far too many former Nazis.

It was another man with links to the Oster plot who further threatened Gehlen's position. With significant opposition building to Gehlen's candidature for the BfV, Adenauer chose one of his aides Ernst Wirmer, the brother of one of the Stauffenberg plotters but again the candidate was vetoed, this time by his main coalition partners, so a frustrated Adenauer bowed out leaving it to Minister of the Interior Robert Lehr, to make the choice which turned out to be the lawyer and anti-Nazi, Otto John.

John had fled Nazi Germany to England after the abortive assassination attempt of 20 July 1944. He would go on to give evidence against Field Marshal Erich von Manstein, one of Gehlen's heroes, at a British military court and later worked for the British in their de-Nazification programme. Knowing that Adenauer did not like John, Gehlen lobbied hard against him. Without explicit reference to the high-ranking ex-Wehrmacht officers in the Org who despised John, Gehlen made the case that John's testimony against Manstein meant that he would never have the confidence of his staff especially given John's sympathy with the wartime Soviet 'Red Orchestra' espionage and resistance group. John had the full support of the British and French, however, who claimed that his opponents inside the OG were nothing more than Nazis acting out of revenge. The Americans kept out of the argument and were content to make it look as if it was the British who had scuppered Gehlen's chances. Adenauer was outmanoeuvred and had no choice but give conditional approval for John's appointment which was formalised in December 1951. As soon as he was in office, John made arrangements to expand BfV activities into counterespionage which would inevitably encroach on OG territory. Unable to challenge John's selection, Gehlen did the next best thing. He met John for conciliatory talks and offered to work with him in a cooperative atmosphere, but he was banking on Adenauer's hostility to John and planned accordingly. He volunteered Albert Radke to represent the OG within the BfV and Radke became his informant there, eventually becoming John's deputy and, along with another of Gehlen's men there, Konrad Gallen, paved the way for what Gehlen hoped would be a future takeover.

The Bundeswehr

> For two decades the mere mention of Gehlen's name was enough to make senior government officials in Bonn clam up and assume the blankest expression they could muster.[60]

After the German surrender on 7 and 8 May 1945, the victorious powers had assumed political control over all of Germany and there followed almost complete demilitarisation and political decentralisation. Then by 1947, sixteen federal states had been created, but there was still no central authority for Germany as a whole. De-Nazification and de-industrialisation followed to eliminate Germany's arms manufacture and other heavy industries but very soon there had emerged serious differences between the Western Powers and the Soviet Union over how to deal with Germany as a nation state. Responding to Soviet provocation, in 1948, the Western Powers approved the Basic Law for the Federal Republic of Germany and on 23 May 1949, the FRG was born but it would still not have full sovereignty for another six years. The Western Allies still had considerable rights over it.

As a partially sovereign state, the FRG had no armed forces of its own but a start was made in 1951 with the establishment of the Federal Border Guard, a paramilitary federal police force. There were moves in both the US and West Germany to include the new FRG in the defence of Western Europe, and the federal chancellor, Adenauer, pointed out the necessity of the FRG having its own armed forces once more, an idea that had been brought into greater focus by the Korean War and the detonation of Joe 1, the Soviet nuclear bomb.

With the blessing of the Western Allies, a secret meeting took place between fifteen former Wehrmacht officers at the Himmerod Monastery between 4 and 9 October 1950 to discuss *Wiederbewaffnung* (West German rearmament – see Appendix 1). The subjects for discussion by this 'shadow' German Joint Chiefs of Staff were the political, ethical, operational and logistical aspects of any future German armed forces with a view to creating a West German contribution to the defence of Western Europe but it would, of necessity, be something fundamentally new without any basis in the old Wehrmacht structures. The proposal was for a ground force of twelve heavily armed divisions with supporting air and naval units all under NATO command to be activated within five years. Their purpose would be to halt any Soviet attack on the river Elbe without resort to nuclear weapons. Following the conference, Adenauer appointed Theodor Blank to the office of the Chancellor's Commissioner for Questions with Regard to the Strengthening of Allied Troops, which became known as the Blank Office. This then became the nucleus of the later Federal Ministry of Defence but was not exclusively entrusted with its formation.

A *Memorandum on the Formation of a German Contingent for the Defence of Western Europe within the Framework of an International Fighting Force*, usually referred to as the Himmerod Memorandum, stated that, since no future

German army would be possible without the historical rehabilitation of the Wehrmacht a number of conditions must be met. All German soldiers convicted as war criminals were to be released. The defamation of the German soldier, including those of the Waffen-SS, would have to cease and measures would have to be taken to transform both domestic and foreign public opinion with regards to the German military. To accommodate the West German government, the Allies commuted a number of war crimes sentences. The modern Wehrmacht was conceived.

Several of Gehlen's senior staff, who had never really been part of his intelligence operations, now began contemplating leaving the OG in preparation for an early return to the military. He invited several of his top men to dinner to discuss the memorandum. They were Heusinger, Wessel, Conrad Kühlein, Horst Wendland, Schreibe, Buntrock and Heinz Guderian, whom Wessel found to be his old self, 'vain, conceited … a political idiot and confused person' fit only to lead a Panzerkorps (Panzer corps).[61] He then held a staff meeting at Pullach to boost morale there.

To make the idea more palatable to the Americans, Adenauer wrote to the commander of US forces in Europe, General Thomas T. Handy, to request that the new Wehrmacht should have a senior American officer as advisor to bring the former German officers up to speed on modern methods and techniques. His main motivation was probably to avoid a resurgence of wartime National Socialist tendencies in the armed services given that it would be staffed by a significant number of ex-Wehrmacht officers.

At a New York conference in September 1950, French Foreign Minister Robert Schuman had told the US Secretary of State Dean Acheson and the British Foreign Secretary Ernest Bevin that he was firmly against any idea of German rearmament refusing even to discuss it in principle. Others in the French Cabinet and the military leadership, however, understood that if Western Europe was going to be able to defend itself against Soviet aggression there would need to be a German military contribution. The question for them was whether or not that was acceptable to the French electorate. Prime Minister Pleven suggested that a European army under a European minister should be made responsible to a European parliament. This meant that there was to be neither a national German army nor a German general staff.[62] Of course, there was still the issue of Soviet reaction to a rearmed Germany led by the very men who had been at the heart of Operation Barbarossa.

On 2 May 1951, the FRG became a full member of the Council of Europe and two months later the Western Powers ended the still-existing state of hostilities with Germany. In the following May, agreement was reached whereby a conscript German army would be integrated into a European Defence Community in 1954 but the French refused to sanction it. However, on 7 June 1955, the GFR would become the fifteenth member state of NATO and the Blank Office would be renamed as the Federal Ministry of Defence with Blank still in charge but there were no actual German military personnel until 12 November of that year when the Bundeswehr was officially created on the 200th anniversary of the birth of Prussian Lieutenant General Gerhard Johann David von Scharnhorst.

The election of Dwight D. Eisenhower to the presidency of the United States in 1952 had come about to a significant extent due to a foreign policy initiative drawn up by his Secretary of State John Foster Dulles, Allen's brother. This had emphasised the need to 'end the negative, futile and immoral policy of containment towards communism' and promised 'a policy of boldness' to free the captive peoples of Europe.[63] At the same time Allen Dulles had become the US director of the CIA. Gehlen assumed that his relationship with Allen Dulles and the new American foreign policy would greatly enhance his position and accelerate the move towards German rearmament.

Von Schwerin, meanwhile, had gone too far and provoked Adenauer into firing him. The official reason was that he had leaked to the press details of his own ideas on remilitarisation implying that he had Adenauer's approval for them, which he hadn't. Adenauer was sure that von Schwerin was acting as a mouthpiece for the British who were anxious to block any move to have the OG incorporated into the German state. For this gross overreach of his authority, he was peremptorily sacked and paved the way for Heusinger and Speidel, close friends since their General Staff College days, to join Heinz's FWHA, part of the Blank Office, and step in with their own ideas.

Von Schwerin saw it differently. He claimed that his position had been undermined in Parliament by Wildermuth, who had been briefed by Gehlen to the effect that von Schwerin had 'exceeded the authority [of his office]' and he had become a convenient scapegoat when the New York conference of the three Allied Powers failed to agree to West German rearmament.[64] Adenauer's political position had become rather precarious, so dismissing von Schwerin offered a welcome distraction.

All this debate over remilitarisation and integration of European military forces left a frustrated Gehlen unable to make any progress towards becoming the governments sole intelligence advisor. Again, he took the opportunity to go to Switzerland to meet Mercier, who came along with two other French intelligence leaders, General Henri

Ribière and Roger Lafont. Then later just before the end of the year, Gehlen spent several days in Bonn deep in discussions with Globke and Blank. Critchfield was unhappy at the way things were going. He couldn't quite work out what Gehlen was up to and relations between the two men became fractious. As Gehlen's bankers, the CIA did not appreciate Gehlen trimming intelligence reports for them and, they suspected, furnishing Bonn with more substantial information.

For his part, Gehlen was very aware that his relationship with Critchfield and the CIA was a serious impediment to his ambitions and Critchfield was, he believed, the main stumbling block preventing him from getting Adenauer full endorsement. Both Wessel and Heusinger were concerned that Gehlen was pursuing a personal agenda that neither of them fully understood. What they did know and had seen from the start of their relations with Gehlen, however, was that he was an opportunist, keen to occupy positions of influence and prestige and very adept at a sort of passive manipulation of those he worked with.

By this time the Americans were developing their own intelligence resources for their anti-Soviet strategy relying less on Gehlen but they were not willing to let the OG go its own way. It was important for them to retain an insight into its operations to maintain some political control over it development. The OG relied on Washington to pay its way but at the same time Gehlen wanted to keep the Americans at arm's length to prevent them finding out too much about the OG internal structure and workings. He wanted to inch his way into the arms of the FRG. Sensing that a crisis was looming for the OG, Gehlen gambled with a blatant and carefully prepared provocation. Throughout his professional life, when faced with a challenging opponent, Gehlen had tended to adopt either a wooing or circumventing approach, sometimes both at the same time but on 28 December 1950 he had a meeting with Critchfield and Heusinger during which he spoke from prepared notes as was anything but conciliatory towards the Americans. He denounced US interference in Zipper and told Critchfield he was rooting out and firing those members of his staff he considered excessively pro-American and rounded off by threatening to resign and leave the OG leaderless.[65] It is hard to know exactly what Gehlen hoped to achieve by this performance, but Critchfield waited ten days to see if there was any further development. When there was none, he asked Gehlen to put his concerns in writing so that he could refer them to his Washington bosses.

This was Gehlen's first serious public outburst criticising Critchfield's handling of the OG and was indicative of his frame of mind. It had the effect of souring relations with some of Critchfield's staff and certainly annoyed Washington when Critchfield report hit the desk there but they considered it to be typical Gehlen bluster and it stirred only a ripple on the other side of the Atlantic. The emphasis there was now on framing the future German intelligence service and there was no particular consensus that there would actually be a place for Gehlen there. Discussion centred on his possible replacement, preferable someone with no political ambitions, and there was talk of possibly moving Gehlen into a military role in the Bonn government. In response, a memo described him as having

> risen ... from the position of a relatively obscure member of the German General Staff to the position of a prime political strategist enjoying the support of conservative political factions, of certain German industrialists, and of influential remaining portions of the German military at the same [as enjoying] semi-diplomatic relations with the major intelligence services in Western Europe.[66]

Analysing their relationship with Gehlen to this point, the CIA noted that he had constantly complained about a lack of US supervision as an excuse for his own leadership shortcomings and at the same time had blamed his failure to stem the tide of uncontrolled growth on US excessive and overbearing demands for more intelligence. Then when he was called on to cut back his operations, he objected and simply demanded more money to make them more efficient. To round off, they said that Gehlen's suggestions for strategic operations were '90% worthless'. While it was conceded that the OG performed to an acceptable level in tactical and military reconnaissance, it was decidedly a 'second-rate' organisation that lacked the ability to carry out sophisticated, traditional intelligence work.

Washington was ready for a showdown with Gehlen. If he wanted their continued support, the CIA said, Gehlen was going to have to 'institute radical changes in personnel, procedures, and attitudes' but that only made Gehlen more determined to throw off the CIA shackles.[67] The man he turned to was the *eminence grise* of the Adenauer organisation, Hans Globke. It was a finely calculated choice.

Globke was one of the most powerful and controversial figures in post-war German life.[68] He had served under the Nazis as a civil servant in the Reich Ministry of the Interior and in 1945 was on the Allies' 'automatic arrest' list. But claimed that he had never been a member of the Nazi Party. During the Second World War, he had repeatedly been in contact with the Gestapo's Adolf Eichmann on Jewish matters in the occupied territories and been involved with drafting the ordinances to enforce the Nuremberg Race Laws of 1935 that discriminated against and humiliated Jews. He claimed that at the end of the war, Gestapo officers had been sent from Berlin to arrest him for his part in the Stauffenberg plot to assassinate Hitler in 1944 but they had been inhibited by the proximity of American forces in the area near Kochel, where his family was then living. His involvement in the attempted assassination of Hitler, however, has never been supported by evidence. A British assessment did not accept that

> Globke's record [was] black enough to prevent his being employed in an advisory capacity under supervision.[69]

A German de-Nazification board of 1947 categorised him as *unbelastet* (unencumbered) and cleared him of any wrongdoing. Gehlen felt sure that Globke was the man to ensure that the tainted past of many members of his organisation would not become an issue when his name was put forward. Globke had appeared at the Nuremberg war trials as a witness up until 1948. In 1949, Blankenhorn introduced him to Adenauer, who took to Globke immediately and had soon established him as his *Staatssekretär* (chief of staff).

Globke was very much in Gehlen's corner and he let Washington know that removing Gehlen would not find favour with the West German administration. To emphasise his point, he made a big show of inviting Gehlen to come to Bonn and brief him on the current situation. This was just at the time that North Korean forces, with Soviet backing, invaded South Korea, which stoked the fires of mistrust about communist intentions elsewhere. Bonn looked again at its stated policy of disarmament and decided that perhaps it was not the prudent course of action.

Although Gehlen had seriously annoyed some of his staff, Critchfield was less antagonistic than might have been expected given the three-hour lecture that Gehlen had given him on 28 December 1950. His time at Pullach had clearly convinced him that Zipper, for all its flaws was well worth preserving and it could only function effectively with Gehlen at its head. He was much more attuned to European sensitivities and security concerns than were his bosses in Washington and it was his belief that the security of Europe was irrevocably tied up with that of Germany. His fear, however, was that there were too many war criminals in the German armed forces who could not be relied upon to work in the best interests of the US. It was in the next generation, he believed, where hope lay for a new dawn of German-US relations and many of those were working with, if not within, Zipper and it was

Gehlen, himself, who could be the bridge between these younger men and Washington. 'I think it would be politically inept of us,' Critchfield would later tell his bosses in June 1951,

> to equivocate in the treatment we give [Zipper] in the United States simply because of our well-documented reservations about [Gehlen].[70]

When asked for his opinion, Globke told Critchfield in a 'direct and emphatic way' that Gehlen would be quite acceptable to the West German government.

Von Schwerin's dismissal allowed Gehlen to set about undermining his other rivals. His first target, and the one he considered not only his deadliest rival but also the most vulnerable, was Heinz. Heinz had built up a group of well-established contacts but he was thought by many to be something of a loose cannon. Nevertheless, he had worked with Dulles's OSS and had become a favourite of French Intelligence who called his reports 'brilliant, highly interesting and important'.[71] The British welcomed the fact that he was positioning himself in opposition to the OG, which they considered to be 'too big, too expensive and too American'.[72] Gehlen doubted that Heinz was capable, on his own, of the level of professional excellence implied by his product and launched an investigation into his networks at the same time as sharing his reservations with Colonel Mercier at the SDECE. He had not missed the chance to drag Heinz into the von Schwerin affair by suggesting that he was also being manipulated by the British.

Unwilling to take his findings directly to the Bonn government who were impressed by Heinz and who might dismiss his objections as mere professional jealousy, Gehlen let it be known, through Globke, that Heinz had been a leader in the *Sturmabteilung* (paramilitary wing of the Nazi Party). Gehlen again exhibited his subtlety, borne of many years of subterfuge, by using John as an unwitting accomplice. Through intermediaries, he hinted to John that the content of Heinz's intelligence strongly suggested that he was being manipulated by the Soviets. This was at a time when Heinz was pushing hard for extra funding to expand his networks. The evidence convinced John who took his suspicions to Globke and Lex at the Ministry of the Interior. When challenged, Heinz told John, 'He will get you too'.[73] He was not wrong about Gehlen trying to do that. Gehlen even managed to convince Globke that John was too much in the pocket of British intelligence, which threatened to derail John's appointment to the BfV, but John was in a much stronger position politically that Heinz.

Heusinger, whom the contemporary historian Johannes Hürter described as a wanderer 'between the worlds of the criminal dictatorship and the democratic constitutional state', was constantly in and out of Adenauer's office and giving a master class in how to play the political game in Bonn but Gehlen lacked his finesse and was facing a crucial moment that would determine whether he would progress or fall by the wayside.[74] Radke, who was supposed to be on Gehlen's side, seemed to confirm US opinion that the bulk of OG counterintelligence reports were worthless and Heusinger advised Gehlen to concentrate his efforts on evaluation, where the OG excelled, rather than intelligence gathering.

Critchfield told Gehlen that, if he was determined to break from the CIA, he was on his own but he would have to slim down the OG considerably because CIA funding could not be taken for granted. Gehlen took his case to Bonn and got an audience with Adenauer. He began by telling the chancellor about OG activities against Germany's eastern foes, but Adenauer cut him short and asked

> *Und wat machen Sie gegen den Westen*? [And what are you doing about the West?]

Gehlen took that to mean Adenauer was concerned about US control of the OG and needed to know more about domestic issues that neither the BfV nor Blank was providing.

Gehlen saw this as his opportunity to promote his own case. He had not the slightest wish to work with his competitors, instead he plotted to destroy them. Professionally he wanted nothing other than complete control and to be surrounded by men in whom he could have total confidence. He drafted a *Proposal for the Appointment of an Advisor to the Federal Chancellor for all Intelligence Issues* leaving no doubt as to who that should be. The OG, he advised, would remain, for the moment, under CIA trusteeship until the FRG gained full sovereignty. Had he been a more astute operator, he would have realised that Adenauer would only protect him as long as it was politically profitable for him to do so. The subtleties of political decision-making, as opposed to the military was never fully appreciated by Gehlen. In Washington, Helms, whose OSO had been formally incorporated into the CIA where he now held a high office, chipped in with a damning assessment. He wrote,

> Gehlen's motivations, his inflexibility, and his preoccupation with military and political questions to the detriment of his intelligence responsibilities, have materially hampered our mutual cooperation.

There were too many 'undesirable qualities' in Gehlen's make-up that might also be reflected in any successor due the responsibilities of the position, of background, and possibly of nationality but it should be possible to find someone 'measurably more cooperative' who was less concerned with protecting his former Wehrmacht buddies.[75] This was problematic, however, given that Gehlen had thrown these men a lifeline, many might well resent any move to replace him, and the morale and efficiency of the whole organisation might well suffer to the point where it became effectively useless. Helms, whose personal view was that Gehlen had outlived his usefulness, proposed a meeting between McCloy, Adenauer and CIA representatives after which, a final decision would then be made depending on Adenauer's opinion as to what to do about him. Meetings followed in Washington in March 1951 between Dulles and Helms. The relationship between Gehlen and Washington was closer than ever to severance with the OG on the point of dissolution. Morale at Pullach hit rock bottom.

Gehlen seemed to have given up all hope of finding a solution through Critchfield and the CIA but he continued to take their money ostensibly on the understanding that he was giving prime consideration to counterespionage against Soviet infiltration in the FRG. His real focus, however, was on getting the approbation of the Bonn government which had recently taken huge steps towards respectability and prestige by being instrumental in founding the European Coal and Steel Community, which led eventually to the creating of the European Union. At the same time, the Federal Republic had been admitted into the Council of Europe. The Soviets reacted quickly to the action in the FRG. In October 1949, the German Democratic Republic was officially announced. These actions in 1949 marked the end of any talk of a reunified Germany.

Gehlen's real problem was that he had no political nous or 'people skills' but fortunately these were not the only requirements for political success, and he had a number of others the most important of which was a belief in the end justifying the means. He had gone to great lengths, despite the occasional confrontation, to keep Critchfield on his side and it was paying dividends now with the CIA man openly advocating support for German military integration into a European front against the Soviet Union and an independent German secret service with Gehlen at its head. His plan was to deliver an ultimatum to Bonn: either recognise the OG as the sole German intelligence agency with Gehlen as its head or see it taken over completely by the CIA but Globke doubted that, even if he had the will, Adenauer lacked the political freedom to implement that.

There was enough support for Gehlen, however, that allowed Globke to arrange for him to address the Federal Cabinet on *Die militärische und wirtschaftliche Lage des Ostblocks; Beurteilung der Gefahr eines Ost-West-Konfliktes* (the Military and Economic Situation in the Eastern Block, Assessing the Dangers of an East-West Conflict). It was a sobering analysis and he returned to his proposal that he be appointed as military advisor to Adenauer but many in the Cabinet agreed that Gehlen and his wartime Wehrmacht associates were the very last people one would want at the heart of young democracy.

When it came down to its legal status, the OG was still completely in the arms of the United States as the occupying power and the whole concept of German remilitarisation was a delicate matter. Critchfield wanted to break the impasse by inviting Gehlen to America both to let Washington see exactly what they were dealing with and also to give Gehlen a more up-to-date appreciation of what the CIA aspirations were in terms of the anti-Soviet operations. For Gehlen this was an opportunity to meet up with old friends like Waldman and Boker but most importantly to meet as many influential people as possible to raise his profile in Washington. The Americans would no doubt have been apprised of a British Foreign Office memorandum bemoaning the fact that there were so many former Wehrmacht officers in staff positions, who were secretly pursuing a vigorous remilitarisation strategy much as had occurred during the Weimar years, and most intelligence agents in the field were Ukrainian or other East European refugees. The general opinion in Britain was that Gehlen's organisation was pretty much under surreptitious Soviet control and could never be considered suitable for adoption as an independent German intelligence service. British Prime Minister Clement Atlee commented that the British should on no account give secret information to Gehlen.

On 22 September 1951, Gehlen and Herre together with eight other OG leaders flew from Rhein-Main to the United States where they were met by Crichfield. Their first meeting was with General Alexander Russell Bolling, the head of army intelligence who praised Gehlen profusely. The meeting with Helms was rather more low-key with the CIA man not wanting to appear too enthusiastic. Gehlen was also able to meet Dulles whom he adjudged to be committed to the German cause but who also urged him to mend fences with the British which was a big ask for both sides given their deep mistrust of each other. In all meetings, Gehlen adopted his default reserved approach by saying very little unless specifically asked for comment.

Dulles emphasised to Gehlen the need for an intensification of espionage against the Soviet Union with specially trained agents. Talks also covered the creation of special forces that might be called upon in the event of a crisis. Gehlen was particularly well placed to launch a recruitment drive amongst the German veterans, ex-members of Vlasov's army and displaced persons camps throughout Germany. Before long there were some 5,000 men being trained by American officers at camps such as Bad Wiesee and Mannheim that would go on to form a CIA private army and the nucleus of the future 'Green Berets'.[76]

A meeting with CIA Director Walter Bedell Smith was short and frosty. He had always resented the way that Gehlen had taken American money and stubbornly resisted CIA control of Zipper. Expectations in that area were changing, however. Others were more willing to accept Gehlen's independent status and saw a future where Zipper could retain sovereignty as a partnership of equals with the CIA. There was a general acceptance that the visit had been beneficial for both sides with a greater understanding of each other's views and a fundamental strengthening of the relationship between Zipper and the CIA. Even Bedell Smith would soften his views and, within a couple of months, express a hope that the West German government would transform Zipper into the official German intelligence service 'in the near future'.[77]

The Stasi

> Within hours Gehlen agents were being rounded up all over East Germany. [78]

On his return to Pullach, Gehlen reported that he had been very well received and gave his staff the misleading impression that he had been given a free hand in matters of domestic policy. Gehlen's position became noticeably more secure when Clement Atlee was replaced as British prime minister on 26 October 1951 by an admirer, Winston Churchill, whose pragmatism allowed him to overlook Gehlen's Nazis who were now allies against the new enemy, the Soviet Union. This gave Gehlen a chance to follow Dulles's advice by softening his attitude to the British and instead holding a briefing for them in November 1951 on the Soviet menace, which was very well received. Gehlen thought that might also sway French opinion and see Paris slackening its opposition to OG's progress towards international respectability.

Then in early 1952, the Soviets sent ripples through the European diplomatic pond.

On 10 March 1952, Stalin surprised everyone by seeming to suggest that he favoured a peace treaty that allowed for the reunification of a neutral Germany. The British and French governments declined to engage with Stalin's offer and demanded free elections across the whole of Germany. By presenting the Soviet Union as the champion of German reunification, Stalin had pulled off a propaganda initiative on a grand scale. Two months later, the Western Powers responded by signing the General (Bonn) and European Defence Community (EDC) treaties indicating a total rejection of Stalin's offer. Adenauer had rejected the idea totally immediately and Gehlen saw an opportunity to ingratiate himself with Bonn by allying himself with that position. The Soviets had failed to hold Yugoslavia and was active in the Middle East, he said. Playing their customary long game, it was likely that, for the moment, they would consolidate their present gains and nibble away at the periphery rather than launch a direct attack against the West. And furthermore, any withdrawal of US forces from Germany was, for him, a totally unacceptable risk.[79]

Gehlen saw it as no coincidence that the Stalin note coincided with a wider organised propaganda campaign against him and his organisation. On 17 March 1952, the British newspaper, the *Daily Express* ran with a headline 'Hitler's General Now Spies For Dollars'. An article by Sefton Delmer mentioned Gehlen by name and suggested that his 'secret organisation' offered 'full protection' for 'plenty of former Nazis, SS men and SD men'. Delmer described the OG as 'an immense underground power in Germany'. Neither did it escape Gehlen's attention that Delmer was a good friend of his rival Otto John.[80] They had worked together during the later stages of the Second World War in the British Office of Political Warfare preparing anti-Nazi propaganda.

The Soviets followed up with a concerted attack to try and discredit and ultimately destroy Zipper thereby sowing discord in the Western alliance. It did not damage Gehlen to any extent on a personal level, given that he had quite good standing amongst Western intelligence agencies, but it had the effect of shining a light on some of the more dubious members of Zipper whose background and supposed political ambitions were easily exploited by Soviet propagandists. The Soviet's exploited the furore that surrounded Delmer's exposé by reopening a wartime Soviet intelligence operation, which Western agencies have called 'Hacke' to add fuel to the fire that had been lit around the OG.

At the end of 1943, some Nazis had seen what they believed to be the inevitability of a German defeat and built up a secret Nazi cadre organisation whose objective was to prepare the groundwork for continuing Reich activity after the defeat. It is believed that, in early 1944, $500,000 in looted gold had been smuggled abroad to Spain, Portugal, Argentina, Japan and Italy. Hacke members were war criminals, fanatics and far-sighted opportunists who saw the handwriting on the wall and moved early to assure their personal future. The Soviets learned of Hacke at its inception. General Semyonovich Abakumov, the head of Smersh managed to exploit SS Colonel Otto Skorzeny who was reputed to have been recruited by Smersh in 1944 and who, for a brief period shortly before the end of the war, attained high rank in German intelligence.

After the Second World War, the Soviets concentrated on maximum penetration of Hacke. Several Nazi war criminals who had been involved in the plot were discovered to be in various eastern European jails. On of these, Albert Förster had been the Nazi Gauleiter of Danzig and was now under sentenced to death as a war criminal in Poland. In 1952, when Förster began cooperating, he was immediately removed from prison and flown to Moscow. Former SS and SD officers in the west were particularly vulnerable to Soviet blackmail, as the Soviets systematically sought out and exploited the evidence of their war crimes guilt. Many of these former Nazis now worked in the West German government and its security services.[81]

At the heart of the Hacke operation was the Stasi. Formed on 8 February 1950 as part of the *Staatssicherheitsdienst* (SSD – State Security Service) with headquarters at 22 Normanenstrasse, Berlin-Lichtenberg, the Stasi, populated by Smersh and ex-Gestapo personnel, was given sweeping powers of covert surveillance of East German citizens and wide powers of arrest in what had become a police state.

In 1942, the German-born communist Wilhelm Zaisser had been appointed by Beria to run an 'anti-fascist' school in Krasnogorsk where German PoWs were vetted to select those who might be 'educated' and returned to hold important administration posts in Germany after the Second World War. Those with special skills such as Abwehr, SS and SD functionaries were of special interest as agents of counterespionage and surveillance. They would be deployed selectively, however, and Zaisser would not be allowed to realise his ambition of leading a German political police force for the occupied Soviet zone. That would be the prerogative of the Soviet Ministry of State Security (MGB) and the Central Administration for Intelligence (GRU). Zaisser's organisation would be allocated a subservient role as

> Kommissariat 5 (K5) with limited powers. After 1946, K5 began to expand its role and responsibilities, primarily by rooting out Nazi war criminals but later was given secret police powers for the legal 'surveillance and suppression of enemies of democratic reconstruction.[82]

The GDR was soon covered by a web of agencies and informers. Along with his cohort of ex-PoW converts to the communist cause, former Abwehr general Rudolf Bamler was summoned by Zaiser. Bamler had served with Gehlen in the 1920 as part of the 3rd (Prussian) Artillery Regiment and later worked with him during the war when he was head of the Abwehr's *Abteilung III*. Others who came from Krasnogorsk with Bamler into the Stasi were former SS-Hauptsturmführer Louis Hagemeister whom became head of the interrogation section, former SS-Untersturmführer Johann Sanitzer and former SS-Scharführer Reinhold Tappert.

Zaiser's first major achievement was in March 1951 when his people arrested one of the leaders of the extremist *Kampfgruppe gegen Unmenschlichkeit* (KgU – Anti-Inhumanity Combat Group). The KgU was being run by the CIA in a particularly unprofessional and haphazard way as an espionage agency with all sorts of hairbrained schemes. The arrest was the trigger for all Stasi agents who had been infiltrated into the KgU to abscond en masse with enough information to fill Stasi cells to overflowing with KgU agents. The Stasi was now ready to turn its fire on Gehlen but Zaiser would not be a part of that.

After Stalin's death in April 1953, Zaisser, rather foolishly, was tempted to become involved in DDR politics on the side of those opposed to First Secretary Walter Ulbricht. On 16 June 1953, two months after Stalin's death, a protest began in East Berlin that, within days, saw almost 1 million East Germans begin rioting across hundreds of East German cities and towns. The Soviet occupation forces declared martial law and employed massive military force to suppress the rioting and support the East German regime. The Stasi was held responsible by the ruling SED for the outbreak of this uprising and giving no warning. Ulbricht took this as an opportunity to force Zaisser out of the MfS and the party. The SSD was demoted from a ministry to a state secretariat with tight state control under Ernst Wollweber but the new man brought with him a new aggressive strategy. Over the following five years, Wollweber would become Gehlen's most determined adversary. Like Gehlen, he was a man who valued anonymity. Although he had been known to the OG for many years as an expert in espionage and sabotage, Gehlen claims to have seen only a single photograph of him in all this time.

Gehlen was taken by surprise by the Berlin uprising and had no strategy to deal with it. Prior to this moment the focus of OG efforts had been Moscow, particularly Soviet foreign policy strategy after Stalin and armament production. Only four days before the uprising, he had been concentrating on presenting a report for Washington on *Thoughts on the World Political Situation* in which East Berlin did not feature. Despite having around 700 active agents in the DDR and a stream of up-to-date information from the growing numbers of refugees indicating an increasingly repressive regime, it had been assumed that the security forces would have been able to contain any opposition movement. Even when it was clear that there was an insurrection, OG staff did not attach any great importance to it, thinking that it may well have been plotted by Moscow to bring pressure to bear on Ulbricht for reasons best known to them. In that case, they assumed that it would be short-lived. It was something of an embarrassment, however, when they were not able to respond to CIA calls for more information about what was going on and realised that Bonn was relying on Heinz and Blanck for information.

On the spur of the moment, Gehlen tried to exploit the disturbances by reaching out to more and more potential agents in the DDR but there had been a breakdown of communications during the crackdown as networks went quiet to avoid being caught up in the security sweeps. When things had settled down and branches opened up again, they proved to be unable to cope with the influx of refugees and many recruits were taken on with little or no background checks made. The consequences of this laxity were not long in becoming manifest.

Operation Hacke had seen many agents infiltrated into the OG, especially Hans Joachim Geyer, aka Henry Troll, a successful writer of detection stories, who had been a member of the Nazi Party since 1928. Geyer had continued to live in the Soviet zone after the Second World War publishing his stories in the FRG. In 1952, he had offered his services to the OG as a courier in the GDR but, unbeknown them, he was arrested in December 1952 and persuaded to act as a double agent (codename Krause, also Grell). After the East German uprising, he posed as a refugee and fled to the FRG where Gehlen gave him a job in the OG Berlin branch, X/9592, officially known as '*Filiale Nordland*'. He was not the only Stasi man the OG took on. In fact, they took on far too many far too quickly without thorough checks being made. It was an incredible blunder that opened the door to a surge of communist double agents who settled into the roles created for them by the Stasi.

Geyer had been promoted to head up X/9592 where he had access to a great deal of sensitive information, all of which he copied and made available to the Stasi. It was a huge security risk given that his wife and family still lived in Falkensee, the GDR. That branch alone ran over sixty informers in the DDR. By 29 October 1953, the stress of working as a double agent final broke him and he fled to the GDR. Before the OG could respond and warn its agents, the Stasi carried out mass arrests, which had already been primed for action in what it called *Aktion Feuerwerk* (Operation Fireworks). Those who avoided arrest suffered crises of confidence and simply stopped acting for the OG or simply fled to the FRG. Stasi agents followed them there and tried to persuade them to change sides.

Wollweber now made a concerted effort to destroy the OG. The fate of the of Gehlen's eastern network hung in the balance and threatened his whole ambition to become institutionalised as a federal intelligence agency. Significant pressure was placed on Rudolf Augstein, the editor of *Der Spiegel* magazine to hold back on an article claiming that the whole of the OG had been destroyed after the mass arrest of its agents. Wessel noted that Gehlen was badly affected by events and seemed to become withdrawn fearing that the poor performance of the OG at this time was damaging his chances of becoming head of a future German intelligence service.

A huge Stasi media propaganda campaign followed to intimidate other OG agents and show the world that it was riddled with Nazis all under American control. The GDR press went into overdrive with condemnation of Western 'gangsters' and celebratory headlines about arrested spies. They produced Geyer at a news conference on 9 November where he read a seven-page script describing how he 'deeply regretted his crimes'.[83] SSD Colonel Hans Bormann then told everyone present that his organisation knew all about Gehlen and his agents.[84]

There followed a series of show trials meant both as an instrument of repression and as a disciplinary measure against the East German population. On 11 November, two men who had been tried and convicted of espionage were beheaded in Dresden. Ewald Misera had been a manger of the Traffic and Service Department in east Berlin and Karli Julius Willi Bandelow a civil engineer at the State Secretariat for Motor Traffic and Roads. Misera had fed Gehlen information about Soviet troop movements and general information about rail traffic in general. Others in his department, Gustav Miecklev and Walter Flentge photographed timetables and details of the senior figures at railway headquarters. Bandelow's speciality was bridges and minutes of conferences for road planning all of which provided important information of routes that were being expanded or fortified for military transports. Between 18 and 21 December of that year Werner Haase, Siegfried Altkrüger, Walter Rennert, Karl-Heinz Schmidt, Rolf Oesterreich, Walter Schneider and Helmut Schwenk, all OG agents, were all brought before the Supreme Court of the GDR and charged with espionage. All were given long prison sentences.

In December, the communist newspaper *Tägliche Rundschau* printed the 'confessions' of the 'guilt' of more than thirty OG agents who had 'applied' to the Stasi for protection. To follow up, Wollweber now recalled some of his own agents, including Gerhard Prather and Gerhard Kapahnke, who had been infiltrated into the OG and paraded them before the world's press as defectors. The trials and executions of Bandelow and Franz Neuegebauer followed. Elli Barczatis (codename Daisy) had been the DDR Prime Minister Otto Grotewohl's private secretary. She and her lover, the journalist Karl Laurenz would be arrested on 4 March 1954, tried, and beheaded.

In December 1953, Gehlen was called up to the Bundestag to appear before the Committee on European Security Issues to explain how he was going to respond to the security lapses that were bedevilling the OG.

His answer was the *Schottensystem* (Bulkhead System) of compartmentalisation designed to protect the identities of its members which was a good idea from a security perspective but resulted in a 'disorganized, opaque and sometimes incomplete' file management system.[85] It would act as an insurmountable barrier between the OG (and later the BND) and anyone who wanted to take a critical look at it. Nevertheless, it was a system that was adopted and carried over as a fundamental principle when the BND was formed, which denied effective scrutiny of its operations. This system would prove to be anything but secure, however, as the Felfe case would show.

Heinz Felfe

> Some of these people might be susceptible to a Soviet approach because of their general sympathies. Others … many of whom were now war criminals … would be vulnerable to blackmail.[86]

A small but elite band of Army Counterintelligence Corps officers led by a bear of a man Thomas Wesley Dale had remained in Germany after the Second World War and formed a somewhat exclusive group that dedicated itself to preventing an authoritarian regime re-emerging but it was from the left rather than the right where they saw the danger. Dale and his two associates, William Parkinson and Daniel

Benjamin, were civilian employees of the CIC. In the minds of these 'strong-minded professionals' who had become 'an elite [but] arrogant, personally abrasive, dangerously independent and paranoid', the German people were psychologically attracted to authoritarian and highly structured leadership.[87] Dale had formed this well-educated and dedicated group into a sophisticated intelligence operation run from Stuttgart, which was called 'Campus'. It was only one of several US intelligence agencies, including those of the army, navy and air force, that were operating in Germany at the time, few of which made any serious effort to cooperate with the others.

Campus produced many reports on the *Heinz Amt* operations but was particularly assigned by CIC to penetrate the OG in 1952 without the CIA being informed. Alfred Bentzinger had been the first leader of Baun's *Dienstelle 114* in 1945 and already at an early stage had connections with CIC. Along with Ludwig Albert, he was passing information about the OG to CIC.

Dale paid particular attention to Gehlen's organisation, which he thought was operating well beyond the limits laid down by the CIA and essentially beyond their control especially in terms the amount of information it was willing to give concerning who it was actually employing. Campus was uncovering aspects of the OG about which the CIA was unaware. OG methods were antiquated, and security seriously flawed, he said. The intelligence Gehlen had produced in the late 1940s certainly filled a gap in US knowledge but as time went on and Soviet security improved the clandestine operations became much less productive to the point where most of what they revealed could have been gathered by non-clandestine methods. When political and economic intelligence began to push military intelligence further down the agenda, the OG showed no inclination, or indeed appeared to have no capacity, to adjust.

Neither did the CIA, itself, escape disdain when Dale cast his jaundiced eye over it. Far too elitist in an ivy-league way, was his opinion, and carrying just a little too much 'leftist' baggage from its OSS parentage. It was the OG's reliance on former Nazis that were coalescing into a clearly defined 'old-boy network' that was becoming the bedrock of the OG that the CIA seemed to be overlooking. In a country that was still struggling to overcome the depredations of defeat and economic catastrophe, all members of this group owed a personal debt to Gehlen for their comfortable circumstances, and it was essentially the ex-SS and ex-SD men who were the most productive of intelligence. Gehlen, of course, could never admit this and neither did the CIA want to look too closely at the issue for fear of what they might find. When challenged, Gehlen usually came back with incomplete or even incorrect information regarding applications for the civil servant status of his employees and the Federal Chancellery did not press him. He would fob them off by saying that there was only about one percent but even they had been de-Nazified and claimed that they did nothing before 1945 that would not be approve of now.

When the OG had been eviscerated by the arrests following the Berlin uprising, Gehlen had set up an internal enquiry, which he kept secret from the CIA but which did not escape the attention of the vigilant Dale, who also chose to keep the secret of what he discovered. Gehlen, and by extension Dale, discovered that a whole group of former Nazis in the Stuttgart area, Hans Sommer, Karl Scheutz, Walter Wollmer, Friedrich Busch and Heinz Felfe, were working for the communists.

Sommer's background has already been covered in this book but his story is not yet complete. He would come play a further part in the events around Heinz Felfe. Busch had been a member of the Nazi Party since 1931. Three years later he joined the Gestapo. After the Second World War, he was arrested for war crimes but disappeared on his way to France in 1947 where he was to face trial. Nothing is known about his whereabouts until he was discovered by Campus working for the OG in 1954. An almost paranoid Dale refused to share his findings with any other US agency.

During his career as a spy, Felfe worked for seven different secret services – the SD, the SIS, the KGB, the CIA and the OG, the BND and finally the Stasi – sometimes for more than one at the same time. The damage he caused to the OG and BND while working for the Soviets was immense. His time at the OG illustrates how agents were infiltrated into opposing security agencies to expose their working methods and intentions. When enemy spies were identified, an attempt was made to 'turn' them into double agents, appearing to work for one side but secretly working for the other. The Felfe episode, however, goes one step further where he plays a double-double game, which effectively paralysed the BND's counterintelligence system.

Born in Dresden in 1918, Felfe started his police career at the age of 13 as a volunteer in a border unit and when he was 17, he joined an SS reserve unit and became a member of the NSDAP a year later. A colleague, Hans-Henning Crome, said of him that he had 'a career fetish' driven by ego.[88] Working in the registry of the NSDAP regional court at 19 he learned how to meticulously study files, which would later help him in intelligence applications. In 1940, at the age of 22, he signed up as an undercover agent for the SD and always 'with his career firmly in mind' began studying law. Through a special program for young promising young people who were particularly loyal to the Nazis, he received his university entrance qualification and was admitted to the SD leadership school in Berlin-Charlottenburg. There, he proved to be the best in the course, although he was the only one without previous experience. He worked completed a law degree and was ready to join the Reich Security Main Office when the Second World War ended.

As an Obersturmführer in the Waffen-SS in the occupied Dutch regions at SD-Branch Enschede, he surrendered to Canadian forces on 31 May 1945. CIA files from that time describe him as an

> average looking individual with no distinguishing physical characteristics. Of the many recorded impressions of him from various stages of his career, certain personality traits dominate: a highly intelligent man with very little personal warmth; a person with a high regard for efficiency, and for authority, but susceptible to flattery; venal; and capable of almost childish displays of vindictiveness. Naturally a devious person.[89]

Taken into British custody, he was led to an interrogation centre near Utrecht, which specialised in the interrogation of former German intelligence personnel. There is some evidence that he was approached at this stage by the KGB. After he returned to Bonn, he began working for British Military Sixth Area Intelligence Office BAOR on 7 July 1947 in the state of North Rhine-Westphalia collecting information on communist student groups at the university there. He met up with Erwin Tiebel, another former SD man who was also working for British intelligence. Felfe also passed on his findings to what later became the *Landesämter für Verfassungsschutz* (West German State Office for the Protection of the Constitution).

After three years, on 14 April 1950, the British terminated his employment for serious personal and security reasons, which included attempts to sell information collected for the British to several other intelligence agencies, two West German news services and to the East German Socialist Unity. He had also 'blown his cover' to the KPD he was supposed to be penetrating and was generally guilty of 'sharp practice' and 'varnishing of the truth', but official reason for his dismissal was his connections with former SS personnel such as Helmut Proebsting and Johannes 'Hans' Clemens. He had actually tried to persuade the British to employ Clemens which did not impress them. Then again in 1949, he tried again after he learned that Clemens had been approached by the Soviets. This time he suggested that Clemens be employed as a double agent but he got no further with the suggestion that he had the first time. By 1950, Felfe was working at the Ministry for All-German Affairs, as an interrogator specialising in refugees knowledgeable on the KVP.

Felfe, Tiebel and the roly-poly, short-sighted Clemens were all Dresdeners 'in body and soul' and had known each since the early 1930s when they were all in the SS Security Service (SD) in Dresden.[90] They later all worked for the RSHA *Amt VI* during the Second World War before Clemens moved to Rome. While he was there, it was alleged that Clemens participate in the murder of 335 civilian hostages, including women and children, in the Ardeatine Caves in 1944. This was one of the worst massacres on Italian soil during the Second World War. He would later be tried and acquitted by an Italian military court in 1948.

Clemens had been approached by a Soviet intelligence agent 'Max' through to his wife, Gerda, with whom Clemens maintained contact despite them having become separated since the war. Gerda had been working for the Soviets (codename Erika) since 1949 and probably earlier. Max had been tracking down Nazi war criminals in the Dresden area and suggested that Clemens help him to locate some of his wartime colleagues. Like many others in his position, Clemens had no job and no money and, although he still held to the Nazi doctrine of Eastern Europeans in general belonging to a lower race of peoples, he considered the proposal and discussed it with his friends, Felfe and Tiebel. Again, Felfe went to the British and this time offered Clemens as a potential double agent and again he got short shrift.

When he first took the Soviet coin on 1 September 1951, he was confident that 'he could end the relationship at some point when it no longer benefited him.'[91] He described his motivations for turning to the Soviets as his transformation into 'an envoy for peace'. In his autobiography, he claims to have recognised

> that the moral superiority of the Soviet Union had its roots in the socialist social system and in Marxism Leninism, the analytical, realistic, scientific and profoundly humane policy of the Soviet Union, in other words, that the future belonged to Communism.[92]

Max knew that both Clemens and Tiebel were on a list of people suspected of having murdered hostages in Dresden and threatened to expose them both to the Americans if they did not cooperate. Clemens's job would be to make contact with his old wartime buddies who were now working for the OG and use them to penetrate the organisation. The fact that Clemens was virtually destitute and his deep hatred of the Americans after their firebombing of his home city of Dresden that had killed some of his family members, easily persuaded him to work for the Soviets who gave him the codename 'Peter' to go with 'Paul', which was their codename for Felfe.

Clemens had excellent connections in the Nazi world going back to the early 1930s and looked up his old friend, Willi Krichbaum, whom he knew to be already working for Gehlen. Krichbaum put him in touch with Hans Sommer, a recruiter for the OG and soon he was on the payroll. Ironically, once taken on by the OG, Krichbaum gave Clemens the exact same sort of job that he was doing for Max. Seeking out other unemployed SS and SD for recruitment to the OG. Two of those he brought to Sommer were Felfe and Tiebel. At one stage in the late 1940s, Felfe had applied to work for the Cologne Water Police who diligently looked for a found a file on him in the Berlin Document Center (BDC) where the Americans kept the NSDAP personnel files. When they discovered his past record, the Cologne agency dismissed his application but the OG had made no attempt to examine Felfe's past. They knew he had worked for the British but had no access to MI6 files.

Once all three were in place, they communicated through Gerda Clemens, who acted as their courier and maildrop. Felfe started work for the chief of Soviet operations, Oscar Reile, and was given the OG codename 'Friesen'. When Reile was moved on, Felfe who had gained a reputation as 'bright, able and outstandingly well-informed' took his place and became the OG Russian expert.[93] He was not popular with his colleagues who found him arrogant but submissive towards his superiors. This had little impact on his OG career, however, and he was soon brought into the fold at Pullach where he came under the direct gaze of Gehlen who formed a very positive opinion of him.

With Soviet help, Felfe began providing the OG with valuable and seemingly authentic intelligence. The operation that really cemented his reputation was an extremely complicated one that involved the East German publisher and senior member of the East German National Democratic Party, Günther Hofe, CIA codenamed 'Lena'. Hofe travelled frequently to the FRG where he passed on intelligence to the OG about East German politics, but in March 1954, he told the OG that he had been recruited by the Soviets to gather information about people in the West German Foreign Ministry. Gehlen now instructed Felfe to turn Hofe into a double agent.

Felfe reported back that Hofe was picking up lots of information from his KGB handlers who were less than scrupulous about what they discussed in his presence and exposed the identities of other KGB agents working in the FRG. In order to keep his KGB handlers in a talkative mood, Felfe suggested that Hofe be allowed to feed them intelligence in return. Gehlen took Felfe to Bonn where they had a meeting with Adenauer to discuss exactly what information Hofe was allowed to pass along. Further talks with government officials involved discussions about what information was not to be released which, in fact, then found its way to KGB headquarters in Karlsrhorst through Felfe. When the KGB wanted information about someone in the OG or the West German government, they gave the name to Hofe who told Felfe. Naturally, the OG was not willing to allow Hofe access to such information but it allowed Felfe to go to the appropriate department and request access to that person's files, ostensibly to find out why the Soviets were so interested in him. He would then pass the information he found out from the files along to the KGB. In a similar vein, Hofe would give the OG the real names of certain KGB officers he had come across. Felfe could then get access to CIA files about these persons and in this way the KGB learned a great deal about what the CIA knew of their operations.

Gehlen was becoming ever more impressed by Felfe and when the OG was reorganised into the BND in 1956, Felfe became deputy chief of the Soviet Operations Section of the counterespionage group. He became so important that officials in the BfV would ask his opinion on counterespionage operations they were contemplating. This knowledge gave him ample opportunity to wreck many BfV operations and conspire in the arrest of Western agents in the DDR.[94]

Felfe received periodic briefings and CIA reports on the Soviet Intelligence Service and their activities in the GDR and the FRG, being privy to several operations on a case-by-case basis. He developed a deep insight into BND operations, policy and administrative procedures. In 1959, he informed the KGB that the BND were planning to tap the Soviet Embassy telephones in Bonn so the Soviets were able to ensure that misinformation was passed along the tapped lines.

In the early 1950s, the burgeoning ranks of former Nazis in the OG was an issue crying out for attention. Many in the CIA were frankly scared that public knowledge of its involvement with former Nazis and war criminals would critically tarnish its image at a time when the Cold War was hotting up. If they thought that they could just close their eyes to it and hope that it might go away, however, the Soviets were never going to allow that to happen. The obvious corollary to Nazis in the OG was Soviet exploitation of them through blackmail. Crichfield went so far as to suggest that the CIC should embed agents inside the OG to root out the Nazis in preparation for its transformation into the BND.[95]

Clare Edward Petty, a CIA counterespionage specialist, was deeply concerned that the OG was an open door for Soviet infiltration into the CIA. He knew that, on 15 February 1954, a 'black-haired and round-faced' man had walked into the American military headquarters in Vienna identifying himself as the chief of Soviet internal counterintelligence, Major Peter Sergeievich Deriabin, claiming asylum. To convince the authorities of his credentials, Deriabin had claimed that there were two KGB agents, known as Peter and Paul, working inside the OG. Then when Petty had learned, a few months later, that during the trial of an OG agent in the GDR information came to light that could only have been obtained from a source high up in the organisation, he started digging for evidence. Gehlen chose to characterise Petty's attack as a move by factions who were jealous of Felfe's successes with the Hofe operation and continued to assign Felfe to the most sensitive counterintelligence operations.

Meanwhile, the CIC had infiltrated Ludwig Albert into GL-V who reported back that Felfe was probably a Soviet spy and one of a clique of 'former SD people [with] rather unsavoury backgrounds'.[96] He had been, in fact, the subject of an internal investigation that had seen Walter Wollmer dismissed but left Felfe in place. Gehlen could not risk his exposure and the inevitable scandal that would follow given that he was on the cusp of transforming the OG into the BND. There was no knowing how deep any internal investigation might delve into the OG and there were far too many Nazi skeletons in its cupboards. A not surprising twist to this story was that Albert was also working for the Stasi who now chose to give him up to take the pressure off Felfe. Felfe leaked Albert's identity as a double agent and he was arrested in May 1955. Awaiting trial, he hanged himself. Whenever a light was shone on Felfe, the KGB chose to sacrifice an agent of lesser importance to protect him. Gehlen and Critchfield would later experience a serious falling out when Gehlen discovered that Albert had also been working for the Americans. Critchfield's final days at Pullach before the CIA closed its special liaison office were difficult for both him and Gehlen but overall, the CIA's relationship with the OG was unaffected by the personal tensions between them.

The CIA claimed to have been suspicious of Felfe since 1952 but it was only in October 1954, that they received the first positive clue when both Felfe and Karl Schuetz were described to them as

> the major suspects in the Gehlen Organization security leak [and] the main organisers and central figures of the SD clique.[97]

Even so, their initial reaction was to downplay the information especially since Crichfield, despite his personal feelings, continued to view Gehlen as

> a very dependable ally in the war against Soviet intelligence and intrigue.

When Dulles visited Pullach in September 1954 he and Gehlen discussed the importance of cooperation between the OG and the CIA in the Middle East where it was known that many former Nazis were employed by Syria and Egypt as military and intelligence advisers. In his memoirs Gehlen says that he

> decided to establish a network of contacts there for the service in order to provide a continuous flow of intelligence reports[98]

and employed a 'few former SS members [with] the full approval' of the United States.[99] In this context, Gehlen approached Skorzeny with a plan for him to go to Egypt with other SS men to train the Egyptian army.

In 1955, a CIA staffer Charles Wheeler had occasion to be returning Felfe to his house in Munich when Felfe unexpectedly invited him in. He thought it odd because Felfe was not the sociable type. He was respected but 'nobody really liked him, not even his fellow Germans'.[100] The size of the house and quality of furnishings for someone on OG pay surprised Wheeler but Felfe told him that he had a generous aunt in the United States. He did indeed have an American aunt but searches found no record of any bequest.

There was a steady accumulation of information in the files of Western intelligence agencies about Felfe but little of it was known to the BND. British MI6 alone had a voluminous file from the days before Felfe joined the OG but none of this came to light until, in 1957, Petty put his findings to Gehlen who agreed to set up his own investigation into Felfe. Gehlen did not see fit to tell Petty that the OG had investigated Felfe some three years earlier when Albert had denounced him and cleared him at that time. It was hard now for Gehlen to even think that Felfe was a 'mole', he had far too much invested in him and the longer he avoided addressing the issue the harder it would be do actually do so. His exposure would be a huge embarrassment for the BND and the CIA and it would not only be the end of Gehlen's career but would cast a pall over his life's work and destroy his reputation leaving his legacy in tatters. Everything he had worked so hard for would be gone. Felfe, however, had manoeuvred himself into a position where he had access to all the most important secrets of even NATO. He had delivered lists of BND agents at Pullach and in the field.

When Felfe was eventually exposed as a spy, it was something of a long, drawn-out process. It began in March 1958, with the receipt of a letter at the American Embassy in Zürich. It was addressed to J. Edgar Hoover at the FBI and signed 'Heckenschütze' (Sniper). The writer offered to give information about communist espionage activities so it found its way onto a CIA desk instead. Other letters followed from the same source but little of any great value was learned until Sniper reported that Polish intelligence was regularly receiving summaries of BND reports from the Soviets. This encouraged the CIA to take Heckenschütze seriously but they kept Gehlen in the dark.

What really got the CIA's attention, however, was Heckenschütze's assertion that two of the six Gehlen officers who had gone to the United States in 1956 were Soviet agents. The CIA opened a case file and called it 'Ujdrowsy'. Soon afterwards they got a call from Heckenschütze on an emergency number demanding that they get him out. He came over at Christmas 1960 with his mistress and introduced himself as Michal Goleniewski, a highly placed officer in Polish intelligence who had worked with the Soviets. He was taken for questioning to ascertain whether or not he was a Soviet 'plant'. Attention again focussed on Felfe, who had been one of the six. The CIA laid their suspicions of Felfe on Gehlen's desk but Gehlen was still stubbornly refusing to admit the possibility that Felfe was a double agent. He had even gone to the lengths of holding a small reception for him to celebrate his ten years of service and presenting him with a plaque inscribed *Für Treue Dienste* (for loyal service).

The evidence continued to pile up, however. An employee of the *Hauptverwaltung Aufklärung* (HVA – Stasi Foreign Intelligence Service), Gunther Maennel, had defected to the CIA and, amongst other information, told them that he knew of a 'mole' inside the BND. He could describe the man and knew that his codename was Paul but that was all. Gehlen was staring at a security failure of such dimensions that it would surely destroy his reputation if it was ever made public but he had no option but to pursue the leads to their natural conclusion.

A BND tap on Felfe's phone revealed compromising conversations between him and Clemens.

On 9 September, Felfe, Clemens and Busch went to Vienna where they were put under surveillance. Clemens had a heavy cold and did not move from his hotel but Felfe took a car on a Sunday morning and drove very fast through the quiet streets making several abrupt turns and running red lights. His followers eventually lost him so they were unaware that he made a rendezvous with his KGB case officer[101] but Phone intercepts were building up a significant body of evidence that both Felfe and Clemens were in contact with Soviet agents. On the morning of 6 November, armed police officers with BND escort were assembled at the BND Headquarters building in Pullach. Felfe had been summoned to the office of General Langkau, a senior BND official, for a meeting and once he was inside the compound, the gates were locked and the telephone lines closed down. Felfe was arrested and Clemens was picked up in Cologne ten minutes later. The following day, Tiebel was taken into custody also. News of the arrests filled the press headlines with a glare of unwanted publicity illuminating Gehlen and the BND which was portrayed as a mixture of Nazis and communists in equal measure. None of this came as a surprise to those who had long opposed the way that Gehlen had run his organisation. It had only been a matter of time, they believed before the skeletons would start popping out of his cupboards.

The three did not go to trial until July 1963 when proceedings were held *in camera*. From the dock, Clemens cursed the Americans who had destroyed his home city on 13 February 1945. He was handed down a nine-year sentence. Felfe told the court his ten years with Gehlen had been like 'dancing at two weddings'. He mocked his former employer by saying that the Soviets had urged him to move departments because 'there were already too many of their agents [where he was]'.[102] He took the opportunity to tell the court that Gehlen's arrangement with the CIA was 'not in the interests of the German people'.[103] Felfe was sentenced to fourteen years in prison but Tiebel, deemed to have been little more than a courier, was given two years hard labour. Under the circumstances, all three sentences were deemed lenient considering what others Cold War spies were being given elsewhere.

The German press demanded Gehlen's dismissal. Heated parliamentary debates threatened to see him removed from office but Adenauer and Globke rallied to his defence with exaggerated, and often untrue, claims about the level of 'only one per cent' of Nazis in the BND and those were at the lowest levels.

After serving about half of his sentence, on 14 February 1969, in a deal negotiated through the East German lawyer Wolfgang Vogel and Jürgen Strange for the FRG, Felfe was to be exchanged for three West German students who had been imprisoned in the Soviet Union on spying charges. That was the story put out for the press but behind the scenes, there was a second concurrent deal. On a cold winter evening on the frontier at Wartha, fifteen male and three female BND agents being held in the GDR were released with the Bonn government paying

DM 80,000 per head as ransom. It was only now that Felfe was taken out of his cell and moved to the border. Crossing the border, Felfe then requested and was granted formal asylum in the GDR. He was awarded a professorship in criminology at the Humboldt University in east Berlin and worked for the Stasi.

Having become one of the senior BND liaison officers working with West German internal security and police services, Felfe was a hugely important agent of penetration in these groups and inflicted considerable damage on them. According to the damage report from the CIA on 7 February 1963, he copied around 15,000 confidential documents and handed them over to the KGB and exposed around 200 spies from the CIA and the OG. An inestimable loss for both secret services. It also includes the following observations:

- Using a high degree of native intelligence and cunning [Felfe] was able to so deeply ingratiate himself with the BND that he attained a position whereby he could initiate, direct or halt any BND operation and later some of the CIA's to the ultimate advantage of the Soviets.
- As a result, the degree of compromise of operations, personnel and facilities in Germany has been very heavy.
- His influence on some members of the BND was of such degree as to permit him at times to dictate liaison policy vis-à-vis the Americans with respect to Soviet operations.
- He was able to keep the Soviets sufficiently current on CIA strengths and weaknesses to allow the KGB wide latitude in countering most of our efforts.

The CIA themselves came to believe that the majority of their tactical sources in the GDR were compromised and under hostile control as a result of his activities.

Meanwhile, on 20 July 1954, while in Berlin, Gehlen's rival Otto John had mysteriously disappeared. His time as head of BfV had not found him short of critics. The CIA said of him that he 'lacked even basic counterespionage experience and had unrealistic expectations' while others found him vain and inclined to keep dubious company. By mid-1954, he appeared unstable and under stress giving rise to a sense that he was no longer up to the job, if in fact he ever had been. Even the British had started to lose confidence in him.[104] He would be regularly briefed about the intelligence activities of other West German agencies while also maintaining a working relationship with other intelligence agencies from the FRG's allies in NATO.

After appearing to be distressed during a ceremony to remember the Stauffenberg bomb plot, John, left in the company of Dr Wolfgang Wohlgemuth who showed up soon afterwards claiming that John had crossed over into the GDR of his own volition. Two days later East German radio announced that John had asked for asylum and had vowed to do all he could to bring about the unification of Germany. John apparently issued a statement criticising Adenauer's remilitarisation policies and condemned his government for the number of former Nazis in its ranks. On 11 August, some three weeks later, John held a press conference, at which he appeared to be comfortable and relaxed, repeating his criticisms of Adenauer and his Nazis with 'conviction and sincerity'.[105]

He reappeared on the world stage some seventeen months later when he crossed back into West Berlin. He crossed at the Brandenburg Gate hidden in a car driven by the Danish journalist Henrik Bonde-Henriksen in an operation organised by Danish military intelligence with the connivance of the West German authorities. From Berlin he was flown directly to Wahn airport near Cologne where he was questioned by the *Bundeskriminalamt* (BKA – Federal Criminal Police). He was quickly brought to trial for treason.

In his defence, he claimed that he had been drugged by Wohlegemuth, lost consciousness in his surgery, abducted by the Stasi and had woken up in Karlshorst. There he had been taken by the Soviets for three and a half months questioning in Moscow. While he maintained throughout trial that he had acted under duress throughout his time in the east, the judge was not convinced. Although the court found him not guilty of treason, they convicted him for 'treacherous falsifications' and handed down a four-year sentence. He would portray this as an act of revenge by judges who had served the Nazi regime, which he had fought as part of the resistance. The head of the KGB, Vitali Tschernjawski later said that John had absconded voluntarily but was subsequently detained against his will.[106]

Analysis of John's motivations incline towards his passionate reaction to the number of former Nazis in the Adenauer administration and the OG, which he could never condone. He saw himself as the conscience of a nation that had failed to rid itself of the scourge of Nazism. Neither was he comfortable with the close relationship between the OG and the CIA, which he believed was a stumbling block to the reunification of Germany. His condemnation of Gehlen for culpability in all this did little to harm Gehlen, however. In fact, John's actions had removed one of his opponents and strengthened his hand immeasurably and hastened his elevation to head of the BND.

Chapter 5
THE BND

Ambition Realised

> the Gehlen Organization had risen to become an 'uncontrolled co-ruler of the German Republic.' It became and remains a state within the state, founded and built by former Nazi functionaries and fascist criminals who recruited and trained its staff and agents without a trace of democratic control over its reactionary operations, involving mass surveillance, provocations, repression and manipulation of political life.[1]

In 1951, the CIA had realised that Gehlen would use every means at his disposal to prevent CIA control over his activities. No doubt, the CIA would have loved to get rid of him but his leadership had become fundamental to the OG and he had made himself too powerful for the Americans to remove even in a country still occupied by the US Army. By the time the OG was formally legalised as the BND in April 1956 and Gehlen's staff officially joined the West German Civil Service, US funds had created a large intelligence bureaucracy that fundamentally undermined the moral high ground of the West by harbouring war criminals in its midst. The OG was also proving to be the least effective and secure intelligence agency in the whole of NATO.

After his dismissal by Adenauer, von Schwerin had continued to remain resident in Bonn and made full use of the contacts he had established there. Not only was he able to maintain strong links with Blank Office but he had also been taken on by the CIA. He was still actively engaged in an unpaid, advisory capacity to certain federal governmental agencies on military issues but was receiving remuneration from the CIA. On top of a monthly salary of DM 750, he got DM 700 for expenses and the use of a Volkswagen car with all petrol and repair costs paid for.[2] In 1951, he had met Kenneth Strong and Allen Dulles where Gehlen's political ambitions were discussed. Reports produced by von Schwerin during the years 1951 to 1953 contain several references to the 'Gehlen problem', in particular Gehlen's penchant for interfering in domestic politics and engaging in a whispering campaign against Otto John. On 30 May 1951, von Schwerin had passed on to the SPD leader Schumacher a damning indictment of the activities of Gehlen accusing him of a grab for power that had already led British intelligence to drop him 'like a hot potato'.[3]

Of particular interest to von Schwerin were reunions of the *Großdeutschland* (Greater Germany) and the Paratroopers' associations and extreme right influences of the *Verband deutscher Soldaten* (VDS – Association of former Professional Soldiers) manifesting themselves within some veterans associations which had just been legalised. He urged the disbandment of Gehlen's domestic, foreign policy and economic intelligence branches. Von Schwerin flew to Washington in 1954 for a meeting with Dulles to address CIA fears that the OG was working completely uncontrolled and had been getting too involved in domestic German affairs. Globke was one singled out for his misuse of the organisation for domestic political purposes.

Uncontrolled growth of Rusty had been a particular issue that, from the very beginning, was the root cause of many problems. It was something that constantly worked against Gehlen's self-styled image of a patriotic German steadfast in pursuit of his country's best interests. Neither were his leaning towards the Americans particularly laudable, however necessary he believed them to be, compared to Baun's fierce but eventual futile, battle for autonomy of the German secret service. Gehlen ceaselessly promoted his own personal agenda at the expense of rigorously controlling and managing of the networks that Baun had created. All this together with Cold War paranoia and Adenauer's championing of his cause had allowed Gehlen to avoid the sort of scrutiny that he would have undoubtedly come under in normal circumstances and would doubtless have resulted in his prompt dismissal.

Reacting to public pressure in the early 1950s, Adenauer and his smaller right-wing coalition partners had the Western Allies release hundreds of German war criminals, SS members, party functionaries and civilian concentration camp personnel, including a number who had been sentenced in the Nuremberg trials. It is clear that, in the early years of the Republic, concerns for the victims of Nazism took second place. In a near total reversal of their previous policies, the Western Powers caved in to the demands of their new ally but won a concession whereby the Adenauer government put on trial right-wing extremist members of parliament and banned the *Sozialistische Reichspartei* (Socialist Reich Party) in 1952. Advocacy of Nazism and justification of the Holocaust were outlawed.[4]

Only now did the OG begin thorough screening of its staff. Analysis of over 3,500 personnel files revealed that around 25 per cent of BND members had been former members of the NSDAP but that was still lower than most West German ministries. Approximately 60 per cent of the full-time BND members had served in the Wehrmacht with a high percentage of former officers. A special tribunal was held where 157 BND members were scrutinised for responsibility for war crimes and, in a bid to placate Bonn, 68 persons were finally dismissed but Gehlen was still sitting on a 'two ticking time-bombs'.[5] The infiltration of the OG by both CIC and the KGB and a conspiracy led by the US Army to discredit him. The Pentagon saw the intelligence situation in Germany as 'chaotic' and it threatened 'unpleasant consequences' for Germany if it wasn't dealt with. They wanted any German intelligence service to be embedded within the Bundeswehr under the command of General Ludwig Cruewell with Heusinger as his deputy.

Hans Speidel, who was soon to be installed as Adenauer's head of *Abt IV* Armed Forces, wrote to the Pentagon rejecting the proposal claiming that the OG had

> provided a near complete picture of the Soviet-occupied zone ... which provides essential information for future military leaders.

Gehlen, he said, was a 'particularly capable and noble character ... of the best type.' On the issue of penetration, he said that 'precautions had been taken by the Gehlen Organisation' and it was a testament to the great value of the OG that the Soviets had made 'unrelenting efforts to discredit' it.[6] Speidel rebuttal held the Pentagon critics at bay for the moment, but it was clear to Gehlen that they were out to destroy him.

When it came down to the creation of the BND, for Adenauer, the issue of personnel was of secondary importance to the need for an efficient espionage and counterespionage service. Adenauer wanted an intelligence service that was on a par with the three Western Powers, which also meant swiftly reducing their special rights on German territory. It was through acceptance of the OG that saw the best hope of doing this. There was huge political will from the Chancellery and the Federal Court of Auditors for the OG to be formalised as the BND, which meant that people like Bentzinger were able to become civil servants with status and remuneration far above their abilities. A schemer 'more cunning than clever' Bentzinger was a particular favourite of Gehlen for the way he tended to uphold morale of those who worked for him, but he was typical of members who crossed over from the OG to the BND without proper scrutiny.

The relationship between Gehlen and Adenauer entered a new phase in December1953 when the OG secured the services of informants in the SPD, including Siegfried Ziegler and its executive secretary at the time, Siegfried Ortloff. Thee most important, however, was SPD Information Director Fried Wesemann who passed on to Gehlen information about the internal discussions, decisions, and personal details of the SPD leadership. Gehlen shared this source with Adenauer, which allowed the chancellor to monitor his biggest political rivals in a party he called his 'mortal enemy'.[7] Over the next ten years, Ortloff verbally passed on almost 500 confidential memorandums to the OG from where they found their way to Adenauer's desk.

Whenever there were important agreements and resolutions in the board, Ortloff reported them to the BND, from the election campaign strategy and planned attacks against the chancellor, from internal conflicts to questions of Western integration and reunification, to the financial situation and foreign policy. Neither was the chancellor passive in this relationship. He requested specific information on political rivals and asked the OG to dig up politically damaging information on his challenger, Willy Brandt. It was this, above all, that put Gehlen in a prime position to take over leadership of the BND. Like Adenauer, Gehlen did not see the SPD as a political candidate or competitor, but as the enemy. In the early 1960s, towards the end of Adenauer's leadership, Gehlen would start to worry that his spying of the SPD could be discovered so, to ensure that the secret stayed out of the public eye, he hired Ortloff to work at the BND, with a high salary while Ziegler, was sent to Mexico, with a comfortable income.

Adenauer tried, in July 1954, to persuade his cabinet to take the OG into the federal government but could not secure sufficient support on account of personal antipathy towards Gehlen from Blank and others. Searching for more political backing, Gehlen now turned to the SPD leader, Fritz Erler, and fed him a few intelligence titbits about the GDR that got his interest. He also started rumours that the CIA were planning to stop funding the OG which had the effect of concentrating minds in Bonn. As it happened, he was not far from the truth. The CIA was rapidly becoming disillusioned with Gehlen and, while they were not prepared to abandon him completely, few in Washington paid much heed to OG weekly intelligence digests.[8] After the Warsaw Pact was created on 11 May 1955 east-west relations hardened but it was seen as a defensive measure and the threat of war receded slightly.

Just one month after he had become head of the German government, Adenauer was invited by President Dwight D. Eisenhower to visit Washington. There, he had meetings with CIA Director Allen Dulles and his brother US Secretary of State John Foster Dulles, both of whom expressed enthusiasm for the idea of the OG becoming the German intelligence service. When he met US Army Chief of Intelligence General Arthur Trudeau, however, he got a different reception. Trudeau held fierce anti-communist views and had always opposed the wartime alliance between the Western Allies and the Soviet Union. Now he was concerned about the rumours of Soviet infiltration of the OG and made clear his views in a private meeting with Adenauer. If the OG was integrated into the German government and NATO, he said, the Soviets would have succedded in burrowing their agents deep into the Western intelligence agencies through that 'spooky Nazi outfit' in Pullach.[9] Adenauer asked Globke to respond to these accusations. He did so through Critchfield. When it got back to CIA headquarters in Washington it was deeply embarrassing for the CIA and Eisenhower but it was not Adenauer or Gehlen who suffered the repercussions. When Gehlen heard about Trudeau's attack on the OG, he went to Adenauer and complaioned about CIC infiltration of his organisation. Making the most of the Trudeau affair, the Soviets turned up the heat with a new propaganda campaign and Delmer came out with a new series of articles about Nazis. Albert's arrest and suicide compounded the issue. Dulles was not amused and came to Gehlen's defence. When the Trudeau-Adenauer incident broke to the press, he appealed to Eisenhower to have Trudeau reprimanded. The publicity caused the CIC and CIA to run for cover. Dale was ordered back to Washington where he was retired from the army and joined the CIA. Operation Campus was closed down. Trudeau was reassigned to a position in the Far East. Nobody in the leadership wanted to upset the aplplecart at this delicate stage of proceedings.

Henry Pleasants, the CIA man who had been entrusted with the supervision of Pullach, had tried to persuade Gehlen to move out of his small flat there and lead a more confortable and relaxed life but Gehlen had resisted until Dulles came up with an offer he could hardly refuse. He had stepped in after the Trudeau incident to mollify Gehlen with an offer of a house in the quiet village of Berg on Lake Starnberg about 10 miles south of Pullach all paid for by the CIA. It was not as grand as the country houses of wealthy German businessmen nearby but it was secluded and had good communications allowing swift access to Gehlen's work every day.

Adenauer came back to the *Bundesrat* (Federal Council) with another proposal, which was accepted and led to the formation of the BND on 11 July 1955 with its mission statement to

> 'collect information abroad which might be of importance to the Federal Government and assist it in taking decisions.'[10]

However, there was no basis in German law for its inception which meant that it could never quite rid itself of the accusations of illegality.

Heusinger was installed as chairman of the *Militärische Führungsrat* (Bundeswehr's military leadership council) and headed up the entire military planning structure responsible to the defence minister. Wessel became head of *G-2 Dienst* and Abwehr *Dienst* (military intelligence and counterintelligence). The protected environment that Gehlen had provided for Heusinger and Speidel away from the public gaze all through the previous decade had served its purpose but not only that, many officers in the new General Staff had been sheltered within the OG also. Naturally, Heusinger saw Gehlen as the right man to head up the BND.

The German Federal Intelligence Service was created on 20 February 1956. Critchfield began relocating his staff from Pullach to Munich and the Star and Stripes of the US flag were lowered over Pullach for the last time on 31 March 1956. Then on 1 April 1956, the BND was officially inaugurated with Gehlen installed as interim chief awaiting legal and bureaucratic confirmation. That would come nine months later.

The former *Heinz Amt* personnel were brought officially into the BND but the new service lost a considerable number of people to the Bundeswehr. These had to be replaced by younger men, but the selection process was now far removed from the erratic and arbitrary process that had existed previously.[11] Gehlen, however, retained his authoritarian leadership style which hindered somewhat a transition towards a modern service whose focus now was on unity. The BND would prove to be little more than a rebranding of the OG and it inherited all of its personnel and structural weaknesses.[12]

Fall from Grace

> Your triumphs remain unsung while your mistakes are trumpeted to the skies.
>
> Reinhard Gehlen[13]

Adenauer lost patience with Gehlen in 1962 over a BND assessment of Germany's defence policy. Gehlen had warned him that any move to expand Germany's military role within the European nuclear defence community would find the German government in direct conflict with the Kennedy administration in Washington. This was seen as Gehlen grossly overstepping the line by interfering in domestic politics and was a cue for Adenauer to start curbing Gehlen's power and influence. Gehlen, already under pressure after the arrest of Felfe, responded by leaking classified information to *Der Spiegel* magazine inferring that Adenauer Minister of Defence, Franz Joseph Strauss, was failing in his duties. A recent NATO exercise, Fallex 62, found the FRG's defence forces to be 'only partially ready to defend the country'.[14]

Der Spiegel owner and editor, Rudolf Augstein, was arrested, the magazine's offices were raided and occupied by the police for several weeks. Adenauer called it an *Abgrund von Landesverrat* (abyss of treason). He summoned Gehlen to the Chancellery for a dressing down and threatened to have him removed from office but could not build a sufficiently strong case against him. In the end it was Strauss who fell after a government reshuffle. The incident is now remembered mostly for producing a shift in public opinion within Germany. Mass protests and demonstrations railed against the traditional authoritarian state heavily tainted with Nazism and demanded more openness and democracy. Clearly, the right-wing character of the BND had effectively made it a political and social counterweight to the emerging liberalisation of the FRG. Its political nature spread it far beyond its core functions of intelligence gathering about foreign countries to include domestic espionage with an anti-liberal surveillance of journalists, writers, politicians and state officials who simply did not conform to the BND right-wing conservative worldview. The problem for Adenauer was that, by now, the BND had become a crucial building block of the FRG directly linked to the process of rearmament and sovereignty intended to integrate the country into the defence partnership of the West. He was anxious to separate the BND from reliance on the CIA in particular to hasten his country's move to complete independence.[15]

Gehlen managed to survive in office but, from this moment, his career trajectory, after many turbulent years, was finally pointing down. Very soon, public outrage at the moral climate within the BND would manifest itself. *Die Welt* would say that

> owing to a catastrophic personnel policy [the BND had provided] a comfortable retreat for both major and minor Nazis.[16]

Gehlen's relationship with Adenauer was badly damaged and it would not take much more to break it completely. Then, a year later, came the Felfe trial closely followed, on 19 July 1963, by Hans Globke's trial *in absentia* in the East German Supreme Court in east Berlin charged with war crimes and crimes against humanity. *The New York Times* reported that the Felfe trial saw 'the destruction of [Gehlen's reputation]'.[17] The Bonn government claimed that it had investigated all charges previously and found Globke had no case to answer and that the East Berlin proceedings were nothing more than a show trial to embarrass the West German government. Globke, far from shying away from the limelight said that 'measures had been taken to ensure that there could be no repetition of [the Felfe] case.'[18]

There had already been a concerted effort by the CIA among others, to keep Gehlen's name out of the reports of the Adolf Eichmann trial in Jerusalem in 1961 to 1962. Globke had been called as a witness, which would have made his role as Eichmann's henchman a matter of public record. Adenauer was desperate to find out which Nazis Eichmann intended to incriminate as part of Germany's elimination of European Jews. In 1960, the Adenauer government had already learned on the CIA to persuade *Life* magazine to delete a reference to Globke in Eichmann's memoirs, which the magazine published. With Adenauer's support, Gehlen was able to persuade the prosecutor in Israel that Globke should not take the stand, but a former Wehrmacht officer Max Merten had stated that Globke personally ordered the deportation of about 20,000 Jews from Thessaloniki in Greece. Gehlen's files record that

> Secretary of State [Globke] agreed to the idea cited, to attempt, regardless of the truth, to present Merten as an agent of Eastern propaganda, on the basis of existing findings.

Only months before, Globke had assisted Adenauer in beginning work on a secret deal to help Israel finance a 'development project' in the Negev desert to develop nuclear weapons but talks had been suspended during the Eichmann trial.

The Israeli intelligence agency, Mossad, many of whose members were Holocaust survivors, had cooperated with the BND after its inauguration in 1955. Prior to that, Mossad showed little interest in the OG, with its high number of former Nazis, believing it to be a private profit-driven organisation. That changed with the new intake of younger officers who had never served in the Second World War and the two organisations began talks after Israel's lightning impressive showing during the Suez Crisis of 1956 made it a military and intelligence power in the Middle East. Gehlen had started looking for new sources of intelligence as the former Baun networks in eastern Europe were becoming outdated and institutionally insecure. Mossad's reputation for worldwide intelligence expertise offered the chance for the BND to tap into new networks. Gehlen guessed that BND links that had been developed with Arab countries through former Nazis would be a useful bargaining tool. Representatives of both sides met in Paris in 1957 and a cooperative relationship developed from there. Already the Israeli Ministry of Defence had permanent representatives openly working in Germany with the Bundeswehr, but the Mossad-BND link remained secret.

The efficacy of this became evident in 1967 when the BND informed Richard Helms, now head of the CIA, that Israel was planning to strike against its Arab neighbours. US Secretary of State Dean Rusk had confidently told the US National Security Council that his ambassador in Tel Aviv assured him that Israel would not go to war. Helms interrupted him to say that he had 'reliable information [from] an allied secret service.'[19] Days later the Israeli struck with what Helms predicted would be 'extreme rapidity' and spectacularly crushed Arab resistance in six days of fighting.

At the beginning of 1961, Gehlen had commissioned Hans-Henning Crome to carry out an investigation into suspected agents of other secret services within the BND. This resulted, two years later, in the formation of a group with the code name *Organizational Unit 85* and led by Crome. Its task was to identify the members of the BND who had participated in acts of violence during the Nazi era or who had worked in the RSHA, GFP, SD, SS or the NSDAP. Checks identified seventy-one people and they were forced out of the BND but, in order to avoid legal disputes, the majority of them received severance payments. Crome's final report of 1 February 1965 noted that members of special units that had been involved in mass executions denied any involvement and even denied having heard anything about the crimes. Crome adjudged these statements to be 'blatantly insincere'. This report, initially distributed to only twenty senior BND officials, was immediately withdrawn, and remained secret until released by BND President Ernst Uhrlau in 2010.

The construction of the Berlin Wall and the closing of East German borders with the FRG came as a political embarrassment to Adenauer and contributed to his fall from power. A catastrophically misjudged attack on Brandt followed by the *Der Spiegel* incident weakened his position to the point where he was forced to resign in October 1963, after fourteen years in office, in favour of Ludwig Erhard. The new administration saw Karl Hohmann given responsibility for the BND but he had little time for or interest in spies who 'do no more than journalists'. Erhard went a step further and declared that he would 'not live under the same roof as [the BND liaison staff]'.[20] This seriously dented Gehlen's hopes of becoming State Secretary of a new independent Federal intelligence authority but by now he was

> a tired man of 61, isolated from the majority of his staff, thinking only in terms of influence and his personal power, burnt out after forty years of uninterrupted toil and badly in need of a rest.[21]

Erhard had resigned in 1966 and Kurt George Kiesinger had been installed as chancellor. Gehlen was already due to be pensioned off but Kiesinger delayed it for another year to give him time to find a successor. When Maurice Picard was accused of supplying information to a foreign power at the end of 1967, it was assumed that the former security chief of the French Ministry of the Interior was working for the Soviets but it turned out that he had, in fact, been supplying intelligence to the BND. It would have come as no surprise for many that all countries spied on their neighbours, whatever their stripe, but sensational press coverage was a different matter especially when it was revealed that Picard had been working for Gehlen for some seven years and had, during the war, collaborated with the Nazis in the Pétain administration. Brandt publicly called for Gehlen to be retired.

Kiesinger's State Secretary in the Chancery, Werner Knieper advised swift intervention to address the many institutional problems in the BND that Gehlen had simply ignored for years. Gehlen was asked for his opinion about who should succeed him. There were two possibilities, he said, Horst Wendland, who was his personal choice, and the head of German military intelligence, Gerhard Wessel. Kiesinger tried to delay the decision even further but, in the end, chose Wessel and having gone that far, went further by commissioning his new State Secretary Karl Carstens to open an inquiry into the BND.

Gehlen was to have one last swansong, however. In spring 1968, he warned NATO that the Soviets were going to clamp down on the Czechs who were showing signs of breaking out of their control and embracing a mild liberalism under Alexander Dubcek. Little notice was taken at NATO headquarters. The general feeling was that it was Gehlen's final expression of his hatred for communism before his official voice would be silenced. Of course, he was proved correct.

After weeks of investigations the report Carsten's people came up with was damning in the extreme. The areas of mismanagement were identified to be,

- Nepotism of the Gehlen clan.
- Gehlen's defective leadership.
- A predominance of inexperienced officers both old and new.
- Misappropriation of funds to serve the personal ambitions of BND veterans.
- Casual treatment of younger BND officials.
- Aversion to publicity and mystery-mongering.

In short, the BND was described as 'a corrupt institution'.[22]

On 30 April 1968, Carstens summoned the senior officers of the BND to complete the inauguration of the new man Wessel. Gehlen stood silently by wearing the sash of the Grand Cross of the Federal Republic Order of Merit with which he had just been presented. Despite being praised for his 'outstanding services', it cannot have been comfortable for him to listen to Carstens call for

> a new manner of working ... less burdened with secrecy [and] substitute cooperation between partners for obsolete hierarchical structures [and] those structural principles effective in the modern world.

It was not the way that Reinhard Gehlen had envisaged the end of his long career.

Appendix 1

ATTENDEES AT THE HIMMEROD MEETING, 4–9 OCTOBER 1950

Wolf Graf von Baudissin (Army)

Hermann Foertsch (Army)

Walter Gladisch (Navy)

Adolf Heusinger (Army)

Johann Adolf Graf von Kielmansegg (Army)

Robert Knauss (Air Force)

Horst Krüger (Air Force)

Rudolf Meister (Air Force)

Eberhard Graf von Nostitz (Army)

Hans Röttiger (Army)

Friedrich Ruge (Navy)

Alfred Schulze-Hinrichs (Navy)

Fridolin von Senger und Etterlin (Army)

Hans Speidel (Army)

Heinrich von Vietinghoff (Army)

Appendix 2
THE STRUCTURE OF *DIE GENERALVERTRETUNG L* IN 1950

- The *GV L* headquarters in Karlsruhe, Gerwigstrasse 36, with sixteen employees.
- The *BV 2600* (North) in Frankfurt am Main, run by Ludwig, responsible for the British occupation zone. It had twenty permanent Org employees, twenty-four agents in and five in East Germany.
- *BV 2601* (South), in Coburg, responsible for Bavaria and Württemberg-Badenas well as the French occupation zone.
- *BV 2602*, later *BV-E* (Berlin), with ten permanent OG employees and twenty-seven agents in East Germany.
- *BV 2603* (Counterespionage), in Künzelsau, Langenburger Str. 35, headed by Oscar Reile, with seven permanent OG employees.
- There were also the special connections *SV Condor* (group of Russian employees), *SV Czardas* (three Hungarian employees with three agents, headed by Paul Hodosy-Strobl) and *SV Polka* (Polish group).
- *Waldkapelle*, an internal security group of the GV, which existed both at the headquarters and at the BVs. The leader of the BV Berlin *forest band* was Kurt Moritz (code name MAUE).

Appendix 3

KNOWN MEMBERS OF GEHLEN ORGANISATION

Members with CIA and (or) OG Code or Pseudonym and OG Number

Albert, Ludwig, CIA and (or) OG code or pseudonym Anders, OG number V-2600

Arlt, Fritz, CIA and (or) OG code or pseudonym Werner, OG number V-2881

Augsburg, Emil, CIA and (or) OG code or pseudonyms Dr Ernst Albertini, Dr Ernst Althaus and Dr Krauss, OG number V-2907

Bernau, Günther Hans, CIA and (or) OG code or pseudonyms Baer, Bracht, Hans Günther Berger, OG number V-3399

Biederbick, Andreas, CIA and (or) OG code or pseudonyms Daniel, Burkhardt, Alfred Brenner and Andre Bach, OG number V-4985

Boehm, Anton, CIA and (or) OG code or pseudonym Otto Von Bolschwing, OG number V-6732

Clemens, Hans, CIA and (or) OG code or pseudonyms Hoffmann, UJfrum and Hans Cramer Hoffmann, OG number V-2665

Deppner, Erich, CIA and (or) OG code or pseudonyms Ernst Borchert and Egon Dietrich, OG number V-616

Didinger, Josef, CIA and (or) OG code or pseudonyms Josef Deichman, Josef Dorner and Hans During, OG number V-13600

Dolezalek, Alexander, CIA and (or) OG code or pseudonym Horst Günther Doehring, OG number V-3002

Domes, Walter, CIA and (or) OG code or pseudonyms Walter Draha and Daniel Wildorf, OG number V-12024

Dorn, Fritz, CIA and (or) OG code or pseudonyms Manfred Peter Dehne and Fritz Traube, OG number V-3376

Erdmann, Fritz Gustav, CIA and (or) OG code or pseudonyms Eller and Fritz Lohrmann, OG number V-2665.2
Feist, Karl Joseph, CIA and (or) OG code or pseudonyms Fritz Korf and Dr Karl Wilke, OG number V-8833
Fiebig, Konrad, CIA and (or) OG code or pseudonyms Konrad Fiedler and Konrad Fischer, OG numbers V-22352 and V-7038
Finsterer, Werner, CIA and (or) OG code or pseudonyms Werner Winterstein, Fritz Weigand and Fritz Kaemmer, OG number V-2354
Flegel, Arwed, CIA and (or) OG code or pseudonyms Migsch, Nietsch, Alfred Friedmann and Hans Hermann Migsch, OG number V-2954
Frank, Friedrich, CIA and (or) OG code or pseudonyms Franke, Kreuger, Krueger, OG number V-14415
Friede, Willy Hienrich, CIA and (or) OG code or pseudonym Frank Pax, OG number V-2835
Froehlich, Kurt, CIA and (or) OG code or pseudonym Gustav Friese, OG number V-2327
Giepel, Walter, CIA and (or) OG code or pseudonym Werner Grunert, OG number V-3348
Gimzauskas, Kazys, CIA and (or) OG code or pseudonym Ulmann, OG number V-15775
Haderlein, Andreas, CIA and (or) OG code or pseudonyms Albert, Albert Halbach, Arthut Hesse and Albert Richter, OG number V-9112
Handrack, Hans, CIA and (or) OG code or pseudonyms Hans Habedank and Rolf Osterreich, OG number V-11760
Heidschuch, Erich, CIA and (or) OG code or pseudonym Eduard Bergmann, OG number V-2620
Helfsgott, Ernst, CIA and (or) OG code or pseudonyms Werner Hassel, Werner Heller and Willi Hillmann, OG number V-7041
Horst, Cornelius van der, CIA and (or) OG code or pseudonym Corny (Conny), OG number V-2951
Kainz, Walter, CIA and (or) OG code or pseudonyms Walter Schade and Korn, OG number V-14801
Karmasin, Franz, CIA and (or) OG code or pseudonyms Fritz Kahr and Fritz Wunder, OG number V-16131
Krassowsky, Werner, CIA and (or) OG code or pseudonym Werner Miller, OG number V-10721
Krichbaum, Wilhelm, CIA and (or) OG code or pseudonym Krug, OG number V-8838
Kurreck, Walter, CIA and (or) OG code or pseudonym Holgers, Kurt Wagner, OG number V-7630

Lienhard, Heinrich, CIA and (or) OG code or pseudonyms Heinz Engelhardt and Heinz Dernburg, OG number V-2026

Lueth, Walter, CIA and (or) OG code or pseudonym Otto Kruse, OG number V-9245

Mailat, Vasile, CIA and (or) OG code or pseudonym Ursu, OG number V-15050

Merk, Kurt, CIA and (or) OG code or pseudonym Walter Peterson, OG number V-12041

Mueller, Franz, CIA and (or) OG code or pseudonym Nettke, OG number V-1721

Murat, Ferid, CIA and (or) OG code or pseudonyms Famine and Cameo, OG number V-11364

Nickel, Siegfried, CIA and (or) OG code or pseudonym Kortmann, OG number V-7048

Nostitz, Eberhard von, CIA and (or) OG code or pseudonyms Justizin, Ernst Keller and Erich Nolte, OG number V-12899

Oebsger-Roeder, Rudolf, CIA and (or) OG code or pseudonyms Ranke and Ropp, OG number V-11728

Offczarek, Emmerich, CIA and (or) OG code or pseudonyms Dr Oskar Eckert, Dr Emmerich Schaeffer and Dr Schreiter, OG number V-7500

Olbrueck, Erich, CIA and (or) OG code or pseudonyms Heinrich Allmann and Erich Pons, OG number V-7902

Otten, Walter, CIA and (or) OG code or pseudonym Günther Holm, OG number V-2837

Panzinger, Friedrich, CIA and (or) OG code or pseudonyms Ujnutlet and Heinz Paulsen, OG number V-1150

Pfahls, Ludwig, CIA and (or) OG code or pseudonyms Ludwig Hoefner, Peter Lindemann and Ludwig Pils, OG number V-7915

Puchta, Adolf, CIA and (or) OG code or pseudonym Alfred Bauer, OG number V-3015

Rauch, Fritz, CIA and (or) OG code or pseudonym Fritz Roemer, OG number V-58

Sander, Hans, CIA and (or) OG code or pseudonyms Hermann Borchers and Hans Franke, OG number V-5850

Schmalschlager, Heinz, CIA and (or) OG code or pseudonyms Avocet, Malt, Heller and Candida, OG number V-67

Schmidt, Martin, CIA and (or) OG code or pseudonym Sydow, OG number V-7501

Schreieder, Joseph, CIA and (or) OG code or pseudonyms Cabolt, Heinz Bauer and Dr Mabuse, OG number V-7627

Schuetz, Carl, CIA and (or) OG code or pseudonym Schuster, OG number V-2978

Schumacher, Hans Carl, CIA and (or) OG code or pseudonym Hans Schubert, OG number V-7025

Somann, Hans, CIA and (or) OG code or pseudonyms Otmar Lange and Otmar Seidemann, OG number V-2950

Sommer, Hans, CIA and (or) OG code or pseudonyms Heinrich Saenger, Herbert Sauer and Heinrich Senner, OG number V-2857

Steinbichl, Wolfgang, CIA and (or) OG code or pseudonym Dr Sill, OG number V-92

Urban, Josef, CIA and (or) OG code or pseudonym Befinal, OG number V-13690

Wellhoehner, Karl, CIA and (or) OG code or pseudonym Karl Woge, OG number V-12643

Woest, Günther, CIA and (or) OG code or pseudonym Haendler, OG number V-21511

Wolf, Erich, CIA and (or) OG code or pseudonym Hans Bauer, OG number V-9107

Wolff, Ludwig, CIA and (or) OG code or pseudonym Ludwig Weber, OG number V-8864

Worm, Ernst, CIA and (or) OG code or pseudonym Parker, Weber, OG number V-3597

Zuber, Ebrulf, CIA and (or) OG code or pseudonym Ackerman, OG number V-3595

Members with CIA and (or) OG Code or Pseudonym

Anders, Heinz, CIA and (or) OG code or pseudonyms Peter Anders, Heinz Schauth and Peter Kirchner

Baumert, Reinhardt, CIA and (or) OG code or pseudonym Helmuth Bachmann

Behnke, Kurt, CIA and (or) OG code or pseudonyms Baldrian and Ujdown

Bickler, Hermann, CIA and (or) OG code or pseudonyms Winkler, Mair, Schmidt and Winkler

Bolschwig, Otto von, CIA and (or) OG code or pseudonym Unrest

Engel, Rolf, CIA and (or) OG code or pseudonym Ebert

Felfe, Heinz, CIA and (or) OG code or pseudonyms Ujdrowsy and Friesen

Fischer, Alois, CIA and (or) OG code or pseudonym Fink

Fumy, Rodolf, CIA and (or) OG code or pseudonym Rudolf Funk

Girg, Walter, CIA and (or) OG code or pseudonym Walter Girk
Glanert, Georg, CIA and (or) OG code or pseudonym Griffiths
Globke, Hans, CIA and (or) OG code or pseudonym Causa-1
Grauer, Gustav, CIA and (or) OG code or pseudonym Grauert
Griesse, Hermann, CIA and (or) OG code or pseudonym Helmut Gantner
Heusinger, Adolf, CIA and (or) OG code or pseudonym Adolf Horn
Hofffmann, Otto, CIA and (or) OG code or pseudonym Paul, Paul Berger
Hossbach, Johannes, CIA and (or) OG code or pseudonym Haehnert
Jansen, Erwin, CIA and (or) OG code or pseudonym Franz Urbanek
Kayser-Eichberg, Ulrich, CIA and (or) OG code or pseudonyms Ujucat-4 and Ulrich Kiel
Krause, Edmund, CIA and (or) OG code or pseudonym Korb
Mueller, Carl Heinz, CIA and (or) OG code or pseudonym Caisson
Parilli, Luigi, CIA and (or) OG code or pseudonym Rohr
Pretzell, Ernst, CIA and (or) OG code or pseudonym Albert Ruhland
Reihle, Orkar, CIA and (or) OG code or pseudonyms Ujdryrot and Reischke
Reiss, Arthur, CIA and (or) OG code or pseudonym Arthur Reiter
Scheidt, Hans, CIA and (or) OG code or pseudonym Gordon
Schmitz, Hans, CIA and (or) OG code or pseudonym Dr Schneiderhan
Schoebel, Hans Erich, CIA and (or) OG code or pseudonyms Gram, Monogram and Peppermill
Starke, Werner, CIA and (or) OG code or pseudonym Werner Stahl
Weiss, Kurt, CIA and (or) OG code or pseudonym Winterstein
Wendland, Major General Horst, CIA and (or) OG Code or pseudonyms Holm and Wendt
Wenger, Erich, CIA and (or) OG code or pseudonym, Cavata-17

Members with V-Numbers Only

Baltrusch, Fritz, V-2665.5
Bauer, Hans, V-9107
Boehrsch, Herbert, V-2713
Busch, Friedrich, V-2982
Dietrich, Wilhelm, V-6628
Duplitzer, Emil, V-11718
Hehn, Jürgen von, V-18526
Hoeher, Wolfgang, V-2996
Kedia, Michael, V-11881

Klaus, Bruno, V-14802
Knoll, Kurt, V-5450
Koerner, Horst, V-14125
Kollenyi, Gyorgy, V-17562
Korzahn, Michael, V-9460.9
Kroeger, Ernst, V-15769
Ledwinke, Karl, V-14401
Makowski, Ernst, V-615
Mast, Heinrich von, V-5300
Metzner, Alfred, V-23411
Moritz, Kurt, V-3080
Ohlbrecht, Helmut, V-2616
Reiser, Heinrich Josef, V-2629
Roth, Georg, V-14410
Schwarzwaeller, Ernst, V-2952
Seibold, Fritz, V-2730
Supper, Adolf, V-20798
Triska, Helmut, V-9134.2
Unglaub, Heinz, V-7043
Vaeth, Walter, V-11540
Vogel, Erich, V-14105
Vollmer, Walter, V-14011
Wildner, Karl, V-21554
Zarp, Christian, V-9136.8
Zenger, Karl, V-2777

NOTES

Chapter 1: Artillery Officer

1. Gehlen, Reinhard, *The Service,* (World Publishing), 1972, p.xxi
2. Cookridge, E.H., *Gehlen, Spy of the Century,* (Random House), 1971, p.14
3. Höhne, Heinz and Zolling, Hermann, *The General was a Spy* (Pan Books), 1972, p.5
4. Cookridge, p.4
5. ibid, p.13
6. Gehlen, p.xxiv
7. Müller, Rolf-Dieter, *Reinhard Gehlen, Geheimdienstchef im Hintergrund der Bonner Republik Die Biografie,1902–1979* (CH Links Verlag), 2018, p.41
8. Cookridge, p.33
9. Müller, p.43
10. *Guide for Teaching in the Army: The Reichswehr Ministry, Berlin 1924,* p.1
11. *Correspondence on this in the Berlin Document Center ('Gehlen') and in the BStU archive, MfS, HA IX/11, FV 5/72, Volume 9, Part 2*
12. Müller, p.80
13. Cookridge, p.61
14. ibid, p.22
15. ibid, p.35
16. Gehlen, p.xxii
17. Müller, p.89
18. ibid, p.93
19. Peter Steinkamp, *On the Problem of Deviance in the Wehrmacht: Alcohol and Drug Abuse in the Troops, Dissertation, Freiburg, 2008*
20. Müller, p.100
21. ibid, p.105
22. Höhne, Heinze and Zolling, Hermann, *The General was a Spy,* p.7

Chapter 2: The War

1. Müller, p.240
2. ibid, p.146
3. Gehlen, p.36
4. Cookridge, p.43
5. Höhne, Heinze and Zolling, Hermann, *The General was a Spy,* p.8
6. Cookridge, p.44
7. *Critical Analysis of German Operational Intelligence,* https: / /www.nsa.gov
8. Thomas, David, *Foreign Armies East and German Military Intelligence in Russia 1941–45* (Journal of Contemporary History, Volume 22, Number 2), 1987, p.274

9. Pahl, Magnus, *Fremde Heere Ost. Hitler's Militärische Feindaufklärung* (Helion), 2012, p.71
10. Müller, p.156
11. Thomas, p.276
12. Halder, Franz, *Kriegstagebuch 1939–42, Volume III* (W. Kollhammer), 1962, p.367
13. *Letter from Goth 4 May 1940 National Archives Washington, T-78/488*
14. Thomas, p.365
15. Reese, Mary Ellen, *General Reinhard Gehlen: The CIA Connection* (George Mason University Press), 1990, p.15
16. Höhne, Heinz and Brownjohn, J, Maxwell, *Canaris* (Martin Secker & Warburg Ltd), 1979, p.471
17. Paehler, Katrin, *The Third Reich's Intelligence Services: Walter Schellenberg* (Cambridge University Press), 2017, p.105
18. Gehlen, p.xxii
19. Müller, p.236
20. Höhne, Heinze and Zolling, Hermann, *The General was a Spy*, p.12
21. Berstein, Vadim J., *Smersh, Stalin's Secret Weapon* (Biteback Publishing), 2013, p.214
22. Gehlen, p.43
23. Thomas, p.264
24. ibid, p.280
25. Gehlen, p.37
26. Kahn, David, *Hitler's Spies* (Macmillan), 1978, p.249
27. Berstein, p.210
28. Kahn, p.210
29. ibid, p.146
30. Höhne, Heinze and Zolling, Hermann, *The General was a Spy*, p.22
31. Gehlen, p.51
32. Höhne, Heinze and Zolling, Hermann, *The General was a Spy*, p.11
33. Schramm, Percy Ernst, *War Diary of the High Command of the Wehrmacht* (Wehrmacht *Command Staff) 1940–1945* (Madison Books), 1991, p.1,275
34. Müller, p.245
35. Gehlen, p.52
36. Höhne, Heinze and Zolling, Hermann, *The General was a Spy*, p.16
37. Gehlen, p.60
38. *US National Archives NA T-78/467*
39. Kahn, p.314
40. ibid, p.312
41. Cookridge, p.75
42. Berstein, p.227
43. Gehlen, p.59
44. Müller, p.252
45. Cookridge, p.76
46. Gehlen, p.56
47. Heusinger, Adolf, *Befehl im Widerstreit: Schicksalsstunden der deutschen Armee 1923–1945* (Tübingen), 1950, p.191
48. Gehlen, p.94
49. Thomas, p.269
50. *FHO Beurteilung der Feindlage vor Heeresgruppe Mitte', 'Zusammenstellung. Teil A', 22*
51. Thomas, p.283

52. *Fremde Heere Ost (I), H. Qu. 29.8.42, Gedanken zur Weiterentwicklung der Feindlage im Herbst und Winter', reproduced in Kehrig, Stalingrad, 550–2*
53. Thomas, p.283
54. ibid
55. Gehlen, p.60
56. ibid, p.68
57. *Abt. Fremde Heere Ost (IIa), nr. 574/43 gkdos., 23.3.1943, 'Beurteilung der Feindabsichten vor der deutschen Ostfront im grossen', 'Zusammenstellung. Teil A', 74–9*
58. *Abt. Fremde Heere Ost (IIa) nr. 1226/43 gkdos, 21 Mai 1943, 'Zusammenfassende Beurteilung der Feindabsichten vor der deutschen Ostfront im grossen', T-78/556/393–398*
59. Müller, p.317
60. Höhne, Heinze and Zolling, Hermann, *The General was a Spy*, p.26
61. Müller, p.320
62. Ridley, Norman, *Hitler's Gold* (Pen & Sword), 2023, p.148
63. Höhne, Heinze and Zolling, Hermann, *The General was a Spy*, p.28
64. Reese, p.15
65. Kahn, p.440
66. Thomas, p.287
67. ibid, p.288
68. ibid
69. Berstein, p.148
70. Müller, p.346
71. Gehlen, p.83
72. Höhne, Heinze and Zolling, Hermann, *The General was a Spy*, p.35
73. Gehlen, p.97
74. ibid
75. Dohna-Schlobitten, Alexander, *Erinnerungen eines alten Ostpreußen* (Berlin), 1989, p.186
76. Critchfield, James H., *Partners at the Creation* (Naval Institute Press), 2003, p.26
77. Gehlen, p.106
78. Boghardt, Thomas, *Covert Legions: U.S. Army intelligence in Germany, 1944–1949* (Center of Military History United States Army, Washington, D.C), 2022, p.264
79. Müller, p.362
80. *US National Archives, 25 February 1945 NA T-78/496*
81. Müller, p.368
82. Gehlen, p.106
83. ibid, p.102
84. ibid, p.106
85. Höhne, Heinze and Zolling, Hermann, *The General was a Spy*, p.47

Chapter 3: Same Foe; Different Friends

1. Gehlen, p.113
2. ibid, p.103
3. Reese, p.9
4. Müller, p.400
5. Gehlen, p.111
6. ibid, p.113
7. Müller, p.406
8. Boghardt, p.267
9. Müller, p.424

10. *Report of Initial Contacts with Gehlen Organisation John R. Boker Jnr: 1 May 1952*, https://www.jewishvirtuallibrary.org
11. ibid
12. Helms, Richard, A *Look Over My Shoulder: A Life in the Central Intelligence Agency* (Random House Publishing Group, Kindle Edition), p.84
13. Reese, p.43
14. Boghardt, p.101
15. Breitman, Richard, Goda, Norman J.W., Nafatali, Timothy, Wolfe, Robert, *U.S. Intelligence and the Nazis* (Cambridge University Press), 2005, p.378
16. Höhne, Heinze and Zolling, Hermann, *The General was a Spy*, p.55
17. Silver, Arnold M., *Memories of Oberursel: Questions, Questions, Questions*, (Intelligence and National Security, Volume 8, Number 2), p.83
18. Gehlen, p.12
19. Boghardt, p.269
20. Gehlen, p.13
21. Mallett, Derek R., *Western Allied Intelligence and the German Military Document Section, 1945–6* (Journal of Contemporary History, Volume 26, Number 2), 2011, p.400
22. *BDN-Archiv, N 13/1*
23. Mallett, p.404
24. *Forging an Intelligence Partnership: CIA and the Origins of the BND, 1945–49*, CIA Historical Staff Center for the Study of Intelligence 1999, p.xvi
25. Boghardt, p.271
26. Müller, p.443
27. Boghardt, p.131
28. Reese, p.66
29. *Die Vierteljahrshefte für Zeitgeschichte, 2016*, (Walter de Gruyter GmbH), 2016, p.202
30. Gehlen, p.107
31. ibid, p.122
32. Breitman, Richard, Goda, Norman J.W., Nafatali, Timothy and Wolfe, Robert, p.375
33. Höhne, Heinz and Zolling, Hermann, p.61
34. Reese, p.72
35. Müller, p.470
36. *Die Vierteljahrshefte für Zeitgeschichte 2016*, p.197
37. ibid, p.200
38. Müller, p.473
39. Gehlen, p.127
40. *Die Vierteljahrshefte für Zeitgeschichte 2016*, p.203
41. ibid, p.206
42. Höhne, Heinz and Zolling, Hermann, p.88
43. *Major-General W.A. Burress, US Forces headquarters in European Theater, to Lieutenant General S. Vandenberg, CIG, Washington, 1 October 194*
44. Boghardt, p.285
45. *Present Usefulness | Operation Rusty 10/06/46*, https://jewishvirtuallibrary.org/cia-relationship-with-nazi-general-reinhard-gehlen-during-world-war
46. Wolf, Thomas, *Die Anfänge des BND* (Institut für Zeitgeschichte), 2016, p.204
47. Reese, p.84
48. Keßelring, Agilolf, *Die Organisation Gehlen und die Neuformierung des Militärs* (Christof Links Verlag), 2017, p.11
49. ibid, p.109

50. *Die Vierteljahrshefte für Zeitgeschichte 2016*, p.211
51. Müller, p.514
52. ibid, p.532
53. Breitman, Richard, Goda, Norman J.W., Nafatali, Timothy, Wolfe, Robert, p.381
54. *Memorandum for the Director, Central Intelligence Group: Subject Rusty, Samuel Brossard, 29 May 1947*
55. Breitman, Richard, Goda, Norman J.W., Nafatali, Timothy and Wolfe, Robert, p.387
56. Wolf, Thomas, *Die Anfänge des BND*, p.224
57. Boghardt, p.275
58. Breitman, Richard, Goda, Norman J.W., Nafatali, Timothy and Wolfe, Robert, p.387
59. Tromly, Benjamin, (Oxford University Press), 2019, p.62
60. Breitman, Richard, Goda, Norman J.W., Nafatali, Timothy and Wolfe, Robert, p.386
61. Müller, p.497
62. *Brossard Report; Memorandum for the Director, Central Intelligence Group 29 May 1947*
63. ibid
64. Müller, p.467
65. Ruffner, Kevin C., *Debriefing of Eric Waldman 30 September 1969 CIA and the Origins of the BND, 1945–49* (CIA Historical Staff Center for the Study of Intelligence), 1969

Chapter 4: The Gehlen Organisation

1. Höhne, Heinz and Zolling, Hermann, p.149
2. Critchfield, p.162
3. Höhne, Heinz and Zolling, Hermann, p.135
4. ibid, p.119
5. ibid, p.91
6. ibid, p.2
7. Müller, p.517
8. Lee, Martin A., *The CIA's Worst-Kept Secret: Newly Declassified Files Confirm United States Collaboration with Nazis*, unpaginated
9. Boghardt, p.279
10. ibid, p.280
11. Höhne, Heinz and Zolling, Hermann, p.69
12. Gehlen, p.145
13. Breitman, Richard, Goda, Norman J.W., Nafatali, Timothy and Wolfe, Robert, p.400
14. Höhne, Heinz and Zolling, Hermann, p.83
15. Breitman, Richard, Goda, Norman J.W., Nafatali, Timothy and Wolfe, Robert, p.390
16. Critchfield, p.100
17. ibid, p.61
18. ibid, p.76
19. ibid, p.78
20. ibid, p.83
21. ibid, p.85
22. Pournelle, Jennifer Rene, *Konrad Adenauer's Military Advisers* (Cornell University Press), 1989, p.24

23. Breitman, Richard, Goda, Norman J.W., Nafatali, Timothy and Wolfe, Robert, p.389
24. Helms, p.88
25. Reese, p.212
26. Müller, p.579
27. Reese, p.111
28. Höhne, Heinz and Zolling, Hermann, p.155
29. Breitman, Richard, Goda, Norman J.W., Nafatali, Timothy and Wolfe, Robert, p.391
30. ibid, p.392
31. ibid, p.399
32. *Wiegrefe Klaus. Braune Wurzelne, Der Spiegel, 14 February, 2011*, p.28
33. Reese, p.215
34. Breitman, Richard, Goda, Norman J.W., Nafatali, Timothy and Wolfe, Robert, p.382
35. ibid, p.383
36. Helms, p.86
37. Lee, Martin A., *The CIA's Worst-Kept Secret: Newly Declassified Files Confirm United States Collaboration with Nazis* (Institute for Policy Studies), 2001
38. Höhne, Heinz and Zolling, Hermann, p.158
39. Reese, p.213
40. Müller, p.581
41. Höhne, Heinz and Zolling, Hermann, p.153
42. ibid, p.162
43. Sälter, Dr Gerhard, *Phantome des Kalten Krieges: Die Organisation Gehlen und die Wiederbelebung des Gestapo-Feindbildes Rote Kapelle*, (CH Links Verlag), 2016, p.59
44. Höhne, Heinz and Zolling, Hermann, p.165
45. Wiegrefe, Klaus, *The Nazi Criminals Who Became German Spooks, Klaus Wiegrefe*, Der Spiegel, 16 February 2011
46. Critchfield, p.158
47. Müller, p.671
48. ibid, p.680
49. Gehlen, p.153
50. Müller, p.597
51. ibid, p.604
52. Höhne, Heinz and Zolling, Hermann, p.172
53. Breitman, Richard, Goda, Norman J.W., Nafatali, Timothy and Wolfe, Robert, p.379
54. ibid, p.394
55. Müller, p.667
56. Searle, Alaric, *Internecine Secret Service Wars Revisited: The Intelligence Career of Count Gerhard von Schwerin, 1945–1956* (https://www.degruyter.com), 2012 p.32
57. Breitman, Richard, Goda, Norman J.W., Nafatali, Timothy and Wolfe, Robert, p.279
58. Höhne, Heinz and Zolling, Hermann, p.177
59. Ridley, Norman, *Reading Hitler's Mind* (Pen & Sword), 2023, p.59
60. Cookridge, p.307
61. Müller, p.680
62. Bradley, Dermot, *The Bundeswehr and German Reunification, 1955–91* (Irish Studies in International Affairs, Volume 3, Number 4), 1992, p.55
63. Cookridge, p.216
64. Searle, p.34

65. Breitman, Richard, Goda, Norman J.W., Nafatali, Timothy and Wolfe, Robert, p.396
66. Müller, p.695
67. Breitman, Richard, Goda, Norman J.W., Nafatali, Timothy and Wolfe, Robert, p.396
68. Rogers, Daniel E., *Restoring a German Career, 1945–1950: The Ambiguity of Being Hans Globke* (University of South Alabama, German Studies Review, Volume 31, Number 2), 2008, p.303
69. ibid, p.311
70. Breitman, Richard, Goda, Norman J.W., Nafatali, Timothy and Wolfe, Robert, p.398
71. Höhne, Heinz and Zolling, Hermann, p.178
72. Critchfield, p.157
73. Höhne, Heinz and Zolling, Hermann, p.180
74. Kellerhoff, Sven Felix, *Wie aus Hitlers General Adenauers Generalinspekteur wurde* (https://www-welt.de), 2022
75. Müller, p.711
76. Cookridge, p.241
77. Breitman, Richard, Goda, Norman J.W., Nafatali, Timothy and Wolfe, Robert, p.398
78. Reese, p.131
79. Ruggenthaler, Peter, *The 1952 Stalin Note on German Unification: The Ongoing Debate* (Journal of Cold War Studies, Volume 13, Number 4), 2011
80. Reese, p.129
81. *CIA Document Number (FOIA) /ESDN (CREST): 02606326 Case Number: F-2016-02521 released 1 March 2019*
82. Höhne, Heinz and Zolling, Hermann, p.189
83. Münkel, Daniela, *State Security: A Reader on the GDR Secret Police* (Department of Education and Research, 10106 Berlin https://publikation@bstu.bund.de), 2016
84. *Akten-Einsichten, Beiträge zum historischen Ort der Staatssicherheit, Herausgegeben von Helge Heidemeyer*, https://publikation@bstu.bund.de
85. Augstein, Franziska, *Der Sauhaufen von Pullach* Süddeutsche Zeitung, 6 October 2016
86. Goda, Norman J.W., *CIA Files Relating to Heinz Felfe, SS officer and KGB Spy* (Ohio University), undated
87. Reese, p.133
88. Kellerhoff
89. *CIA Document Number (FOIA) /ESDN (CREST): 02606326 Case Number: F-2016-02521 released 1 March 2019*
90. Hechelhammer, Bodo V., *Spion ohne Grenzen* (Piper Verlag), 2019, p.14
91. ibid, p.105
92. Felfe, Heinz, *Im Dienst des Gegners: Autobiografie* (Verlag der Nation), 1988, p.195
93. Reese, p.145
94. Messenger, David and Paehler, Katrin, A *Nazi Past: Recasting German Identity in Postwar Europe* (University Press of Kentucky), 2015, p.281
95. ibid
96. ibid, p.282
97. Breitman, Richard, Goda, Norman J.W., Nafatali, Timothy and Wolfe, Robert, p.402
98. Gehlen, p.344
99. ibid, p.203
100. Reese, p.151

101. *KGB Eploitation of Heinz Felfe CIA File Approved for Release: 2022/08/01 C02603913,* p.87
102. Reese, p.168
103. Cookridge, p.344
104. Fenemore, Mark, *Victim of Kidnapping or an Unfortunate Defector? The Strange Case of Otto John* (Cold War History vol 20 issue 2), 2019, p.5
105. ibid, p.11
106. ibid, p.20

Chapter 5: The BND

1. *'How Former Nazi Official Reinhard Gehlen Erected a State within a State in Post-War Germany', Wolfgang Weber,* 27 December 2017, https:www.wsws.org
2. Searle, p.40
3. ibid, p.48
4. Schiller, Kay, *The Presence of the Nazi Past in the Early Decades of the Bonn Republic* (Journal of Contemporary History, Volume 39, Number 2), 2004, p.288
5. Nowack, Sabrina, *Sicherheitsrisiko NS-Belastung: Personalüberprüfungen im Bundesnachrichtendienst in den 1960er Jahren* (Berlin), 2016, p.291
6. Critchfield, p.181
7. *'German 'Watergate': Chancellor spied on Rival Party,* The Washington Post, Dan Rosenzweig-Ziff, 8 April 2022
8. Reese, p.176
9. Cookridge, p.315
10. Höhne, Heinz and Zolling, Hermann, p.183
11. Müller, p.901
12. Wolf, Thomas, Die Anfänge des BND, p.225
13. Gehlen, p.279
14. *Krewel, Mona,* (23 March 2014), *'Spiegel Affair', Encyclopædia Britannica*
15. Wolf, Thomas, *Methods, Topics and New Sources in Contemporary History Research on the German Foreign Intelligence Service* (German Historical Institute Moscow), 2019
16. *Die Welt,* 24 July 1963
17. Höhne, Heinz and Zolling, Hermann, p.229
18. ibid
19. ibid, p.236
20. ibid, p.230
21. ibid, p.231
22. ibid, p.239

BIBLIOGRAPHY AND SOURCES

Alvarez, David and Mark, Eduard, *Spying Through a Glass Darkly*, (University Press of Kansas), 2016

Berstein, Vadim J., *Smersh, Stalin's Secret Weapon*, (Biteback Publishing), 2013

Boghardt, Thomas, *Covert Legions: U.S. Army intelligence in Germany, 1944–1949*, (Center of Military History United States Army Washington, DC), 2022

Boker, John R., *Report of Initial Contacts with Gehlen Organisation*, (https//www.jewishvirtuallibrary.org)

Bradley, Dermot, *The Bundeswehr and German Reunification, 1955–91*, (Irish Studies in International Affairs, Volume 3, Number 4), 1992

Breitman, Richard, Goda, Norman J.W., Nafatali, Timothy, Wolfe, Robert, *U.S. Intelligence and the Nazis*, (Cambridge University Press), 2005

Cookridge, E.H., *Gehlen, Spy of the Century*, (Random House), 1971

Critchfield, James H., *Partners at the Creation*, (Naval Institute Press), 2003

Dohna-Schlobitten, Alexander, *Erinnerungen eines alten Ostpreußen*, (Berlin), 1989

Durning, Marvin B. and Massie, Robert K., *World Turned Upside Down: U.S. Naval Intelligence and the Early Cold War Struggle for Germany*, (Potomac Books), 2007

Felfe, Heinz, *Im Dienst des Gegners: Autobiografie*, (Verlag der Nation), 1988

Fenemore, Mark, *Victim of Kidnapping or an Unfortunate Defector? The Strange Case of Otto John*, (Cold War History, Volume 20, Issue 2), 2019

Gehlen, Reinhard, *The Service*, (World Publishing), 1972

Goda, Norman J.W., *CIA Files Relating to Heinz Felfe, SS Officer and KGB Spy*, (Ohio University), undated

Halder, Franz, *Kriegstagebuch 1939–42, Volume III*, (W. Kollhammer), 1962

Hechelhammer, Bodo V., *Spion ohne Grenzen*, (Piper Verlag), 2019

Helms, Richard, A *Look Over My Shoulder: A Life in the Central Intelligence Agency*, (Random House), 2003

Heusinger, Adolf, *Befehl im Widerstreit: Schicksalsstunden der deutschen Armee 1923–1945*, (Tübingen), 1950

Höhne, Heinz and Zolling, Hermann, *The General was a Spy*, (Pan Books), 1972

Höhne, Heinz and Brownjohn, J., Maxwell, *Canaris*, (Martin Secker & Warburg Ltd), 1979

Kahm, David, *Hitler's Spies*, (Macmillan), 1978

Kellerhoff, Sven Felix, *Wie aus Hitlers General Adenauers Generalinspekteur wurde*, (https://www-welt.de), 2022

Kellerhoff, Sven Felix, *Dieser Agent spitzelte für sieben verschiedene Geheimdienste*, (Welt), 2022

Keßelring, Agilolf, *Die Organisation Gehlen und die Neuformierung des Militärs*, (Christof Links Verlag), 2017

Lee, Martin A., *The CIA's Worst-Kept Secret: Newly Declassified Files Confirm United States Collaboration with Nazis*, (Institute for Policy Studies), 2001

Mader, Julius, *Die graue Hande*, (Kongress-Verlag), 1961

Mallett, Derek R., *Hitler's Generals in America: Nazi PoWs and Allied Military Intelligence*, (The University Press of Kentucky), 2013

Mallett, Derek R., *Western Allied Intelligence and the German Military Document Section, 1945–6*, (Journal of Contemporary History, Volume 26, Number 2), 2011

Messenger, David and Paehler, Katrin, A *Nazi Past: Recasting German Identity in Postwar Europe*, (University Press of Kentucky), 2015

Müller, Rolf-Dieter, *Reinhard Gehlen, Geheimdienstchef im Hintergrund der Bonner Republik Die Biografie,1902–1979*, (CH Links Verlag), 2018

Münkel, Daniela, *State Security: A Reader on the GDR Secret Police*, (Department of Education and Research, 10106 Berlin, https://publikation@bstu.bund.de), 2016

Nowack, Sabrina, *Sicherheitsrisiko NS-Belastung: Personalüberprüfungen im Bundesnachrichtendienst in den 1960er Jahren*, (Berlin), 2016

Orbach, Danny, *Fugitives, A History of Nazi Mercenaries during the Cold War*, (C. Hurst & Co.), 2022

Paehler,Katrin, *The Third Reich's Intelligence Services: Walter Schellenberg* (Cambridge University Press), 2017

Pahl, Magnus, *Fremde Heere Ost. Hitlers militärische Feindaufklärung*, (Helion), 2012

Paine, Lauran, *German Military Intelligence in World War II, The Abwehr*, (Military Heritage Press), 1984

Reese, Mary Ellen, *General Reinhard Gehlen: The CIA Connection*, (George Mason University Press), 1990

Pournelle, Jennifer Rene, *Konrad Adenauer's Military Advisers*, (Cornell University Press), 1989

Ridley, Norman, *Hitler's Gold*, (Pen & Sword), 2023

Ridley, Norman, *Reading Hitler's Mind*, (Pen & Sword), 2023

Rogers, Daniel E., *Restoring a German Career, 1945–1950: The Ambiguity of Being Hans Globke*, (University of South Alabama, German Studies Review, Volume 31, Number 2), 2008

Ruffner, Kevin C., *American Intelligence and the Gehlen Organisation, 1945–49*, (CIA Historical Staff center for the study of Intelligence), 1997

Ruffner, Kevin C., *Debriefing of Eric Waldman 30 September 1969 CIA and the Origins of the BND, 1945 –49*, (CIA Historical Staff Center for the Study of Intelligence), 1969

Ruggenthaler, Peter, *The 1952 Stalin Note on German Unification: The Ongoing Debate*, (Journal of Cold War Studies, Volume 13, Number 4), 2011

Sälter, Gerhard, *Phantome des Kalten Krieges: Die Organisation Gehlen und die Wiederbelebung des Gestapo-Feindbildes Rote Kapelle*, (CH Links Verlag), 2016

Sälter, Dr Gerhard, *Phantome des Kalten Krieges: Die Organisation Gehlen und die Wiederbelebung des Gestapo-Feindbildes Rote Kapelle*, (CH Links Verlag), 2016

Schiller, Kay, *The Presence of the Nazi Past in the Early Decades of the Bonn Republic*, (Journal of Contemporary History, Volume 39, Number 2), 2004

Schramm, Percy Ernst, *War Diary of the High Command of the Wehrmacht (Wehrmacht Command Staff) 1940–1945*, (Madison Books), 1991

Searle, Alaric, *Internecine Secret Service Wars Revisited: The Intelligence Career of Count Gerhard von Schwerin, 1945–1956*, (https://degruyter.com), 2012

Silver, Arnold M., *Memories of Oberursel, Questions, Questions, Questions*, (Intelligence and National Security, Volume 8, Number 2), 1993

Thomas, David, *Foreign Armies East and German Military Intelligence in Russia 1941–45*, (Journal of Contemporary History Volume 22, Number 2), 1987

Tromly, Benjamin, *Cold War Exiles and the CIA: Plotting to Free Russia*, (Oxford University Press), 2019

Weber, Wolfgang, *How Former Nazi Official Reinhard Gehlen Erected a State within a State in Post-War Germany*, (https:www/wsws.org), 2017

Wolf, Thomas, *Die Anfänge des BND*, (Institut für Zeitgeschichte), 2016

Wolf, Thomas, *Methods, Topics and New Sources in Contemporary History Research on the German Foreign Intelligence Service*, (German Historical Institute Moscow), 2019

INDEX

Abakumov, Semyonovich 173
Acheson, Dean 162
Adam, Wilhelm 18–19
Adenauer, Konrad 147, 149–155, 157–166, 168–170, 172, 183, 187, 189–198
Aigner, Viktor von 7
Albert, Ludwig 178, 184–185, 194, 203
Altkrüger, Siegfried 177
Anger, Kurt 20
Armin, Friedrich Sixt von 21
Attlee, Clement 170–171
Augsburg, Emil 143–144, 146, 203
Augstein, Rudolf 176, 196
Auner, Kurt 144

Bamler, Rudolf 9, 174
Bandelow, Karli Julius Willi 123, 176–177
Barczatis, Elli 177
Baum, Anna 2
Baun, Hermann 34, 39–40, 60, 73, 76, 78, 81, 85–87, 90–95, 97–105, 107–110, 112, 114, 117, 119, 125–126, 129–130, 138–139, 141, 144, 148, 154, 178, 191, 198
Beck, Ludwig 19
Belov, Pawel 66
Benjamin, Daniel 178
Bentivegni, Franz Eccard 'Benti' von 29, 65
Bentzinger, Alfred 101, 119, 178, 192
Beria, Lavrentiy 47, 67, 173
Bevin, Ernest 162
Bissell, Clayton L 85, 87–88, 91
Blankenhorn, Herbert 155, 157, 166
Blomberg, Werner von 13, 18
Blücher, Franz 155
Bock, Fedor von 27, 63–64
Boehrsch, Herbert 144, 207
Boker, John R. 81–83, 85, 88–89, 170
Bolling, Alexander Russell 170
Bolschwing, Otto von 144, 203
Bonde-Henriksen, Henrik 189
Bormann, Martin 12, 60, 128
Bormann, Hans 176
Bossard, Samuel 107, 112–115, 134
Brachmüller, Hans 146
Brandt, Willy 193, 198–199
Brauchitsch, Walther von 18
Brockdorff-Rantzau, Ulrich von 8
Brunner, Alois 144
Burress, Withers A. 'Pinky' 106
Busch, Friedrich 179, 186, 207

Carr, Henry 124
Carstenn, Friedrich 134
Carstens, Karl, 199–200
Chamberlain, Neville 19
Chamberlin, Stephen J. 115
Chikalov-Almazov, Alexander F. 113
Churchill, Winston 77, 96, 171
Clay, Lucius D. 97, 129–130

Clemens, Johannes 'Hans' 180–182, 186–187, 203
Critchfield, James H. 133, 135–144, 146–148, 151, 153–158, 164–170, 184, 194–195
Crome, Hans-Henning 179, 198
Cruewell, Ludwig 192

Dale,Thomas Wesley 177, 178–179, 194
de Gaulle, Charles 150
Deane, John R. Jnr. 93, 99, 103–105, 107, 109–112, 115, 140, 154
Delmer, Sefton 172, 194
Deppner, Erich 143–144, 203
Deriabin, Peter Sergeievich 184
Deutsch, Valentina 47
Dill, Sir John 14
Dingler, Hans-Jürgen 109–111, 119, 122, 129
Dulles, Allen W. 84, 91, 107, 133, 144, 163, 167, 169–171, 185, 191, 194
Dulles, John Foster 163, 194

Eckstein, Theodor 5, 12
Eckstein, Ernst 13
Eisenhower, Dwight D. 82, 87, 163, 194
Erdmann, Kurt Wilhelm Gustav 17
Erhard, Ludwig 198
Erler, Fritz 193

Felfe, Heinz 143, 177, 179–187, 188, 196–197
Fiebig, Konrad 143, 145, 204
Filbert, Albert 29
Filitz, Gerda 47
Flentge, Walter 176
Foertsch, Hermann 111, 135, 137, 201
Förster, Albert 173
Freytag-Loringhov, Baron Wessel von 69
Fritsch, Werner von 18
Fromm, Friedrich 11
Füner, Herbert 88, 100

Galloway, Donald H. 106, 135, 138, 142
Gehlen, Reinhard 1, 13, 22, 25, 33, 40, 47, 55, 63, 68, 70, 76, 87, 97, 133, 152, 195, 200, 209–210, 216, 218–220
Gehlen, Benno Erwin Felix Walther 1–3
Gehlen, Johannes 2–3, 6
Gehlen, Max 1, 3
Gehlen, Arnold 3
Gehlen, Katharina Margarete 13
Gehlen, Felix Christoph 17
Gehlen née Wiede, Luise 1
Geyer, Hans Joachim 175
Geylener, Gaugraf Johannes 1
Giskes, Hermann 119
Globke, Hans 151, 165, 197, 215, 219
Goebbels, Joseph 64–65
Göring, Hermann 18
Göring, Frans 132
Graver, Bill 139
Grotewohl, Otto 177
Gruschwitz, Max 6
Guderian, Heinz 24, 132, 162
Guse, Karl 144

Hagemeister, Louis 174
Hajek, Bozena 125
Handy, Thomas T. 162
Harnisch, Rudolf 113
Hasse, Werner 204
Hays, George P. 158
Heinemann, Gustav 155
Heinz, Friedrich Wilhelm 159
Helms, Richard 101, 134, 198
Hencke, Andor 8
Hengelhaupt, Erich 66
Herre, Heinz Danko 31
Hess, Rudolf 12, 128
Heusinger, Adolf 16, 110, 201
Heydrich, Reinhard 9, 144
Hickson, H. 80
Hiemenz, Horst 87

Hillenkoetter, Roscoe H. 115
Himmler, Heinrich 18, 33
Hinrichs, Hans 87
Hitler, Adolf 8, 14
Hodosy-Strobl, Paul 144
Hofe, Günther 182
Hohmann, Karl 199
Hönlinger, Roman 101
Hörner, née Markiewitz, Helene von 10
Hundhammer, Alois 153

Imhoff, Klaus 122

Jerabek, Vojtech 125
Jobke, Karl Otto 134
Johannes, Heina Paul 132
John, Otto 152, 156, 160, 172, 188, 191, 216–217
Jost, Heinz 34

Kaiser, Jakob 153
Kalman, Ivolia 47
Kapahnke, Gerhard 177
Kauder, Richard 43
Kayser-Eichberg, Erich Ulich 146, 207
Keuner, Dieter 121
Kharitonov, Fyedor M. 37
Khrushchev, Nikita 42
Kiesinger, Kurt George 199
Kinghofer, A. 80
Kinzel, Eberhard 25
Kirkpatrick, Ivone 158
Kleinkamp, Rudolf 128, 132
Klose, Hans-Helmut 124
Kluge, Günther von 11
Knieper, Werner 199
Koehler, Willard 115
Kohler, Kurt 105
Kopp, Klara Elisabeth 10
Koska, Jaromir 126
Krassowski, Werner 144
Krebs, Hans 74
Kreidl, Rudolf IX
Krichbaum, William 'Willy' 144, 182, 204
Kurreck, Walter 145

Lafont, Roger 164
Lahousen, Erwin von 69
Lammers, Heinrich 12
Langkau, Wolfgang 9
Laurenz, Karl 177
Leahy, William D. 91, 95
Lex, Hans Ritter von 149
Lindemann, Georg 8
Lindemann, Fritz 14
Liss, Ulrich 38
Longin, Ira (Iliya Lang) 44, 47, 86
Loßberg, Bernhard von 16
Lossow, Hans von 105
Lovell, John Raymond 90
Lucid,Tom 139, 146
Lütgendorf, Karl Freiherr von 88, 100

Malyshkin, Vasili Feodorovich 65
Manstein, Erich von 16, 20, 54, 60, 160
Makowski, Ernst 144
Marogna-Redwitz, Rudolf Graf von 44–45
Marshall, George C. 133
McCloy, John Jay 159, 169
McKibbin, Alexander 124
Meily, John J. 44
Mellenthin, Horst von 9, 111, 132, 137
Menshinsky, Vyacheslav Rudolfovich 14
Mercier, Marcel-André 153, 163, 167
Miecklev, Gustav 176
Milch, Erhard 18
Misera, Ewald 123, 176
Molotov, Vyacheslav 42, 96
Moos, Arthur 101
Münchhausen, Georg-Heino Freiherr von 48

Neuegebauer Franz, 177
Noack, Ulrich 132
Nolte, Heinrich Eduard 25, 205

Oesterreich, Rolf 177
Ollenhauer, Erich 149
Ondarza, Herbert von 11
Oriola, Ralph Graf von 20
Ortloff, Siegfried 193
Oster, Achim 157
Oster, Hans 157, 159
Otten, Walter 144

Paget, Sir Bernard 14, 15
Parkinson, William 177
Paulson, Agda Torborg 3
Paulus, Friedrich von 25, 37–38, 43, 48, 53, 55, 68
Petersen, Ernest 32
Petty, Clare Edward 184–185
Philby, Harold Adrian Russell 'Kim' 102, 125
Philp, William R. 'Rusty' 81, 84, 93, 99, 106, 134
Picard, Maurice 199
Pleasants, Henry 139, 194
Porter, Marian E. 81
Prather, Gerhard 177
Proebsting, Helmut 180

Rabenau, Friedrich von 1
Radke, Albert 160, 168
Reile, Oscar 182, 202
Rennert, Walter 177
Ribbentrop, Joachim von 33, 65
Ribière, Henri 164
Richter, Herbert 123, 204
Rittberg, Karl-Heinrich Graf von 78
Rittner, Andre 139
Rohleder, Joachim 119
Rönne, Alexis Freiherr von 32–33, 38, 64–66, 68, 70, 78
Rosenberg, Alfred 33, 63–64, 67
Rosvall, Toivo 139
Rusk, Dean 198

Sanitzer, Johann 174
Schellenberg, Walter 29, 34, 47, 60, 66, 70, 72, 78, 109, 210, 218
Scheutz, Carl 179
Schlandt, Ernst 144
Schmalschläger, Heinz 35, 60, 91, 205
Schmidt, Fritz 144
Schmidt, Karl-Heinz 177
Schneemilch, Otto 10
Schneider, Walter 110, 123, 136, 177
Schoeller, Albert 87, 100
Schultz, Joseph 44, 86–87
Schumacher, Kurt 150, 153, 191
Schuman, Robert 162
Schwarzwalder, John J. 80
Schwenk, Helmut 177
Schwerin, Gerhard Graf von 157–158, 163, 167, 190–191, 214, 219
Seydlitz-Kurzbach, Joachim von 110
Seydlitz-Kurzbach, Walther von 9
Seydlitz-Kuzbach, Herta Charlotte Agnes Helene von 12
Seydlitz-Kuzbach, Friedrich Wilhelm von 12
Shtemenko, Sergei 62
Sibert, Edwin L. 82–88, 91–93, 97–99, 101–107, 111
Sichel, Peter M.F. 131
Silver, Arnold M. 86–87, 212, 219
Sima, Horia 144
Skorzeny, Otto 70, 72, 77, 173, 185
Slute, Benjamin 155
Smith, Walter Bedell 'Beetle' 83, 87, 171
Somann, Otto 144
Sommer, Hans 132–133, 179, 182, 206
Souers, Sidney W. 95
Speer, Albert 55
Speidel, Hans 137, 163, 192, 195, 201
Stalder, Fred 139
Stalin, Josef 33, 37, 42, 46–47, 52, 56, 59, 63, 65–67, 71- 73, 172, 174–175, 210, 215, 217, 219
Staudinger, Max 145
Stauffenberg, Claus von 15, 32, 68–69, 159–160, 166, 189
Stein, Herbert 132
Stephanus, Konrad 87

Stewart, Gordon M. 155
Strange, Jürgen 187
Strauss, Franz Joseph 196
Strik-Stirkfeldt, Wilfried 63–65, 67
Strong, Kenneth 16, 87, 158, 190
Stülpnagel, Carl-Heinrich von 14–16

Tappert, Reinhold 174
Tellkamp, Eberhard 134
Tiebel, Erwin 180–182, 187
Tölle, Kurt 121, 122
Tresckow, Henning von 16
Trudeau, Arthur 194
Truman, Harry S. 91, 94–95, 131
Tschernjawski, Vitali 189
Tukhol'nikov-Sokolov, V.P. 113
Turkul, Anton 44, 47, 86
Tymoshenko, Semyon K. 37

Uhrlau, Ernst 198
Ulbricht, Walter 174–175
Urban, Herbert 5, 7
Urban, Josef Adolf 145

Vacarescu, Joachim 144
Vaernewyck, Katherine Margarete (Käthi) von 2, 128
Vandenberg, Hoyt S. 106, 115, 212
Vinishkiy, Vladimir 45–46
Vlasov, Andrey Andreyovich 63- 67, 70–71, 73, 88–89, 94, 101, 113, 124, 171
Vogel, Wolfgang 187

Wagner, Otto 44–45, 86.
Wahl-Welskirch, Roland von 47
Waibel, Max 150
Waldman, Eric 89, 94, 97–98, 101–103, 106–107, 109, 112, 114–115, 128, 130, 137, 139–140, 154, 170, 213, 219
Walsh, Robert L. 130
Wehner, Herbert 149
Wendland, Horst 119, 162, 199
Wesemann, Fried 193
Wessel, Gerhard 31, 33, 40, 48, 58–59, 61, 63, 69–70, 74, 76, 78–80, 85, 91, 93–95, 97, 99, 104, 109–110, 111, 114, 119, 131, 137, 162, 164, 176, 195, 199–200
Westphal, Siegfried 16
Wheeler, Charles 185
Wicht, Adolf 65–66, 132
Wildermuth, Eberhard 137, 163
Winter, August Otto 16, 78
Winter, August 111
Witzelben, Erwin Erdmann von 16
Wohlgemuth, Wolfgang 189
Wollweber, Ernst 174, 176–177
Worgitzky, Hans-Heinrich 21, 131

Zaisser, Wilhelm 173–174
Zeitzler, Kurt 49–50, 52, 55–56, 63
Zentner, Walter 121–122
Zhukov, Georgy 46, 96
Ziegler, Siegfried 193
Zkilenkov, Georgi Nicolaievich 65
Zykov, Mileti 65